acclaim for F

"Dorothy Ellen Palmer's *Falling For* ... tice movement that doesn't ignore Disability Justice. Through painfully honest and laugh-out-loud storytelling, Palmer delves deep into personal, genetic and societal memory, showing us that it's possible to uncinch ourselves from the lies we've been told about ableism and disability. A moving, informative and magical read."
– Farzana Doctor, author of *All Inclusive*

"Dorothy Palmer spent a life trying to fit in – to shoes, and with her classmates and colleagues. She was born with congenital anomalies in her feet, and while she tried to hide from what was wrong with her, she frequently fell. After a lifetime, Dorothy Palmer finally accepted herself as a disabled woman, and her need for mobility aids. Profound and engrossing, *Falling for Myself* details a strong woman's search for herself and for disability acceptance across Canada."
– Jane Eaton Hamilton, author of *Weekend*

"Dorothy Ellen Palmer writes to 'channel shame into solidarity, anger into analysis, denial into delight and loss into love,' and this book – full of insight and wild humour, fierce activism and vital intersectional analysis – marks her stellar success. She calls all of us to imagine a world beyond the limits of ableism and a movement where all of us have room to move."
– Sonya Huber, author of *Pain Woman Takes Your Keys, and Other Essays from a Nervous System*

"At the very start of her memoir, *Falling for Myself*, Dorothy Palmer tells us that we may laugh. She writes, 'But as you chuckle, remember this: Funny fat women are always angry. We're taught to aim the punchline at ourselves and smile. Not this time.' Fair warning. Palmer's storytelling carries her sharp intelligence and sparkling humour throughout her reflections on a lonely childhood, living as a disabled woman in an ableist world and the costs of being an activist. This is not 'inspiration porn.' Palmer also does not want or need the reader's pity. We respect her too much for that. Instead, we are moved, entertained and provoked to examine ourselves. By telling us her stories, Palmer invites us to examine ours. Also, you will laugh and laugh."
– Carrianne Leung, author of *That Time I Loved You*

"This book reads like a map of exposed nerves. It is a raw, detailed rendering of a disabled woman's life that, in the end, offers a beautifully discomforting and necessary gift of unapologetic, even gleeful defiance."
– Adam Pottle, author of *Voice: On Writing with Deafness*

"Look out, Canada, this memoir has the most fierce account of what it really means to be a disabled person that you are going to read, this year or any year. Whether she's destroying the myth of Tiny Tim's cheerfulness or explaining why the word *bastard* should exit your vocabulary immediately, Dorothy Palmer looks squarely at injustice and refuses to let it define who she is."
– Julie Rak, author of *Boom!: Manufacturing Memoir for the Popular Market*

"If you care about social justice and equality, you must read *Falling for Myself*. In a searing memoir that is both moving and funny, Dorothy Palmer comes out of the closet as a disabled person and challenges all of us to bring down the walls – from inaccessible spaces to ableist language – that exclude and oppress huge numbers of people who are struggling against the ableism imposed by our culture and society."
– Judy Rebick, author of *Heroes in My Head*

"In her luminous memoir, Dorothy Palmer vividly renders in-depth reflections and examination of adoption, disability, the body, ableism and difficult knowledge. She untangles intricate knots which bind these to ideal femininity, race, place, heteronormativity and Canadian institutions of the White identity as a systemic buttress for the nation. Her nimble prose, enmeshed with sensitive wit firmly lodged in the critical consciousness of dissent and power, locates resistance through a purposeful examination of 'the disabled closet . . . opened from the inside.' A constant occupant within the closet are angst-ridden Canadian discourses and fears of nonconforming bodies, minds, imaginaries and understandings of what and who is centre and other; beauty and monstrous; seen and the abjected; rewarded and or subjected to punitive subjection; which bodies are deemed normal and which rendered feral and hyper-Other. Palmer skillfully navigates these affective layers of a Canadian WASP familial history in which the state plays a colossal role managing disability as pathology, confusion and shame, thereby naturalizing the reduction of disabled folx to 'Almost Human.' That 'no body be left behind,' for Palmer, is to demand that critical disability consciousness must address desire to not be deemed as heroic or brave, but radically 'ordinary' and 'a disabled whole.' Palmer's struggle, epiphanies and revelations, storied through striking, clear prose, is a *must-read* primer for those seeking to engage Palmer's real 'target of this story: ableism.' To truly get at the root, one must look deeply – at the family history level – into how normative ideas of Canada, the nation, state and ableism actually weaponize and repress relevant knowledge which is situated and too often obscured between repressed desire, shame, adoption, disability, struggle, resistance and dissent."
– Margo Tamez (Kónitsąąii gokíyaa dindé | 'Big Water Peoples' | enrolled Lipan Apache), author of *Raven Eye* (Willa Award)

Falling for Myself

ALSO BY DOROTHY ELLEN PALMER

When Fenelon Falls

Falling f&r Myself

a memoir

Dorothy Ellen Palmer

WOLSAK
& WYNN

Cover and interior design: Marijke Friesen
Author photograph: Zekar Photo
Typeset in Adobe Garamond
Printed by Ball Media, Brantford, Canada

Ideas, passages and chapters from this memoir have been published in the following: *All Lit Up; Alt-Minds; Don't Talk to Me About Love; Little Fiction, Big Truths; Many Gendered Mothers; Refuse: CanLit in Ruins; Suffering and the Intelligence of Love in the Teaching Life* and *Wordgathering: Journal of Disability Literature.*

The passage from *When Fenelon Falls* is reprinted with the permission of Coach House Books.

10 9 8 7 6 5 4 3 2 1

The publisher gratefully acknowledges the support of the Ontario Arts Council, the Canada Council for the Arts and the Government of Canada.

Wolsak and Wynn Publishers Ltd.
280 James Street North
Hamilton, ON
Canada L8R 2L3

Library and Archives Canada Cataloguing in Publication

Title: Falling for myself : a memoir / by Dorothy Ellen Palmer.
Names: Palmer, Dorothy Ellen, 1955- author.
Identifiers: Canadiana 20190166541 | ISBN 9781989496039 (softcover)
Subjects: LCSH: Palmer, Dorothy Ellen, 1955- | LCSH: Palmer, Dorothy Ellen, 1955—Health. | LCSH: Feminists—Canada—Biography. | LCSH: Political activists—Canada—Biography. | LCSH: People with disabilities—Canada—Biography. | LCSH: Adoptees—Canada—Biography. | LCSH: Social justice—Canada. | LCSH: People with disabilities—Civil rights—Canada. | LCSH: Adoption—Canada. | CSH: Women authors, Canadian (English)—Biography.
Classification: LCC PS8631.A449 Z46 2019 | DDC C818/.603—dc23

Dedicated to the lives and living legacies of
Stella Young and Audre Lorde

and when we speak we are afraid
our words will not be heard
nor welcomed
but when we are silent
we are still afraid

So it is better to speak
remembering
we were never meant to survive.
— AUDRE LORDE, "A LITANY FOR SURVIVAL,"
THE BLACK UNICORN

I am not a snowflake. I am not a sweet, infantilising
symbol of the fragility of life.
I am a strong, fierce, flawed adult woman.
I plan to remain that way in life, and in death.
— STELLA YOUNG, FACEBOOK

CONTENTS

By Way of Introduction

My father raised stud guppies. Beautiful male fish with fantails like monarch butterflies. He bagged them up and pimped them out to other guppy enthusiasts, who paid a stud fee in hopes of their own handsome offspring. Father found his twelve-tank calling thanks to me. He'd originally purchased neon tetras and angelfish. But I'd leaned too close, lost my balance, fallen into the tank and pulled plants, pink gravel, fish and the burbling little Diver Dan filter all onto the floor, where none survived. My mother spanked me. The next day, my father bought guppies.

We all have one true gift to offer the world, and now you know mine: I fall down. Repeatedly. Spectacularly. Like the pope, I'm forever kissing the ground. I trace my history by the scars on my body, by the times and places I've fallen.

At birth, I fell from an unwilling womb into the arms of the Children's Aid. Falling far short of my adoptive mother's expectations, I spent my girlhood on my knees, apologizing for bloody leotards. When corrective surgeries failed to correct much of anything, I fell on crutches, in walking casts and off my freshly cut feet. I fell at double dutch when my orthopedic Oxfords failed to jump, and at university when my unisex workboots stopped working. I married a good man in my twenties; in my thirties, I fell for a boy pretending to be one. In a heart-cracking moment as a new mom, I smacked the sidewalk with my first-born in his Snugglie. To the delight of my grade ten drama class, I once fell right off the stage. I spent my forties fighting not to need a crutch and my fifties resisting a walker. A face plant into a moving streetcar changed my mind. At sixty-three, my walker and I collided with a kilted, hammer-throwing highlander at the Fergus Scottish Festival. When he stepped over my face to help me up, it settled the pressing question of Scottish manhood and gave new meaning to the phrase *getting off scot-free*.

But if you're expecting an inspiring tale about the importance of getting back up, you'll be disappointed. Here's my truth: I'm a faller and will always be one. Falling makes me bloody furious, and it makes me furiously bloody proud. Now that I understand exactly what makes me fall, I know what I can, and can't, do about it. I'm learning to retrace my scarred history, to channel shame into solidarity, anger into analysis, denial into delight and loss into love. After half a century of falling down, I'm falling up. I'm falling for myself.

Thanks to a pair of enemies who have become my long-standing friends. Please let me introduce them to you.

My left foot, Herkimer, at size 2.5, is flexible and finely boned. Frail, fussy and bossy, he's my nattering C-3PO. A full size smaller at 1.5, my fat right foot, Horatio, is my martyred workhorse. He's plodding, persistent and as stubborn as a fridge magnet. Since there are two of them and one of me, I'm frequently outvoted. Especially lately. My red hair has gone grey. My disability is degenerative. With each passing day, I'm less spring and more chicken. The congenital anomalies in my feet that we once called *birth defects* are complicated by a creeping, whole-body arthritis. Despite surgery and meds, I'm in constant pain. When I fall on my knees, I don't hear angel voices. I do hear cursing. Usually mine.

But for most of my life I could pass in the walking world.

From my shoes up, I looked "normal." Just another little red-headed girl. Blue-grey eyes behind glasses, some Jackson Pollock freckles and a toothy smile. Pushing past pain, I could impersonate an able body, fake a reasonable facsimile of the gait of my peers. And my tongue was always quick on its feet. I improvised. I blamed limping on a ninja thumbtack. I passed falling off as clumsy, or one teensy drink too many. When asked about childhood operations, I lied; I claimed the knife had cured me. Because I could pass for normal, I couldn't pass up the chance for a normal life. I refused to be "demoted" to the humiliation of being seen as disabled.

This is how you become an imposter in your own life: you fake a role until it is your life.

To secure a role in the walking world, I pushed my true-born self into what the disability community calls "the disabled closet." My adoption framed my closet. My girlhood insulated it. Religion pounded in the nails. I made it fashionably cozy in my twenties, then spent the next thirty years ensuring no one picked the lock. But here's the Catch-22 of closets: the longer they're locked, the more they demand to be opened. They're claustrophobic. Inevitably, they start to smell a little funky. Craving human company, the hand reaching for the key is your own. How fitting. In my ripe old age, I'm coming out of the disabled closet.

"Almost Human" is a role I refuse to play. I'm a disabled whole.

I am not "so lame." I'm splendidly lame. Magnificently lame.

In short, all four foot ten of me won't be telling you an inspiring tall tale about defeating or overcoming disability. Mine can't be hidden, halted or healed. We all need to stop falling for the double lie that disabled people can be healed and should want to be healed. Instead, I'll do my best to air out my closet and redress my aging body. A life in pain is both delicate and resilient. In all its shrivelling personal loss, I have found collective joy. I long to show you the extraordinary ordinariness of my life.

Here's what is inspiring: in my lifetime, all kinds of closets have been pried open from the inside. I've worked all my life to be on the

right side of that history, to add my two cents to that joint wealth. I'm
thankful every second for the generations of disabled activists who've
worked for decades to change history. To honour their gift, I'm exposing my unclad truth, hoping you'll get naked with me. I've made so
many mistakes, we can get dressed down together. But as you chuckle, remember this: Funny fat women are always angry. We're taught to
aim the punchline at ourselves and smile. Not this time.

Let's all name the target of this story: *ableism*.

It's a word I didn't learn until my fifties, when I met the online
disability community. Like all *isms*, ableism wields both a carrot and
a stick. As a world view created by and for abled people, ableism normalizes, values, rewards, privileges, entitles, enriches and empowers
those deemed to have socially acceptable "healthy and normal" minds
and bodies. Ableism shames, marginalizes, impoverishes, silences,
punishes, incarcerates and kills disabled people. *Internalized ableism*
made me a liar for half a century. It's the weaponized shame I aimed
at myself, as I spent every waking moment denying and hiding my
disability. Desperate to belong in the walking world, I kept reaching
for the carrot and running from the stick.

Today, I know any aim I take at ableism must be double-barrelled,
must target both the discrimination and the privilege. That's no easy
task because ableism is systemic: built into all beliefs, behaviours,
buildings, language and laws. It's intersectional: in its hierarchical
ranking of worthy to worthless bodies, ableism reinforces all other
forms of hatred and oppression.

How do I live in a disabled body, in a world that labels me
unworthy?

Once a redhead, always a redhead: if you're looking for feisty,
you've found me.

This memoir charts the slow repossession of my birthright – a
righteous, red-headed anger. For your entertainment pleasure, I'll
journey back to the days of Ed Sullivan to tell my perpetually improvised running joke: *Holy Shit, It's Saturday Night and I'm Still Alive.*

It's the uncomfortable humour I trust. It's purposeful; it's the laughter that empowers change.

Herkimer, Horatio and I invite you come trip with us down memory lane.

Welcome to our remembrance alphabet, our recollection in twenty-six letters. Here are all the words I learned to unlearn, fall by fall. Then painstakingly rearranged, step by step. I'm respelling each letter of my life in my body to extend a loving touch to all the somebodies like me.

Won't you please join us?

A is Always for Almost

In my first baby picture, I'm no baby; I'm almost three years old.

In brand-new Sunday best, I'm wearing my first costume: the ensemble my parents brought to court. They want me to look nice for the judge, and for posterity – for the photo of "the day we brought you home." It's the winter of 1958. My parents, Marguerite Isobel Stobie Palmer and Robert David Palmer, have just signed my adoption papers. The judge banged his gavel and the Toronto Children's Aid caseworker put their re-clad, renamed daughter into their arms. The photos are in black and white, but I remember my ensemble in living colour. From head to toe, I'm the blush pink of a newborn rose.

It's February. I'm plenty warm. My bonnet is a rich, quilted velveteen. Three pink rosettes with minty green leaves embellish the white ribbon on the crown. Like every well-dressed girl in the 1950s, my bonnet matches my coat. It's the same pink velveteen, sporting the same white ribbon trim and identical rosettes on the collar and cuffs. Of course, my coat matches my dress; it's also velveteen, with an ornately embroidered yoke of festive holly green, trimmed with the same minty leaves and rosebuds. I have pink mittens, hand-knit by my new mother. They dangle on a pink string, attached to my coat collar with a pink safety pin. When she covers my mouth with a pink scarf, I smile. Of course, I do; I'm a good girl.

This outfit is the first set of big girl clothes, and the only set of new clothes, I've ever owned. The white leotards are my first pair of tights. I'm concerned that these strange new people do not seem to think I need a diaper, but I do not complain. Even my underpants have rosebuds. In each detail, my mother has chosen deliberately and well: pink and green in exactly the right shades to makeover nobody's child into her little girl. When she wrapped my auburn curls around her finger, they fell in place like Shirley Temple's ringlets.

But two things ruin the picture: the left one and the right one.

My shoes.

When my new father slipped an ensemble-completing pair of unwearable pink shoes into his overcoat pocket, my new mother sighed. I had to wear my baby booties. Curved over sideways, with broken laces, they matched my feet. When my new mother laced them up, she seemed to think their sides could be pulled together. Trying to close the gaps my shoes require on either side of their tongues, she tied them too tight. Looking down from my perch in her arms, I remember the perfect flashing points of her pink high heels.

When we reached 26 Delma Drive, a tiny wartime bungalow in the Toronto suburb of Alderwood, she set me down on the grey living room carpet where I promptly peed my new pink panties. It worked. She removed my shoes. Until I turned eight, my parents and I giggled at that story whenever we looked at my "coming home" photo. Then they had their own children.

My mother was born in 1920, my dad in 1922. They married at thirty-three and thirty-one, late for the times. Choosing adoption only after multiple miscarriages, I always assumed age put them so far down the priority list that they got a slightly older, slightly damaged baby. In 1959, they adopted again, photographing my brother in his snazzy coming home outfit. In 1960, my mother told five-year-old me they were going back to Children's Aid to get my sister.

And I believed her.

How I loved that baby. My Judith Ann. My sister. My real sister.

Months later, in a medically documented phenomenon, nearing menopause and after adopting, my mother got pregnant. She didn't tell me. I came home one day at lunch and my baby sister was gone. Judith was always in her carriage on the front porch. I grabbed her carriage and took off. As I ran, I prayed. I begged God not to take my family away from me. Not again. When I finally lifted the blanket, of course God was laughing at me. I didn't deserve a sister.

When I came home without her, my mother's tears were already dry.

She said, "Don't worry. Another family will love her just as much as you do."

"That's not true. Nobody could love Judy more than me. Can't we please get her back?"

"No, we can't. But I'm going to tell you a big girl secret. Your father and I are going to have a better baby, a baby of our very own. Won't that be lovely?"

She smiled at me like she expected me to be happy for her.

"There is no better baby! Judith is my sister. My real sister!"

"What? No, dear. We just told you that to make you feel better. This baby is our real daughter. If it's a girl, we'll call her Judy, too. So, sit down and eat your SpaghettiOs. And don't worry. Soon, you won't even remember that there was another baby."

I didn't even try to reach the toilet. I stood up and threw up. I can still see the tablecloth, a cheery blue gingham with tiny white baby bones floating in the red of baby's blood.

Mother handed me a dishcloth, swivelled on her stiletto and went to lie down.

Now that I'm a mother, I can feel the devastation of her 1960 Sophie's Choice. Given her history of miscarriage, told she could not both care for an infant and carry one, she made the only choice legally and medically available. I date the worst of my sleepwalking to that choice.

Talk about a cruel irony. You'd think my silly feet would welcome the rest. Instead, I've walked in my sleep from the time I could walk. I wake up mid-stair, barefoot in my nightie, to find things moved or missing. Over sixty years, I've shined my shoes, made sandwiches, knitted, ironed and rearranged furniture, all in my sleep. Much like the truth I'd never been toilet trained, I imagine my sleepwalking was something Children's Aid conveniently forgot to mention.

On my first night in their home, Dave and Peggy Palmer discovered their sleeping child could indeed pee the bed, drip down the hall, unlock the front door and greet the snow in a sodden sleeper. That first night, they saved me only because the neighbours heard me screaming.

After repeat performances, once they believed I was truly asleep and not just willful and wild, my father installed a chain-link sliding lock, one set over his head that I couldn't reach. Awakened by the sound of me yanking on the door like a mini Jacob Marley rattling her chains, they took me back to bed, shaking their heads with all the incredulity of Ebenezer Scrooge.

In 1960, when my mother's daughter started kicking, I stepped out every night.

In the escape of sleep, I sought escape. I pulled a kitchen chair to the door and unlocked it. My father came after me; my mother couldn't get out of bed. A prescription of total bedrest for high-risk pregnancies was common then, but that never got explained to eight-year-old me. My aunties and all the neighbour ladies treated me with the forced joviality that alerts any child. Even more alarming was the unheard-of expense of Mrs. Devenish, a cleaning lady, brought in because my mother must not pick anything up, including her two children. I came home from school for a daily fifteen-minute visit with my mother. Then, exiled from her room, I spent the evening alone in mine, straining to hear through the walls to be sure she was still breathing.

This is what I believed beyond reason: unless I was a very good girl, my mother was going to die. I trained myself to silence, convinced that any disturbance from me would kill her. Only once I was asleep did I dare try to escape. After a difficult delivery, my mother gave her beloved blood daughter my missing sister's name.

A year later, once I'd finally begun sleeping through the night, my mother got pregnant again. In 1963, when a woman in her mid-forties who nearly died in her first confinement risks a second child, she is either brave and life-affirming or selfish to the core, so desperate for her own biological spawn that she's willing to leave her chosen children motherless. I know that's not fair, given women's lack of choice in 1963. I equally know this was unfair: my eight-year-old mind quite logically concluded this: I'd disappear next. My parents sent my sister Judith back the first time. Now it was my turn. My mother was willing to die to replace me.

This is how I spent the year I turned eight and she turned forty-three. I stopped sleeping. To stay awake, I chanted the alphabet and dug my nails into my knees until they bled. No one noticed. My knees were already bloody. But it worked. The Children's Aid kidnappers who took my sister, they couldn't get me. If I stayed awake, I could scream. That summer, in a delivery that very nearly took her life, my mother birthed my baby brother.

We became a forced-fit family: two natural children, and by default, two unnatural ones.

Exactly one month later, the first political event that I'd remember all my life occurred. On September 15, 1963, the Ku Klux Klan bombed the 16th Street Baptist Church in Birmingham, Alabama, killing four little black girls at Sunday school. As an avid attender of Sunday school, it told me the world wasn't safe for any girls anywhere. When JFK was assassinated two months later on November 22, 1963, I concluded that kidnappers, bombers and assassins lurked on every corner. When my dad said what I imagine many white, suburban parents said to reassure their children, "That violence is far away, not here in Canada," I knew better than to believe him.

I know what you're thinking: Why did no one get counselling for a child caught in this recursive trauma? That assumes anyone saw trauma. No one did. Fifty years ago, child psychiatrists were rare, reserved for the demonstrably disturbed. I'd joined the Baby Boom Dream Team: a suburban nuclear family. What could I possibly need to talk about?

In secret, I told my own creation story, only to myself: "Once upon a time, a man and a woman wanted a baby. First-best babies come from a woman's tummy and the hospital. They had to settle for one from the second-hand baby store. When they saw they could get first-best babies after all, of course, they loved them more. First-best babies have kissable toes."

My coming home photo paled beside those of my parents' tiny perfect newborns. My velveteen lost its sheen. When my dirty, broken booties came home with me, they ruined everything. My disability, my second-best-ness, has always been inextricably enmeshed with my adoption. They embody the same shame, tar me with the same dirty brush. They required the same hushed tones, or preferably, no words at all. I can't separate them. I've come to believe they can't be separated. My intersecting almosts have always been messy, tangled like my curly red hair, knotted into the snarls of love and loss I felt from the day I entered my parents' home.

Daddy put down his newspaper each night, used his own wide thumb like a shoehorn to help me pull on my slippers. When I asked him why even slippers hurt, he affirmed my feet were "different." He said he hoped I'd "grow out of it," but if I didn't, they'd have me "fixed." I knew when they "fixed" the dog, they reached between his legs and whacked the spunk out of him.

This was not encouraging. I was already bloody. My knees incessantly scabbed.

My mother saw my "clumsiness" the same way she saw the fact I still wet the bed: as a selfish campaign to make more work for her. In an era when girls couldn't wear pants to school, she kept me in knee socks until the worst of winter. When I wore leotards, mashing my knees to jelly on a daily basis cost her money. I must not be rewarded with new leotards. She made me wash out the blood with Javex, made me stand beside her mending chair to watch as she shoved her darning ham down the throat of my leotards, positioned it under the hole and wove grids of thread to patch it. Mother was as tired of mending and re-mending my tights as I was of wearing them mended. When most annoyed at me, she wove scarlet grids into what our 1960s WASP tongues unthinkingly called my "flesh-coloured" tights.

On the Sunday night she announced it was time for me to learn to do my own darning, my mother guided my needle through a grid of her own making and attempted to be kind.

"Now that you're a big girl mending for yourself, Dorothy, I'll try not to lose my temper about how much you fall. I hope you know that having little feet is very feminine. Nothing to be ashamed of, not at all." She patted my hand. "But never take your shoes off in public."

This confused me. I knew no good girl would ever take her top off in public, but I'd seen plenty of barefoot children of both sexes. "But why aren't my feet normal?"

Mother's hands froze. "You can ask Dr. Ridley. When you turn eighteen."

She reclaimed her needle. Told me to go watch Walt Disney and stay put for Ed Sullivan.

My parents likewise told me I was adopted. They replayed roles that began and ended in cameo, no backstory necessary. Mother reprised her line, "It's absolutely nothing to be ashamed of, dear," adding, "But you must never speak about it to anyone, for any reason."

I hope she was embarrassed for me.

I knew she was ashamed of me.

Until I became a mother, it never occurred to me that my questions made her sad. It never occurred to my parents to explain their feelings, or to ask about mine. In the 1960s, we had no *Dr. Phil*, no *Oprah* and no Internet. Beyond Dr. Spock's 1946 *Baby and Child Care*, which my mother had read to tatters and rebound with duct tape, there were no self-help books. There was absolutely no one to advise first-time parents of adopted, disabled children. In further handicap, both my parents came from deeply wounded families.

My mother's mother, Ellen Sarah Morgan Stobie, retreated into herself after the death of her fifth and favoured child. I'd been told some of the story: my mother's baby brother died in a car accident. She was five. His death was her first memory. She remembered the automobile, a long black boat of a thing, a Packard like her chum Janie Packard. It had four fat wheels and one strapped to the side. She remembered climbing up on the running board, how her older brothers and her sister poked at the beige canvas roof with their fingers. She was too short to reach it. She said when Grandpa rolled over the embankment, everyone crawled out laughing.

Until they saw a lacy white bonnet under the car.

But, as happens so often in family history, a half-truth tells less than half the story.

It wasn't until I began researching for this memoir that I understood the cruel, recursive coincidence of their loss. I had to check and double-check online records to be sure I wasn't imagining it. My grandma was born September 6, 1881. On her forty-third birthday, September 6, 1924, she gave birth to her last child, christened James after my grandpa but nicknamed Fronty. Two years later to the day, Grandpa took the family for a celebratory drive.

Baby Fronty died on September 6, 1926.

It was my grandma's forty-fifth birthday.

It was Fronty's second birthday.

My mother's birthday fell days later, on the last day of September.

Year after year, how could it ever have been a happy day for any of them?

My grandmother never forgave my grandfather. In full karmic circle, some forty years later, Grandpa Stobie died when a wound he'd received in a car accident turned septic. Put all that poison and loss in a novel, no one would believe it. In real life, it kept bleeding.

My mother kept one memento from that childhood: a china doll, clad in Fronty's christening dress, painted lips smiling but cracked in the head. She never said it, but I believe it: two babies died that day. Neither mother could hold on to them. I once overheard my mother telling a friend that she believed her mother would have preferred it if Fronty had lived and she, the expendable second daughter, had died.

My mother and her mother never bonded. Personal history, and their moment in history, both worked against them.

My grandma, born in 1881, wouldn't let my mother ride a bike because it was unladylike. She couldn't attend university for the same reason. My mother read non-stop and remembered it all. She graduated high school first in her class, won a provincial biology award, and hoped to be a doctor. Instead, she watched her parents pay for her brothers' degrees while she got told to earn her keep. She always denounced her parents' refusal to pay for a daughter's education as old-fashioned and unfair. She let her father off scot-free. She blamed her mother entirely.

I found it hard to believe that her mother and my grandma were the same person.

It is true that my Victorian grandmother valued femininity and decorum. Every strand of her waist-length, iron-grey hair got tightly braided and wound into the bun at the nape of her neck. But, alone with me, she literally let her hair down. She let me brush it, braid it and style it at will. And her closet held magic: scarves, beads, hats with bows and mysterious veils, and a rainbow of soft shirt-dresses with neat pearl buttons. She loved navy blue with swiss dot and tiny floral patterns. They all smelled of lavender. Best of all, she played with me. Festooned in floppy hats and jewelry, we attended the Royal Ascot horse races. We met at Harrods for high tea.

I never tired of bedtime stories from the London of her girlhood, tales that bolstered my love for Sherlock Holmes. She played Watson to my Sherlock. She played Moriarty and Irene Adler. Unlike the cross-dressing Irene, she never wore pants. When I asked why, she shrugged. "Trousers are for men and little circus monkeys. Not that one can always tell the difference."

My mother thought Sherlock Holmes was both silly and for boys.

My mother wallpapered my bedroom with pink ballerinas twirling on pointe shoes.

She thought she was doing a better job than her mother because I owned a bike. When she insisted that I leave my training wheels on, it wasn't out of concern for me. She didn't want neighbours seeing me fall in the street anymore than they already did. I never played in her closet; I'd have been spanked. I did sneak in to stare at her high heels, a precision army ranked by height and colour on three shoe racks, but I never tried them on. A broken ankle I could risk, but if rolling an ankle ruined one of her lovely shoes, I wouldn't sit down for a month.

In retrospect, my mother and hers did have one thing in common: the ultra-feminine face they showed the world. They kept their upper lips stiff and impeccably lipsticked. Maintained decorum, no matter the cost. My immigrant grandfather, whose father dug coal in Scotland, did very well with a company that became CIL. After Fronty's death, the Depression took every dime. The grieving Stobie family left a home overlooking Grenadier Pond in High Park for a tiny house in Swansea. Mother went from having a tailor to mending her sister's off-the-rack hand-me-downs. When loss is your leitmotif, you overcompensate, you cling to what remains.

Today, we'd call my grandparents hoarders.

Back then, we called them Scottish.

Jammed from floor to ceiling, my grandparents' Port Credit basement held every jar, egg carton, bit of string, bread bag, elastic band and *National Geographic* they had ever owned. Everyone kept tinfoil during the war; they kept keeping it, in a giant ball approaching the size of a Volkswagen. This penny-pinching, Scottish girlhood did not prepare my mother for the throwaway, rule-breaking 1960s. When I asked about my adoption, she did what her mother had done: she shut down. She only once admitted why. She'd been told by a well-meaning Children's Aid worker that if she did a good job as a mother, I wouldn't ask any questions. She saw my questions as proof of her failure and responded with her mother's retreat.

Then she regifted me with the worst wound of her childhood: the loss of a beloved baby sibling. When my mother gave up baby Judith, was it like losing baby Fronty all over again? Did she feel guilty about haunting my childhood with the ghost that ruined hers?

I'll never know. I do know when I lost my mother, I found hers.

Perhaps Grandma Stobie embraced her less-loved daughter's less-loved daughter to heal us both. She stepped up when she saw my mother favouring her own babies, repeating her own mother wound and distancing herself from me. When Grandma met me, I was a few months older than Fronty when he died. Perhaps she saw a baby returned. She showered me with all the affection she never showed my mother. They could barely look at each other, but Grandma couldn't get enough of me. I often stayed the weekend, baking, sewing, skipping up to Woolworth's lunch counter at Dixie Mall for grilled cheese sandwiches with extra dill pickles. I knew she loved me best of all. I had the most presents under her tree. All my cousins, aunts and uncles said it: "Dorothy is Grandma's favourite."

As I near the age she was during those fondly remembered Christmases, I realize this: Grandma didn't drive. To shop for presents, my mother had to drive her. I like to imagine them chatting over tea and crumpets in Eaton's, discussing a Chatty Cathy doll and a dollhouse.

Someone bought both, meaning the Christmas generosity I always attributed to my grandmother belongs in part to my mother. The older I get, the more I believe this: most people – even your parents – do the best they can, most of the time.

Of course, none of that helped a limping eight-year-old in 1963.

I kept falling. On grass. On gravel. On sidewalks. On nothing. On each and every day. And the more my mother darned, the more she stitched in silence. The more I fell, the more I felt her disappointment. Her silence didn't silence my fears. It made me furtive. As I lost my mother, I shifted my need for her to a mystery woman – my birth mother. I knew I began with shameful secrets. I knew her story and mine began with papers kept under lock and key.

So, I resolved to read them.

Beginning with Bible and Bastard

In the darkest depths of her underwear drawer, my mother kept a lacy scarlet girdle, garnished with naughty black ribbons. I hope she wore it, but suspect she never did. My Sherlock sleuthing revealed what it did contain: the key to her desk. In 1964, at age nine, I found my *Non-Identifying Information* from the Toronto Children's Aid:

You were born on June 23, 1955, at St. Michael's Hospital, in Toronto, time of birth, unknown. Your birth weight was most likely 7 lbs. (although also on record is another document listing your birth weight as 5.5 lbs.). You went directly from hospital to a private foster home which had been recommended to your natural mother by a public health nurse. In August of 1955, you came into the care of the Children's Aid society. You were placed in one of our foster homes. The following November you were rushed to the Hospital for Sick Children with acute bronchitis. You were discharged from hospital in December and placed in a third foster home.

(There is no explanation as to why you could not return to your previous foster home.)

A month later your foster mother had to request your removal as her children had been injured in a car accident and needed all her attention.

You were moved to a fourth foster home but in April 1956 again went to the hospital for investigation of fibrocystic disease. After a week there you went to Thistletown Hospital, a convalescent centre. You were discharged to a fifth foster home in May 1956. The following October you were readmitted for further tests for fibrocystic disease as the April tests were incomplete. All tests proved negative and in November you were returned to your foster home. Eventually, you were placed for adoption.

Your natural mother is described as in her mid-twenties, of medium height with a slender build, hazel eyes, a fair, freckled complexion and straight brown hair. Her worker found her to be a very tense, anxious person who found it difficult to make deep and satisfying relationships with people, although she could get along on a superficial level with business associates. She found it extremely difficult to discuss her present situation or even acknowledge that she was pregnant. Her manner of speech and action was very thoughtful and pronounced. She enjoyed debating and public speaking as well as more domestic pursuits such as crocheting, sewing, reading and some bowling.

She began school at five and completed Grade 11 at age sixteen, followed by a year's commercial training. She was a bright student in the top half of her class all through school. She was a conforming child who tried hard to please but did not take part in extracurricular activities. After leaving school she worked as a stenographer. A routine psychological testing showed her to be of bright-normal intelligence. Her physical health was good but since high school she had experienced serious emotional difficulties resulting in depression and insomnia.

She was the eldest of two children whose parents separated when she was a young child.

Her mother is of Scottish origin, but born in Canada. She had a Grade 8 education plus one year of normal school and taught school at one time. She was interested in keeping up her home and also did excellent painting. She is described as tall with auburn hair. She suffered from nerves and is described as a tense, unhappy woman who placed a great deal of responsibility on her eldest daughter. She dominated your natural mother who spent her life trying to make up to her mother for the father leaving the home. Your natural mother did not know much about her father except that he was born in Canada of Scottish descent and was a farmer. He died after the family separated. The cause of his death is not known. Your mother's sister is said to have had excellent health and enjoyed hunting, painting, basketball and swimming. An outgoing, carefree girl who was happily married.

Your natural mother came to the Children's Aid a few months prior to your birth. She explained she was pregnant by a man whom she had dated a few times but could not remember anything about the circumstances leading to the pregnancy. She had been hospitalized for depression and insomnia and received numerous shock treatments which affected her memory. Since then she had met and married another man. Her husband knew of the pregnancy and they had married earlier than planned on the condition that she place you for adoption. The husband felt he could not accept another man's child and that it would place too great a strain on the marriage. The Society did work with them for several months in an attempt to see if they might reconsider, but it became apparent that your natural mother was very dependent upon her husband and both were becoming increasingly upset at the delay. You were therefore made a Permanent Ward of the Society in January 1956.

The only information concerning your natural father was that he was thought to be employed as a bricklayer. The Society made several attempts to interview him but messages left with his mother were not acknowledged. We do not know if he was aware of the pregnancy. Your mother's husband was of Scottish origin and worked in a bank. He was very protective of your natural mother and anxious to have your future settled so they could begin a new life elsewhere.

A letter is on file from the hospital where your natural mother received therapy, stating that she had recovered when she left and that it was felt her condition would not affect your mental health. From the date of her admission it would appear that she was not pregnant during her hospitalization. On reading the entire record I am left with the impression of a very unhappy, emotionally fragile woman who could not accept the situation in which she found herself and was at the same time trying desperately to protect a new marriage. She felt it would be selfish and unfair to keep you under the circumstances.

There is no possible way I can ever explain to you, to anyone, the Holy Grail Golden Ticket Full House Rummoli Jackpot Lottery New Testament Eureka Final Jeopardy Answer of finding my *Non-Identifying Information*. This was my first real baby picture. Of course, I stole it. It was mine. I also took the medical forms under it. Reports from two stints in the hospital and a convalescent home, Thistledown, where repeated tests for cystic fibrosis came back negative. These reports gave me another treasure, one it was against the law for me to have in 1964.

My birth name: Susan Gail Johnston.

I date the birth of my red-headed anger to that moment.

The thieves in the night took more than my sister. They had stolen my name.

That night, I burned an undercover flashlight until I could recite every word of my story. Once memorized, no one could take it from me. Years later, reading *Fahrenheit 451*, I instantly understood that the only safe place to keep a story is in your head. Especially if it's your story, one you'd been told you had no right to read. At dawn, I hid it again. I'm not the first little girl to know a nail file is also a screwdriver. When you unscrew the round metal cap of the pink roll-up blind in your bedroom it opens to a tube, custom-made to conceal papers rolled-up like a treasure map. A blind your mother touches each morning when she – wait for it – lets in the light.

Mother did not confront me about my theft. Asking about my purposefully purloined papers would mean having to admit they existed. When I discovered she had re-hidden her key somewhere even more private and unfindable than a girdle, I knew she knew my papers were missing. I knew she knew that I knew that she knew. And we both knew we'd say nothing.

I broke that silence only once, that same 1964 summer at the cottage. Truth had a place in the private world of early morning swims with my dad. Awakened by birdsong, we watched the lake shimmer black, indigo, then summer sky blue. We swam at dawn because this was something, the only thing, my father remembered doing with his father.

Back in 1919, a farmer gave my grandfather the Reverend Robert Cecil Palmer a patch of then-worthless land in payment for a summer ministry. Part rock, part swamp, without road or electricity, it sat just off Highway 35 on the eastern shore of Balsam Lake, at the swing bridge in Rosedale. Family lore says that Grandpa built the cottage by hand until August of 1934, when he cemented the last rock in the chimney, stood up, keeled over and died. My dad was eleven.

In the Great Depression, my father lost his father, his home and his childhood. Forced to leave her comfortable Rosedale, Toronto, home for the only job anyone would give a widow with four young children, Grandma Palmer ran a logging camp boarding house up north in Timmins. All the kids had to work. My minister grandfather graduated magna cum laude from Cambridge; my father had to leave school at twelve. Dad spoke of this only once. When I graduated high school, he told me his one regret in life was that he couldn't pass the basic reading test to qualify for the Servicemen's Readjustment Act of 1944. Known as the GI Bill, it provided benefits to World War II vets, including free university tuition. He wanted to be a psychologist, wanted to know "what made people tick." With no father and no education, everything my dad knew about being a dad, he had to teach himself.

We swam at dawn to remember his dad.

We swam because Mother did not.

The more the cottage receded, the more we relaxed. When your feet are under water, you look like any other girl. The lake welcomes you every morning, just as you are, without pity or judgment. The lake does what parents are supposed to do: it holds you up. Warm, playful, safe. Waves lap over you like rolling hugs and kisses.

"Are you tired yet, Pooch?"

"No, Daddy. Just a little longer please."

We were finally far enough away that all we could hear were the loons. No wailing infant. No whining three-year-old still pretending to be my sister. When I tired and went under, his large, sure hand plunged down and pulled me up. I clung to his neck as he swam for home. He could help me, I could accept it, because it was private between us.

"Tell me again why you picked me."

He laughed. Loved telling this story. "Because you had red hair, just like mine. Because I figured that when I went bald, you would give me some of yours to glue onto my head."

"Daddy, do you ever wonder about my other mommy and daddy?"

In his pause, I hear pain, but no accusation. In his answer there is courage.

"No, Pooch, I don't. But I take it you do?"

"Sometimes. I wonder why they didn't want me?"

"Well, troubles happen. Your mother and I, we wanted you very much."

Truth blurts out before I can stop it. "Not as much as she wants her own babies."

My father pulled me around in front of him. He cradled my chin to keep me afloat.

"Look at me, Dorothy. The day we got you was the happiest day of my life. Nothing. Nothing in this world will ever beat the day you came into my life and made me your dad. That's how it was and always will be. I promise you that, Pooch. Forever and for always."

For that, I'm forever thankful. Of course, it also meant I couldn't ever ask him about my adoption again without feeling like an ungrateful brat. But at least he didn't lie. He didn't try to claim I made my mother's happiest day by peeing on her carpet.

In self-consolation, I gave my *Non-Identifying Information* a nickname: my NII. It became my first script. I whispered it on my knees when I pretended to be praying. At the cottage, I'd climb the balsam tree that was my cousins' tree house and declaim to the wind. I microanalyzed each word, comma and period. I saw my NII – likely written in haste by an overworked clerk with a grade ten diploma – as Holy Writ. Invoking The Sacred Script of the Real Me, word by word, I laboured until I gave secret, hidden birth to my natural self. It was not an easy delivery; I was doubly defective, both lame and a bastard. But at least this little girl had a real mother. A woman who liked public speaking, handicrafts and bowling. Just in case I might someday get to meet her, using my script, I began rehearsing to be her daughter.

I ransacked Peggy Palmer's library, memorizing everything I thought would make me a good public speaker. I began with her huge *Reader's Digest Book Club Book of Modern Poetry*. Should you ever need a rousing rendition of "Evangeline," or "The Cremation of Sam McGee," I'm your girl. I memorized long passages of my first bible, *Little Women*, my scripture of hope that somewhere out there, mothers loved their daughters and sisters loved each other. In Louisa May Alcott's honour, I added passages from her neighbour Thoreau's account of Walden Pond. I can still spout whole speeches from Lincoln, Churchill and JFK. Every birthday, I begged my parents to go bowling, a sport like all others, at which I proved an abject failure. All balls aimed straight for the gutter. But I didn't care.

I memorized the face of every woman there.

I knew I lived without my real mother because it was my fault and His will. Preteen me took The Lord Thy God seriously. I was a minister's granddaughter. At the cottage, I attended St. John's Anglican, his tiny, white, wooden church, where he was the sole sleeper buried behind it. In Toronto, I visited Alderwood United three times a week: Tuesday for Explorers, Thursday for choir practice, then Sunday school and the service. Longing to be good and do good, I took the Explorers' motto, "Be doers of the word, and not hearers only," very much to heart.

When I graduated from Explorers to Canadian Girls in Training, Mother said it sounded like a bunch of prison inmates and complained that dues raised from a dime to a quarter was "good money wasted." Incarcerating girls, or at least this redhead, was a running "joke" in my family. Our cottage drive took us past the "Home for Bad Girls" in Lindsay. Without fail, my mother kindly offered to drop me off. It's little wonder that in Explorers and CGIT, I earned every star for good effort and behaviour. I sang every hymn by heart, with my whole heart.

My mother loved to sing, but she never heard me sing. Each Sunday, she stayed home with her children. My dad attended my every performance, singing tunelessly at full volume, loud and proud in the very first pew. But despite his encouragement and my constant exposure, I never caught the Jesus bug. I blame it on the "Suffer little children" line. What kind of saviour wants kids to suffer? I did like the bit where Mary Magdalene washed his feet with her hair. Knowing nothing of harlot symbolism, I loved the painting where she brandished a giant blaze of red hair. Best of all, I loved Jesus' bent feet. I gazed up from the choir loft, enjoying the twisted, turned-in way they got nailed to the cross. His feet looked like mine. I'd wonder, secretly hope, that God gave his son deformed feet. Just maybe, Jesus said, "Suffer little children to come unto me," because he knew suffering. Because he loved children who suffer. Children like me.

But, beyond that secret affinity, quite likely precisely because I had to keep that affinity a secret, I couldn't embrace the Son of God. I was way too afraid of his father. Jesus may have gallivanted around Galilee healing the blind and the lame, but a vengeful Jehovah kept making more of us. I saw my feet as His punishment. When my pious Aunt Muriel gave me a Bible with a concordance, where I could research words like *disabled* and *bastard*, my preteen mind leapt from NII to Holy Writ in the most self-condemnatory misinterpretations possible.

Like the Gospels of Matthew, Mark, Luke and John, I thought each book bore the name of its blessed male author. I figured some of these guys wouldn't be much fun at a bowling party. When Leviticus 21:17 ruled that none of the "generations that hath any blemish" could "approach to offer the bread of his God," I knew he didn't mean pimples. He kindly listed which blemished people would defile the altar: "a blind man, or a lame, or he that hath a flat nose . . . or a man that is brokenfooted, or brokenhanded, or crookbackt, or a dwarf, or that hath a blemish in his eye, or be scurvy, or scabbed, or hath his stones broken."

I spent days ruminating on these mysteries. Assuming I could still walk in my twenties, assuming some man might want to marry me, I concluded broken-footed me couldn't walk down the aisle with my dad because I'd defile the altar. Maybe I could get married in the church basement? It would be a shorter walk. Refreshments would be handy. While I resented being cast out to consort with scurvy dwarves, given my knees, I reluctantly accepted kinship with the scabbed. But I had no idea how broken stones figured into it. You're in the bloody desert. Why the devil couldn't you just reach down and pick up some unbroken ones?

But it was no joke when I got banned from heaven.

In 23:2, Deuteronomy declared, "A bastard shall not enter into the congregation of the Lord, even to his tenth generation." Each time I did the math, I got the same answer. Some future relative, some two hundred years after my death, might enter the pearly gates, but none of their family would be waiting. As for the issue of a tainted womb, I could accept my damnation. But it seemed a tad uncharitable to condemn all my unborn babies' unborn babies, up to my great-great-great-great-great-great-great-grandchildren. Why did a supposedly loving God ban all of us from heaven for what one long-dead woman had done?

A woman none of us had ever met. But who was I to judge?

Sunday school logic said my birth mother was "a bad girl."

A fallen woman with a daughter who kept falling.

In one of my many dreams about her, she won a beauty pageant with a red silk banner gracing her breasts, "Miss Toronto Whore of

Babylon, 1954." I knew her sin made me an abomination, made me as bad as she was. Maybe worse. Because even she didn't want me. Because of my feet. They were my bastard blemish, my mark of Cain, the reason her new husband couldn't accept me. If I'd been born normal, she would have kept me.

If I'd been born normal, I'd be good enough to be loved by my own mother.

Of course, when you and I read this today, it's heart-rending nonsense. It only makes sense if you're a child with no one to ask, and that was me. Grandma Stobie and I could discuss everything but one: my adoption. I liked my Alderwood United minister, the Reverend Warren, but confiding in him would have been unspeakably selfish. He had a beautifully frail wife, a woman so timid I never heard her speak. She had spaceship blue eyes and white blonde hair the ethereal consistency of milkweed. Together, they had a young son with what my mother called "a devastating dwarfish deformity." I'll admit it, I've inherited two things from her: a profoundly puerile penchant for triple alliteration and a tendency to be just a jot judgmental.

Beyond my mirror, Billy was the first disabled child, the first disabled body, I'd ever seen. The medical term for his disability is *osteogenesis imperfecta*, a genetic disorder meaning "imperfectly formed bones." I couldn't bring myself to look at him; I had to force myself not to stare. He was maybe two feet long. I'm not sure how old he was. I have no idea if he went to school – it never occurred to me to ask. I didn't see another kid; I saw a freak. Stumpy. Barrel-chested. Compacted. As if the Jolly Green Giant had crushed him like a pop can. The whites of his eyes, a telltale blue, made him as scary as the alien kids in *Village of the Damned*.

I needed him to stay alien, so no one would guess I was like him.

I wanted to grow up and I knew he wouldn't.

Billy had to remain a baby. In the early 1960s, there either were no adapted wheelchairs or the Warrens couldn't afford one. In summer, they pulled Billy in a little red wagon, a step up from the baby carriage they used in winter. In the only moments he got to be a real live boy, on the flat terrazzo floor of the church, Billy pushed his tiny, wheezing body around on a skateboard. Lying chest down, he could use his palms to propel himself along. You'd hear him before you'd see him; his whirling wheels slid right underneath the pews. He didn't fall off the skateboard only by virtue of being strapped to it with one of his reverend father's leather belts. I'd see him cinched in to save his little life and think, "There but for the grace of God go I."

One of my Sunday school teachers kindly explained that grace: "In the olden days, an abomination like Billy would be killed at birth as the devil's spawn. Or his parents would sell him to the circus, where people would pay a penny to stare at him." She shrugged. "At least he'd eat; he'd earn his keep." She smiled. "For centuries, having a deformed child would have disqualified a man as a minister. Today, our minister thrives, despite his burden. Praise God."

I told myself I was a cut above other kids because I never called Billy names, not even behind his back. In the suburbs of the '60s, we had endless slurs available. In insult and in casual conversation, they hit me like snakebites. I didn't feel them individually; I absorbed the full weight of their venom collectively. I lay awake at night squeezing their poison back out of me in an order of my choosing, alphabetizing every nasty one: abnormal, batty, birdbrain, boot-baby, crackpot, crazy, cretin, cripple, cuckoo, daft, defective, deformed, deranged, dimwit, dolt, dunce, dummy, eejit, feeble-minded, four-eyes, freak, fruitcake, gimp, harelip, hysteric, imbecile, idiot, invalid, jerky-turkey, KO'ed, lameo, limpy-gimpy, looney, lunatic, maniac, mental, midget, mongoloid, moron, nitwit, nuts, nutbar, oaf, pea brain, poo brain, psycho, queer, retard, schizoid, simpleton, slow, spaz, stupid, tard, village idiot, whacko, wingnut, yob, yutz and ziotard.

But I wasn't innocent. Some of these words came out of my mouth. I used them to side with abled people, to keep them from being used on me. But I never used the word *bastard*. It hurt me every time, and I heard it non-stop. "Silly bastard," "dumb bastard," "bloody bastard" and "you cheeky little bastard" flew daily from the potty mouths of my British family, adults who also affectionately called their children "stupid little buggers." I told myself it was normal. I didn't understand it as I do now: it's a hammer of rape culture. A bastard is a child of an unwed mother. We have no term, let alone slur, for an unwed father. Unwed fathers get off scot-free.

I never threw stones at Billy, but the words hurled by the world hurt us both.

I never made the sign of the evil eye, like I saw older Italian women do when they saw the Warrens in the street. I simply avoided the skateboard. If Billy rolled my way, I ran away. On Sundays, I watched Reverend Warren preach "God's healing love," certain that deep in his soul he knew himself to be a liar. I pitied him for having to raise Billy, for having to be seen with Billy. I figured if you had a son like Billy, you sure didn't want to talk to any stupid, selfish, whining little brat of a girl who could stand up from your ministering and walk herself home.

The God that damned both Billy and me as unholy burdens banged the final, finishing nails into my closet. Shame, spun as finely as Mrs. Warren's hair, sealed any and every crack.

Concerning Crinolines, Crutches and Castings

In 1962, I entered an experimental enrichment class that asked a progressive question: What happens to working-class/lower-middle-class kids who accelerate, take grades three, four and five in two years? I know what happened to me: I got sick. Colds, relentless stomach flu and a life-threatening bout of pleurisy: an infection of the lining of the lungs. I remember waiting for the ambulance while laid out on three kitchen chairs, thinking, "But I don't want to die under an umbrella with a Vicks vaporizer blowing in my face."

My left lung never fully re-inflated. I still wheeze. When Dr. Ridley ordered exercise, I happily went swimming. When I got repeated ear infections, Mother used peroxide. Scar tissue and a virus eventually led to a full loss of hearing in my left ear. That felt normal. Everything on my left side is weaker: my left foot, lung, ear and eye. The fingernails on my left hand are smaller. When I learned that *left* in Latin means *sinister,* dirty and evil, coming from *the bar sinister* in heraldry, a bar slanting to the left-hand side of a coat of arms which denotes – you guessed it – bastardy, it all made a perfectly sick sense to me.

After the birth of their daughter, my parents informed me they were "sending me to a specialist." I heard, "to the slaughterhouse." In truth, I don't know why they waited so long. My feet had stopped growing: one just over, one just under eight inches. At the cottage on the dock, a poetic cousin kindly called them "pink Plasticine blobs with tacked-on raisin toes."

In equal kindness, my mother gave me the news while breastfeeding her daughter.

"Don't worry. We'll do whatever can reasonably be done to fix you."

My biggest concern wasn't being fixed – the dog and I had little expectation of that. I feared that the good Dr. Ridley might mention my feet to his five lovely daughters, all of whom played high-status roles at CGIT. I watched them carefully for weeks before I concluded they were not a pack of she-wolves sniffing in my direction. But mean girls weren't the only things that could kill me. Whenever I think about my childhood X-rays, I'm thankful to be alive.

In 1963, X-ray machines beamed like lighthouses and growled like rusty lawn mowers. Today, X-rays are instant. Back then, you had to hold still as sickly blue-green light seeped up your body, glowering around the room. I told myself that at least the glowing light was blue, not green like the kryptonite that killed even Superman. Today, you get a lead pad to shield you from scatter. In 1963, naked me got multiple shots per foot, per visit. I got yelled at for not staying still long enough while the technician hid behind an iron wall with a little window like a submarine. I had over sixty childhood exposures to radiation, and can't count the number since.

For each film shoot, mother and I took a bus and a subway to the old Medical Arts Building at Bloor and St. George, today the University of Toronto Jackman Humanities Building. Mother began each trip smoothing her second-best white gloves, reminding me that ninety minutes in transit was an inconvenient expense. If she was in a good mood, we'd play *Jeopardy*. When she watched it on TV, she played along and aloud. I thought every mother could get every answer right. For nine years, en route to appointments, we played our own version, creating categories and answering in the form of a question. Rather than speak to each other, we spoke to a host who wasn't there. In my youth it was Art Fleming, but the host in my head will always be his successor, He Who Made Smart Sexy, the Game Show Mustachioed Greek God: Alex Trebek.

"I'll take *Knitting and Purling* for ten dollars, Alex."

"Okay, Alex. Can I have *Towns on the Way to the Cottage* for fifty dollars, please?"

When my mother was in a bad mood, it would have been real jeopardy to open my mouth, but when we arrived, electromagnetic radiation wouldn't melt in hers. She always told the receptionist the same thing: "A long trip downtown is well worth it to fix my little girl."

On my first visit, when I pulled off my socks, the X-ray technician gasped.

He didn't see a frightened child. He saw a bratty child actress refusing to cooperate in her close-ups. As if a job with Alfred Hitchcock depended on it, he began shooting my feet as directed. I aced the first pose, pressing my feet flat on the tacky black plates. I managed the second, arches up, after four retakes and what he called "snivelling." With each repositioning, he took longer to stroll into his protected room and push the button. By the third pose, I was sweating, nauseous with pain. My sweaty feet kept sliding off the X-ray plate.

He threw my socks at me and sneered. "Wipe your little piggy hooves dry."

He began twisting my feet, arches down on the plate. It wasn't that I was too tired or in too much pain to do it. My bones couldn't do it. Full weight, he forced me down.

When I screamed, mother rushed in, took one look and slapped my hand. "For goodness sake, Dorothy! Stop the caterwauling. Do you want people to think you were you born in a barn? Apologize. Now. He's a professional. He's only doing his job."

In the name of science, my mother held me down.

White gloves leave purple bruises.

I didn't want to meet a specialist with a sadist for a sidekick. I had no idea he'd be the first, first-best thing about me. Dr. Robert Bruce Salter, CC, OOnt, FRSC, FRHSC, was not only an impressive possessor of titular alphabet soup, he was Head Orthopedic Surgeon and Surgeon in Chief of Sick Children's Hospital, and the world's foremost inventor of surgical techniques to correct rare birth defects like mine. In 1969, he won the medical Nobel Prize: the Gairdner Foundation Award for Medical Science. He was inducted into the Order of Ontario, the Order of Canada and the Canadian Medical Hall of Fame. The first time I saw him, I gasped. Tall and bespectacled would be kind. Nerdy and Lurch-like was more accurate.

And I loved him. Some people are born to work with children. They relate to kids without artifice, with a relaxed grace and warm sincerity. As respectful as Mary Magdalene, Dr. Salter always asked permission to touch my feet. I was his priority. Mother's questions were tolerated; mine mattered. When she answered for me, he'd say, "Okay, Dorothy, let's hear the expert opinion." He was the first man, the first human being, I trusted to tell me the whole truth.

On my first visit, in sugar-white gloves, my mother held her own hands. Dr. Salter put my X-rays up on his giant light board and smiled. "Dorothy, here are your extraordinary feet. Please let me introduce them to you."

Patiently, slowly, with the detailed thoroughness of an anatomy class, he taught me the names of my bones, explaining the ones I had that everyone had, the ones I didn't have and the ones I had that no one on the planet had. I see it still: red cap on blue pen, tapping grey bones.

"A normal human foot has twenty-six bones: seven tarsals or ankle bones, five metatarsals or foot bones, and fourteen phalanges or toes. Dorothy, your left foot has three tarsals, three metatarsals and two fused bones unique to you. Your right foot has three tarsals, three metatarsals and three fused bones. Your tiny toes have two bones each. So, instead of twenty-six bones each, your left foot has eighteen and your right has nineteen. Your muscles and ligaments are likewise unique. They pull your feet over, like permanently twisted ankles."

Mother twitched. "That's exactly what I was afraid of. She has clubbed feet."

Dr. Salter looked only at me. "No, Dorothy, you don't. A clubbed foot can't place itself flat on the ground. With effort, with considerable pain, you can force your feet down. One in a thousand babies have clubfoot. Your birth defects are more complex and much rarer."

He pulled my X-rays from the screen then moved to sit beside me.

"Here's the skivvy, Princess. I don't know how many years you'll walk for. Maybe into your thirties or forties. That's up to your feet, not to you or to me." Still smiling, he patted my hand. "But we can be hopeful on three fronts: I can reduce your pain. I can improve your stability. You will walk better for longer. But to do that, you'll need an operation. Several, in fact. And understand this, Princess. It's experimental. There are no guarantees."

When you're a kid, once you hear the word *operation*, it doesn't matter what gets said next. All following words buzz in an incomprehensibly foreign language. I vaguely recall him defining a triple arthrodesis as a procedure fusing three joints. When he calmly announced I'd need an operation every two years, when he began detailing removable metal pins and implanted staples, I had two choices: tune out or barf. I retreated. Built a chant in my head: "Knifed at nine. Severed at eleven. Thwacked at thirteen. Filleted at fifteen. Slit at seventeen." I squinted at his homely, old face. Would he live long enough to do all this slicing and dicing, or die when I was only half cut? I tuned back in long enough to wish I hadn't.

"I'll begin with the left foot. It's the weakest. I'll try to make it last the longest. Cut apart the fused bones to improve range of motion, install staples for pain reduction and stability. File abutting bones so they can articulate more like the joints of a normal foot."

Articulate? A crazy man wants to cut me open.

A man who thinks feet can talk.

My mother took this lunacy straight in her chair, poised, attentive, accepting.

"She didn't walk when we got her. They called it 'failure to thrive.' Said she might be retarded. She falls so much, it's embarrassing. After all your work, will she pass for normal?"

As Dr. Salter stacked my X-rays, one trembled. Like a bone-grey dove, it fluttered from his hands. I offered it back to him and he answered my mother while smiling at me.

"Your daughter's feet, Mrs. Palmer, have virtually no cartilage."

I knew that word from Health Class. "Like in the rim of our ears?"

"Yes, Princess. Connective tissue, like gristle. Between joints, cartilage acts as a shock absorber. It cushions impact. You limp because, without it, every movement registers as pain."

"Is that why she's always complaining that her feet hurt?"

For the first time, Doctor Salter looked directly at the very pretty Peggy Palmer.

"Your daughter is in pain. All the time. Sitting or standing. Worse when walking. Unbearable by nighttime. I can insert metal staples as shock absorbers. I can prescribe medication. But imagine this." He pushed his knuckles together, grated them hard. "These are her bones. Without cartilage, they're grinding themselves into splinters."

My mother averted her gaze. He dropped his hands and reached for mine. "So you didn't walk until three. So you limp and fall down. So what? You know what, Princess? None of that matters. The longer I'm in this business the more impressed I am by kids like you. I'm very proud of you, Dorothy. I don't know how you walk at all."

Facing my mother, he waited. When she said nothing, he tugged on my braid; he winked.

All the pieces of my life flew together. I wasn't a lazy, lying, clumsy excuse for girl. It hurt. He said so. The sanest man in the world. He could cut me anywhere he wanted.

My mother made the sound in her throat reserved for my brother when he picked his nose. "Excuse me," she said, "I'm wondering about high heels?"

It was only a flash, but I saw it: the disgust on my good doctor's face. It marked the moment when it first occurred to me that my mother might not be the Anointed Arbiter of All Things. Maybe, just maybe, sometimes, she might even be wrong.

For years, I believe I'm the only one he called Princess.

His lovely, ugly face was the last thing I saw before anaesthetic. "Sleep safe, Princess." And the first sight fighting the fog? His high-ridged forehead like Roddy McDowall in *Planet of the Apes*. "Rise and shine, Princess."

In my first recovery room, I'm reported to have said my foot had a toothache. I don't believe it. I think mother made it up to make cutting me cute. To trivialize it. To reassure herself. To make it easier for her to bear. There's no comparison. A toothache stops hurting. My feet kept hurting long after they were drilled. I remember that first awakening, pulled from sleep to the screams of my now articulate left foot. For those of you who may have been wondering, no, I did not name my feet. Their names are no cutesy attempt to domesticate pain, to create a pair of pets.

As soon as they could articulate, my feet self-identified; they chose their own names.

Herkimer whimpered for two days before saying anything intelligible. I'm sure he picked the most prissy, persnickety name he could find. He loved referring to himself in third person, a self-pitying tactic I immediately recognized years later in Harry Potter's Dobby the house-elf: "Poor Herkimer. He doesn't like the nasty stairs. Herkimer needs to sit down. Or he will fall down." Horatio took his name from a book Grandma Stobie gave me about Horatio Nelson, a much-injured British Navy captain who bravely fought sea battles, despite suffering lifelong seasickness. Since articulation, Horatio and Herkimer have battled about where to go, how to go, if they agree to go and who goes first. Their bickering dialogue scripted the medical theatre that ran in reruns every two years: Surgery. A cast for six weeks. A walking cast for six more weeks. Physiotherapy for six months. Walk on. Then trash that script, recut its subject and repeat.

All three of us hated being cast in casts.

A cast itches like red ants on steroids.

It makes its own cheese: creamy goo you can see down the sides but can't reach to wash. It stinks, even if you're like me and have little sense of smell. By six weeks, a cast is a chemical weapon lugged around by crutches. Only my mother saw a bright side: with one foot in a cast, she had to buy only one pair of shoes. Casts had no silver linings for me. Putting my full weight on one foot made me want to chop them both off. With each operation, it grew harder to shut out Herkimer and Horatio's endless prattle, each trying to convince the other to do what he so obdurately did not want to do: hold me up to swing my crutches while his partner lay idle.

A walking cast improved neither their bickering nor the production of stinky cheese.

For the next six weeks, the newly cast foot complained that being forced to walk again was too soon and too cruel. The foot that had been waiting for its partner to pull its own weight belittled the other for malingering. This split me clean in two. I couldn't help Herkimer without hurting Horatio, and vice versa. When my walking casts came off, my feet emerged as scarred, mushroomy versions of their former selves. Then the real production began. Learning to re-articulate, to renegotiate the act of walking, took a year each time to get script agreement in triplicate. All three of us wanted to put words in the other's mouths and direct the show.

As for those high heels my mother asked about? The only shoes that ever graced her feet?

The only high heels I've ever worn don't come in pairs; they're the single, stumpy rubber plugs on my walking casts. The first one I wore did serious damage. Sick Kids is a teaching hospital, but the supervising technician had his eyes glued on the attending nurse. His trainee, who had more zits than all my teenage cousins combined, saw cast replacement as a race he must win. He slashed my old cast with a zippy electric pizza wheel, then cracked it open with a giant set of salad tongs. He told me to look away; I didn't. Chucks of old scab and flesh went flying as he yanked out my metal stitches with pliers. I knew Dr. Salter had implanted my first stabilizing rod, but I was unprepared to see it jutting out of my tender pink heel like the Last Spike of the Canadian Pacific Railway. A spike hammered halfway in.

It wouldn't get pulled out for another six weeks, when my walking cast came off.

The trainee covered my scar with breathable dressing, wrapped my foot and leg with flannel, and set a thin pad of gauze under the rod in my heel. I remember wondering if there was enough padding under that poked-out rod, but I said nothing. What did I know? Still in racing mode, he popped a sterile rubber cap over the rod and quickly wrapped warm, wet plaster of Paris over the cap, around my foot and up my calf. He attached my ugly, one-inch high heel, punched my shoulder and proclaimed, "Arrrrg, Matey! Now you're a Peg-Leg Pirate for sure!"

"I'll take *The First Time I Nearly Punched an Adult Back* for one hundred, Alex."

Boys were pirates; I was a girl. I wanted pretty party shoes.

I already had a peg leg.

His plastering skills proved as flimsy as his "joke"; his cast lasted two weeks. I couldn't figure out why it hurt so much. Mother told me to stop being a baby. Then a squishy pink spot appeared on the back of my heel, began melting the plaster from the inside out. It took another week of my parents staring at the growing stain to be convinced: yes, it was blood, and no, I wasn't making it up for attention. At further expense and inconvenience, we travelled back to Sick Kids. Not only had the intern failed to properly pad my heel, he hadn't made the hole around my stabilizing rod big enough. When I put weight on my foot, the metal rod had hit the hard plaster edge of the hole. The supervisor watched the recasting, but didn't apologize.

Even in the new cast, Herkimer kept insisting that, like the final sword thrust at Jesus, the metal rod was impaling him. And he was right. Six weeks later, when it came time to remove the cast, they discovered why I was in pain. Pressing the hard edge of the first, misapplied cast, the rod had bent inside my foot. The two weeks I'd walked on it had put so much pressure on the tiny hole drilled through my bone that the bone cracked.

It took three men to hold down a nine-year-old girl.

They got the bent rod out, but then had to operate to repair the damage. Six months of physio got Herkimer and Horatio to cooperate on stairs without throwing a tantrum and dumping me down them. We developed a complex telepathic code, ranking each step on the pain scale I learned in physio. Like chess, I taught myself to make a move, while plotting two moves ahead. My feet became my bosses. My terrorists. My sulky children. This is how we negotiate stairs.

ME: Okay, boys, we're at the top of seven stairs. No treads. One railing. On the left.

HORATIO: I always take the first step. Make Herkimer do it this time.

HERKIMER: Herkimer did it once. Herkimer hated it. Herkimer won't do it again.

ME: Grasp railing. Lean on Herkimer. Lift Horatio. Force him down.

HERKIMER: Pain: lateral edge. Scale: 6/10.

HORATIO: Pain: tarsal articulation. Scale: 8/10.

ME: Confirm balance. Lift Herk. Bend Horatio's knee. Aim. Set teeth. Drop. Breathe.

HORATIO: I can do six more, if you go slowly.

Me: C'mon feet, don't fail me now. It's only the second step.
Herkimer: Herkimer says sit down. Or he'll make us all fall down.

But after learning to walk again, I didn't get party shoes. I didn't even get girls' shoes. In the mid-1960s, white canvas tennis shoes, made dazzlingly so by daily liquid shoe polish, were the height of tween fashion. To church and parties, we wore white patent leather, embellished with bows and rhinestones. What did I get? Gimp shoes. Heavy black leather. Not shiny. Not pointed-toed. Thick black laces. Fat flat heels. Boys' orthopedic Oxfords. Ugly as sin.

To prevent my feet from rolling, orthotic inserts were out of the question. Herkimer and Horatio need all the room in a shoe they can get. One of the fleet of international groupies shadowing Dr. Salter said, "Let's build up the outside instead." My already ugly Oxfords got sent to a freak factory that kindly added a wedge of fibreglass. Like water wings for a girl who can't tread land, they jutted out a full inch down the side of my shoe, from baby toe to heel. On black shoes, my new gimp wings were red. Of course they were. I cried until I couldn't.

Windy Hillcrest said I couldn't come to her party because of my shoes.

My mother said they looked like bleeding caskets.

After one look at my shoes, my grandmother announced that they simply would not stand. When she learned that Fosters, the orthopedic shoe store that sold my Oxfords, also sold custom-made dress shoes, we rode three buses there and back, enjoying every second.

We told no one until the magic slippers were safely on this Dorothy's feet.

When my mother accused her mother of spoiling me rotten, Grandma snorted.

"Peggy, go home and count your high heels. If you have under twenty pairs, I'll eat this child's second pair of shoes with a knife and fork." When Mother protested the cost, Grandma shrugged. "I'm not sorry. You should be. You can't take them back. I'm keeping the bill."

I slept with my slippers under my pillow until I believed I'd get to keep them.

On party days, if I strapped them on first thing in the morning, the swelling would be low enough to let me buckle them up. Herkimer and Horatio protested, but the straps held. I knew my shoes looked fat and stumpy compared to the dainty dress shoes of my girlfriends, but for the first time in my life, I could be seen at a party in both a dress and shoes befitting one.

Unfortunately, like Cinderella, I always had to leave early.

These were the first of many shoes that tugged at my scars. Shoes that made me bleed.

The instant my white socks saw red, I made my excuses. Sometimes, girls pointed and giggled. As I limped home, I ate every treat in my grab bag. If I got a little toy, a flower ring that squirted water, or a plastic puzzle game that dropped tiny silver balls into a clown's smiling mouth, I hid it in the sewer to retrieve later, correctly predicting that when Mother saw bloody socks, she'd confiscate my grab bag as penalty for ruining yet another pair. She'd give my candy to her children who didn't cost her a fortune. If I told her there were no grab bags, she'd tell me she didn't believe me and dock my allowance. Frilly white socks joined my leotards in Javex. They stayed stained, soured pink. But blood was a small price to pay to be a girl with friends.

I told myself it could have been worse: at least I wasn't a boy. Girls weren't expected to like sports, let alone play them. I was expected to applaud and cheerlead for every boy I knew. But I didn't have to don smelly jerseys to chase balls large and small, or strap knife blades on my feet to chase a chunk of rubber over the ice with a stick. I took every escape from that sweaty nonsense I could. Girls couldn't wear pants, or shorts, to Sir Adam Beck Public School. We carried our gym shorts back and forth for Girls' Physical Education, which consisted of doing the hokey-pokey and tossing beanbags. When you repeatedly forget your gym shorts, when you hide them in the sewer so that, oh dear, you have to exercise in your crinoline again, you're safe. No one expects you to make any movement that might, heavens no, show your panties.

In my 1960s' suburban girlhood, the divide between boys and girls was ironclad and uncrossable. And I thanked sweet baby Jesus for it. Boys yelled. Boys ran everywhere, all the time. Boys shoved each other to the ground and got up laughing. They tolerated school knowing their real lives took place outside it: playing Red Rover, capture the flag and all-season road hockey. Boys who couldn't participate in the daily rough-and-tumble had nowhere to hide. They had to make the team, or get cut from play. Our homophobia wasn't hidden. A boy interested in music or the arts better keep it to himself, or keep running. At recess, you saw "nancy boys" in only two places: playing with younger girls or alone, pushed up against the chain-link fence with their nose in a book, hoping said book would keep said nose from getting punched. It seldom did.

As a girl, there was less contradiction between my disability and my expected gender role. We ceded the grassy playground without question or loss, spent recess on the small strip of asphalt reserved for us. Thanks to good hand-eye coordination and planted feet, I could hold my own at bouncing a ball tied into a nylon stocking. I could skip double dutch with gritted teeth, each jump a cleaver to my feet. But anything was better than jumpsies – a game that has gone the way of the dodo and Chatty Cathy dolls, and is of no loss to me. Two girls hold a homemade chain of elastic bands, raising it in incremental heights: ankle, kneesies, arm's length, waist, underarm, chinsies, earsies, head and sky high. The trick to jumping over was to catch the chain with one foot and stretch it down, to twist, while twirling your other foot over it.

There was a thin, long-haired blond boy named Barry who never got out, not even at sky high. He could cartwheel without his hands, churning his feet up over all our heads. When he won, he'd blush and giggle. The boys would have nothing to do with him, except to yell, "homo," and beat him up several times a year. In 1963, it would never have crossed my eight-year-old mind that he might be gay or transgender. I'd never heard either word. I thought when the boys yelled, "homo," they meant Barry was like homogenized milk: childish, more a baby than a boy. My girlfriends and I gave him a temporary recess refuge, but we never defended him.

I was often asked to play jumpsies, because I'd get out at kneesies.

To avoid bloody kneesies, I often took myself out, volunteering to hold the end, hoping to go all recess without falling. Horatio rolled more than Herkimer, but they both dumped me onto the same spot: the crests of their own knees. I still have the scars, shiny patches, like palimpsests, like reptilian scales. Mother sighed at new holes in my leotards, ripped darning out and redid it.

"Honestly, Dorothy. I wish I had a nickel for all the times you've made me waste a good hour of my life like this, just because you won't even try to be a more careful girl."

She was wrong. I was ultra-careful. And I was a very, very good girl. I was the kind of girl who came from school to play school. I followed all the don't get dirty, play dolls and tea party, sit still, colour pretty pictures and be quiet, quiet, quiet, rules. Boys did sports; girls did sitting. Everything I liked to do required hours of it and I had excellent teachers. Grandma bought me my first sewing machine. My mother was an expert knitter. She could glance at a full baby's layette – blanket, bonnet, booties, dress and sweater – and reproduce it, from memory. I never appreciated her skill. Like clearing the *Jeopardy* board, I thought all mothers could knit. And I devalued her twice: I learned every handicraft in my NII, imagining my birth mother beside me. Wondering what stitches might please her. If she liked the same iris shades of blues and purples that I did. Wondering if my work would be good enough, hoping I'd be good enough. Praying that I'd someday get to meet her.

Instead, I got a book mother. Miss Abigail came to the Alderwood Public Library when I was about eight years old. She asked me what I liked to read about and didn't blink when I answered, "Orphans." When she handed me *Madeline*, by Ludwig Bemelmans, I didn't tell her I used to fantasize about running away to Paris, to live in that old orphanage covered in vines, home to Madeline and twelve little girls in two straight lines. I told her I'd already read the whole series when I was a child, thank you very much. When she recommended *Heidi*, *Eight Cousins* and *Rose in Bloom*, and I'd read them all, she held out her hand like I was grown up.

"I'm so pleased to meet another reader. I hope we'll read lots of books together."

I visited the Alderwood Public Library twice a week, eager to share my every idea about books with my beloved Miss Abigail. She offered me home and refuge. Made me believe that a life of the mind could be lived in books, that the physical world was merely the obstacle course I took to get there. I told her I was adopted, but never gave her any specifics. Something about her tightly wound bun, sensible shoes and lack of a wedding ring told me her take on bastardy might be wanting. I also feared being honest would backfire.

Most grown-ups thought that people with broken bodies also had broken brains. If I told her about my feet, she'd quite logically think there might be something wrong with my brain. She might stop letting me into the teen section. That's where she kept Sherlock Holmes. Him, I would not risk. In Sherlock, I found the only father figure I could count on to take action. He'd never hide in the basement. He had no time for guppies. Sherlock wouldn't give one whit about my feet. He'd see only a kindred spirit, ready, willing and able to play any mental game afoot.

Miss Abigail and I argued only once, over *Anne of Green Gables*.

I was nine and on crutches. She loved the book and insisted that I should love Canada's also-adopted, also-red-headed national heroine.

I hated her. I thought she was a faker and a fraud. I never believed the romantic fantasy she told about her missing parents. I told Miss Abigail that Anne's anger against the teasing Gilbert was misdirected, that it was dead wrong that she had to hide her real anger about being adopted just to be accepted by snotty Avonlea. Concluding that I had outgrown the teen section, for my birthday in 1965, at age ten, Miss Abigail gave me an adult library card, far earlier than legally, or arguably morally, advisable.

But despite how much I trusted her, I never asked her for books about disability.

Saying it would "inspire me," a well-meaning Sunday school teacher gave me the first and only book I ever read about another disabled kid: *Karen*, a 1952 memoir by Marie Killilea. I cried for days. In the tribute by a mother to her daughter with cerebral palsy, I saw the lengths a loving mother would take to spend time with, help, love, delight in and advocate for a disabled daughter. I threw the book in the sewer and lied. I told my teacher I'd lost it. I said I hadn't read it. I wasn't going to discuss how inferior it made me feel. Not with her. Not with anyone. I wasn't going to let anyone else in Alderwood read it, in case they saw the Karen in me.

The only disabled children I ever saw were all angelic. They graced my television twice each year. Every Christmas Eve, in tears, I watched the black-and-white version of *A Christmas Carol*, vowing to be as good as sweet Tiny Tim. On Labour Day weekends, I watched living Tiny Tims: "Jerry's Kids," on the Jerry Lewis telethon for muscular dystrophy. For more years than I'd like to admit, I crept down to the TV in the basement and fed my hungry soul with three days of "inspiring" kids in wheelchairs. Their lovely faces, their undying gratitude while dying, moved me to blubbering inconsolability. When Jerry sang, "You'll Never Walk Alone," I sang with him. When Jerry raised millions of dollars, I whispered, "Thank you." I snuck back upstairs, telling myself that if I tried harder to be good, my mother might think I was worth something.

Decades later, I realized these children were being exploited in what disabled activist Stella Young would call "inspiration porn": using disabled people as props to provoke the pity that makes abled people feel good about themselves. Inspiration porn makes abled people feel grateful not to be us, and feel warm and fuzzy about charitably reaching down to help us.

As a child, I fell hook, line and sinker for the lie that as a disabled adoptee I was a double charity case. I didn't understand how the sentimental adoption narrative mimics inspiration porn. It cast my parents as charitable heroes for taking in burdensome baby me. I did know I was supposed to be nothing but grateful. I choked back even the slightest taste of Anne's red-headed anger, knowing it would make me less deserving of their charity. I see it so clearly now: adoption and disability double-primed me to a childhood of terror, to fearing I did not deserve the charity I loathed but could not possibly live without.

It took a lifetime to embrace my red-headed birthright.

Thanks to an adult interest in genealogy and DNA testing, I learned that red hair crowns less than 2 percent of the planet. Those with the red-haired genome feel pain more acutely and need more anaesthetic. In scientific basis for Anne's red-headed temper, we often have high blood pressure. The medication I take controls mine most of the time. But I was raised to deny my red-headed self. Taught to see anger not as a healthy response to harm or injustice but as only one thing: my own failure. Proof I wasn't trying hard enough to be good. My mother's white-gloved bruises made the limits of her charity clear. I couldn't be an angry girl if I wanted to be a good girl. I had to be a good girl if I wanted to be her girl.

If I kept my nose in a book, I could keep my mouth closed.

When I got my glasses, my ability to read improved immediately. Prescribed shortly after the fall into the fish tank, my glasses disappointed my mother almost as much as my bloody tights. Before the advent of plastic lenses, my glasses were Coke-bottle-bottom thick. But I liked them: cat's eye frames sparkling like sun on Balsam Lake sand. Mother said I mustn't worry if people said they weren't attractive. That pep talk got reinforced by adults who thought "Men seldom make passes at girls who wear glasses" was an acceptable thing to tell an eight-year-old.

I ignored them all. As for men looking at me, I didn't want anyone to do that.

In the stardom of my first operation, when first cast as "the poor wee thing," I'd received plenty of attention, flowers, cards and chocolates. I got a whole box of Nancy Drew mysteries from my dad's Employee Association. By my second operation, stardom waned. I got half the well wishes. By my third, I wondered what I'd done wrong. Had I been insufficiently grateful? It did occur to me that the novelty had simply worn off. My audience had moved on.

But I also feared they'd discovered my secret life as a child porn star. I was eleven.

Mother drove me to Sick Kids that day, and only at the last possible second, when she hit a different button in the elevator, did she inform me we were headed down, not up.

"You're going to do something fun today. You're going to make a movie."

"Why? I don't want to. What for?"

"It's for science. It's so they can study how you walk. To show other doctors."

"But I don't want —"

"Don't be so selfish, Dorothy. I already said you'd do it."

Hoping for Hollywood, I got a damp, dingy room in the basement. A circle of floodlights glared on a swept and prepped terrazzo stage, covered in sheets of brown paper. It was a solo command performance, but extras hovered in the wings: Dr. Salter and his understudies. Without explanation, a nurse stripped me naked. Hefting a paint roller, she spread the bottoms of my feet with India ink. For the first of what would be many times in my life, I met a delusional director. "Okay, honey. Forget we're all here. Forget we're all watching. Just walk normally."

My mother stood silent in the wings watching her daughter, a girl with the first swelling of breast buds, limp in the nude. Fall spread-legged in the nude. Be gawked at by a room full of smoking men. A haze of yellow smoke wafted under the floodlights.

Like fog. Like scum.

I said nothing all the way home. I didn't cry until I closed the door to my room.

I told no one. I never confronted my mother.

She couldn't have known that what she made me do in 1966 would today be considered child abuse. It would never have occurred to her that she'd pimped me out, cast her own daughter in another kind of pornography. As for the idea that my movie might get sold, without Sick Kids' permission, for something other than medical purposes, that was truly inconceivable.

We had no language for perverts then, but I'm furious now. Somewhere out there, slobbering men – jerks who get off, not just on kiddy porn but on kiddy porn with a freak fetish – may still be jerking off to illegal, bootleg copies of a tiny, naked redhead, struggling to walk on scarred, deformed feet. And failing, and falling. Again, and again.

Discovery, Denial and Duplicity

Canada's Centennial Year, 1967, began in grade seven and ended in grade eight.

I began Franklin Horner Junior High at eleven, loving my symmetry with the Centennial symbol: a stylized maple leaf of eleven triangles, one for each province and the NWT. On January 1, on TV dinner trays in the living room, I heard the first broadcast of the song the CBC commissioned from Gordon Lightfoot: "The Canadian Railroad Trilogy." That year, I saw the first Caribana parade, marvelled at the impossible height of the new TD Bank Tower, and cheered with my dad when the Toronto Maple Leafs won the Stanley Cup. In truth, it didn't seem like a big deal; I figured it would happen all the time. I was more impressed with our Centennial celebrations. Alderwood United sang in a mass choir at the opening of Etobicoke's Centennial Park and its ecological wonder: a hill made of garbage. I embroidered Centennial tea towels, planted trees and time capsules, proudly wearing the gold Centennial pins issued to every child.

I still have mine. I'd intended to wear it for Canada 150, but chose not to do so.

In 1967, I watched Chief Dan George's "A Lament for Confederation." I memorized it, loving this line: "So shall we shatter the barriers of our isolation." I took it because, at age eleven, I assumed it was free. Because I loved Centennial year, and everyone told me it was mine. In what I'd later see as white, colonial privilege, the only Canadian history I knew told me the whole country was mine. In the preoccupation of pre-puberty, the only barriers I cared about were mine. TV touted Centennial multiculturalism, but in junior high, if you got labelled "different," you were dead meat.

There is no animal on the planet more vicious than a pretty, white preteen flexing her new-found mean-girl muscle. This predator doesn't attack at the first scent of weakness. She circles. She taunts, snaps and teases. Draws blood and relishes its taste. She takes all the time she wants before dashing in for the kill. Because she leads a willing pack.

This is the class Centennial project I've never shared: the hunting of Rosamunde.

She looked like a target: a timid bone rack of a girl with greasy hair. Her skin riddled with sharp, creamy pustules that pushed up out of her face like fork tines. The first slur we reached for was "that dirty Kraut kid." We began mangling her German surname, one we'd pronounced since kindergarten. All girls kept an emergency Kleenex. One. In our pockets. But Rosamunde had a giant, plastic bag bursting with them. And – it looked like it, we were soon sure of it – they were all used. The boys stole it and threw Kraut Cooties all over the playground.

All her dresses were hand-me-downs. With parents who'd weathered the Depression and wartime rationing, we all wore them. But Rosamunde's were soiled, crumpled, stained and patched. Repeatedly, poorly, downright comically, patched. Not the discrete, iron-on patches our mothers used, but emblazonments of crudely cut cloth, blobs of contrasting colours and textures that made no attempt to belong. I remember a large, brown corduroy patch straight from her little brother's pants, sewn on the tummy of a faded flower-print dress. The boys called it her "German belly button" and tried to yank it off.

We were good girls. Nice girls. We never touched her patches. Behind her back, we held our noses and made farting noises.

The sound of smelly, sour Kraut air escaping.

In every junior high, the prettiest girl controls and dispenses the carrots and sticks. Windy was the first to change her name, from a similar one to that of the girl in the Association's 1967 hit song. She brought three of her old dresses, displayed on hangers, and gave them to Rosamunde. Noting her generosity, not that anyone could miss it, our teacher made Windy Student of the Week. Instantly, all the girls began competing to be seen giving Rosamunde, the poor thing, the most dresses. The best dresses. Ones they could boast they no longer needed.

My mother looked at me like I was asking for the fridge.

"No. Anything you can still wear, Missy, you will wear. Period."

Our Good Sisters of Charity Act lasted maybe two weeks, until Rosamunde showed up in one of Windy's dresses with a patch on it. It was tiny. A red patch on a red dress, set discretely at a worn-out elbow. A defect Windy no doubt knew about when she so generously gifted said dress. This patch was tasteful, necessary and unobtrusive. It was also unforgivable.

Windy sniffed. She circled in. She drew a willing pack in with her.

She began with Rosamunde's hair: "It could be pretty. Maybe. I'll bring you some leftover shampoo." She brought a wrapped present with a fancy bow, telling Rosamunde she couldn't open it until we gathered at recess. It was a bar of Sunlight soap. Offering to clean Rosamunde's glasses, Windy flourished a Kleenex from her own pocket. "See, dear? This is what they look like when they're clean." She invited all us girls to help find all the dirt. On cue, one of Windy's many male admirers swooped down from the playground. The boys obligingly passed the filthy glasses from shirttail to shirttail, until forced to return them at the bell.

Rosamunde took her seat, and took it like she deserved it. That sealed her fate. Someone, I never knew who, whispered, "Rowwsa-munnnde." The whole class joined in. When nobody stopped us, we had no reason to stop ourselves. We groaned it out non-stop: "ROW-WWWWWWWWSAAAAMUNNNNNDE." She got it at lunch and before and after school. Our teacher heard us. Teachers in the hall and on yard duty heard us. They said and did nothing.

After days of this stalking, Windy herded the girl pack and attacked.

I'd heard it was going to happen – we all knew precisely where and when it would happen – in the park, Friday, right after school. I went straight home. To establish my alibi, I asked my mother the time. I didn't see the swarming, but heard the blow-by-blow so many times it still feels as if I'd been there. They started pulling at patches and finished by ripping her clothes right off. They broke her glasses and ground them beneath their lovely shoes.

What would I have done had I been there? Not a damn thing. What condemned Rosamunde for me wasn't her patches, her pimples or even her snotty Kleenex bag. It was her lazy eye. It rolled up, bounced and rolled down. Her thick black glasses, so clearly cheap, boys' glasses, failed to tame it. Despite a row of spelling stars and perfect math tests, ignoring the fact we'd all been accelerated for a reason, my classmates called her "a gimpy moron," a "total retard." Bobby Gimby might be singing about Ontario as "a place to stand and a place to grow," and a year later, our new prime minister, Pierre Elliott Trudeau, would invite immigrants to "build the Canadian mosaic," but Rosamunde's heritage, poverty and disability made her an alien species, one we treated worse than our pets.

We believed we could bully her without guilt or consequence.

And we were right.

In staging her attack on a long weekend, Windy had chosen deliberately and well. Come Tuesday morning, our teacher had moved Rosamunde's desk to the back corner. His choice or hers, we neither knew nor cared. Perhaps he hoped if we didn't see her, we'd leave her alone. Or, if he didn't see us not leaving her alone, he wouldn't have to intervene. If anyone ever got in any trouble for stripping a girl naked in a public park, I never heard about it.

I didn't think about Rosamunde again until I heard a rumour she dropped out of high school. It was only then that I admitted what I'd always known: she was poor. Hers was one of the tiniest houses in Alderwood, wrinkled by peeling paint, practically on the railroad tracks. I'd always known the way we treated her was unchristian and just plain wrong. But it was only when I began writing her story, some fifty years later, that it all clicked in.

Why didn't we see the obvious?

Her patches were sewn on by a child.

Rosamunde was the only girl in her family. Her mother was dead.

From age ten, a little girl had been getting top marks, while housekeeping for her father and three brothers: washing, ironing and mending for all five of them. My choir sang at the funeral. Windy's mom, a Sunday school teacher, loaned Rosamunde a pair of Windy's white gloves. As an elder, Windy's dad passed the collection plate for the family. I threw my dime at its metal bottom, hoping it sounded more like the quarter Windy donated. Windy's dad set the plate of five-dollar bills on the altar, pulled out his wallet and casually dropped a twenty.

I remember the cheap cardboard coffin. I didn't know they made such things. I remember Reverend Warren praying "for all who have died of asthma." I watched Billy, solemn on his skateboard, and a pale little boy beside Rosamunde, wondering which one we'd pray for next. When Rosamunde handed her wheezing brother yet another Kleenex, I saw the bag for what it was. For years after her mother's funeral, a fearful sister had carried extra Kleenex to come to her baby brother's rescue. As if having extra Kleenex could save him.

Today, I feel the weight of her bullied childhood. I long to tell her, "I'm so sorry."

I need everyone to hear this: it's long past time to share the blame. We were smart kids who should have known better, but we were still children. My teachers, my choirmaster, my Sunday school teachers, Reverend Warren and all our neighbours with full view of the park had no such excuse. Grown adults, adults paid to be role models, saw and said nothing. When bystanders look away, they're not neutral; they're enablers. They're ensuring two things: that the abusers win this time, and that there will be a next time. Of course, that's exactly what happened.

The girl who targeted me was Windy's best friend, the almost-as-pretty, newly named Lindy. Under her old name, she'd been my friend for years. In grade six, she'd nominated me for Red Cross Class President. I'd won in a landslide. If it was a pity vote for a Tiny Tim on crutches yet again, I did a good job reading the *Red Cross Student News* and distributing buttons. If we were a nickel short, I figured no one would guess my mother had refused to give me one.

Lindy and I had no childhood grudge, no new beef. But upon entering junior high, she had graduated to the ultra-cool: one of the first to have miniskirts, pierced ears, black eyeliner, black fishnet stockings, pointy black shoes with junior heels and the most desirable accessory of all: a boyfriend. If the fight had been planned, it was news to me. No bullying preceded it. I think it likely Lindy simply wanted to impress said boyfriend, one Ricky B. He was the kind of boy who skipped out of grade nine to look all bad-boy impressive to girls two years his junior. When we hit high school, we realized no girls their own age would be seen with them. But that day, we were grade seven kids graced by the presence of a cool, older boy. A boy who smoked.

Lindy challenged me at the lunch bell. "You and me, Palmer. Today. Now. Or else."

While I might have preferred "or else," she rallied the pack to prevent it. The friends I walked with every day never materialized. A crowd did. At the train tracks, Lindy took out her pierced earrings, grabbed me by the hair and threw me to the ground.

It's still a blur. A battering of contradictions. Betrayed, yet expecting betrayal. And frozen, frozen, frozen. Unable to move. Believing I didn't deserve it; knowing I did.

She sat on me. When she started to punch, I shielded my glasses. If they got broken, my mother would do worse. Truly worse, without glasses, I couldn't read. Inexperienced at roughhousing, I did the only thing I could think of to protect my feet: I lifted my legs and wrapped them around her waist. As bad luck would have it, I was wearing a wide-pleated flannel skirt. When I lifted my legs, it fanned out on the ground, revealing my panties and garter belt in all their shoddy, mended, second-hand splendour. The crowd pointed. They hooted. I left my body, floated above it. A girl with a cool Twiggy haircut punched an unmoving little redhead.

One who took each punch without making a sound.

When it became clear I wasn't going to fight back, the crowd jeered. They felt cheated. They began to drift away. Calling me "a total lameo retard," my attacker declared she'd won and got off me. She started to leave, paused, then returned.

She leaned back, took aim and kicked Horatio full force with her pointed shoe.

I screamed. That's when I cried. Somebody threw my bike down on the railway tracks. Somebody else went and got it for me. I couldn't ride it home. I limped home, throwing up repeatedly from the pain in my foot. I told my mother I had another stomach flu. I went straight to bed and stayed there. None of my friends phoned that night. Not one.

When I came back to school, at least my teacher hadn't moved my desk. My girlfriends slowly drifted back, without apology or explanation. No girl ever spoke to me about it again, but the boys never stopped talking about it. For years, boys said, "Hey, remember when Lindy beat you up? When everybody saw your garter belt and your panties? Man, that was so funny!"

I have no idea if the school ever called my parents, or if they ever heard in any other way. All I know is that I never told them. Why didn't I give them the chance to comfort and defend me? Because I knew they wouldn't. Because I'd learned what people were really thinking.

On March 5, 1967, my best friend's father went to the Toronto-Dominion Bank at Brown's Line and Horner Avenue, three blocks from my house, waited for his brother to leave the bank, shot him, then shot himself. The initial horror, the disbelief that it happened in safe, sleepy Alderwood, quickly morphed into something else. Not a murder; "a mercy killing." My friend's uncle had been diagnosed with inoperable cancer. Neighbours sighed, then shrugged.

"Nobody wants to see a loved one suffer. It's a kind of kindness, isn't it?"

"There's something honourable about being man enough to do that."

My own father said, "My generation has seen too many men die in agony. I hope someone would have the courage to put me out of my misery."

From this I gleaned two critical things: a life in pain isn't worth living and if it's "kind" to put people out of their misery, no one better know I was in misery.

To cheer me up after my first brush with death, Mother took me somewhere she wanted to go: Expo 67. We toured the pavilions in companionable silence, pored over brochures and played *Man and His World Jeopardy*. To paraphrase *I Seem to Be a Verb*, the title of the famous book by the futurist designer of Expo's geodesic dome, Buckminster Fuller, it was during our trip that for one moment Peggy Palmer "seemed to be a verb," not just my mother.

In the crowded Pakistan Restaurant of the United Nations Pavilion, a young couple arrived pushing a wheelchair. Mother whispered, "Oh, dear. Spastic and non-responsive."

Everyone peered at the freak and looked away. Except my mother. She stood up and said, "Please join us." She led an animated conversation, about exhibits, about current political unrest in Pakistan. She praised the young mother on the skill with which she'd sewn her "lovely sari."

But when the trio departed Mother pressed a Kleenex to her tears.

"That poor woman. That child must break her heart, over and over again."

Did I break her heart? I'll never know. I wouldn't have said she had one.

Her one moment's sympathy for a child not her own never extended to me. When I needed money for things my little siblings did not – for school trips, CGIT dues, a bra and then sanitary napkins – I took her eye-rolling annoyance as proof she didn't think me worth a cent. I'd never ask her if looking at me broke her heart. I'd never tell her I'd been in a fight, or how the words *mercy killing* terrified me. She'd think I started the fight. She'd berate my self-pity. She'd say if I didn't stop talking nonsense, she'd mercifully kill me herself.

At the end of grade eight, we saw two murders none of us alive at the time would ever forget: the assassination of Dr. Martin Luther King Jr. on April 4, 1968, and a short two months later, the murder of Robert Francis Kennedy, on June 6, 1968. Bobby died two weeks before I became a teenager. In that spring of double death, it felt as if all the light in the world had been snuffed out. In naive solidarity, I vowed to carry on the fight somehow, someday.

That September, I entered grade nine and discovered girl power. The previous winter, girls at Alderwood Collegiate had decided that the "no pants" rule had to go. They secretly picked a date, spread the word and showed up en masse in pants, correctly assuming no one could suspend them all. Thanks to their solidarity, I could wear my bell-bottoms and pantsuits. I could wear my wide-suspendered hot pants: navy blue corduroy with little red rosebuds. Hot indeed. Thanks to my grandmother's mentoring, I sewed all my own clothes. She loved my blouses with long, pointed collars and billowy sleeves with three-button cuffs. She even loved my mod pantsuit. Straight out of an Austin Powers movie, "Yeah, baby, yeah!" It was "so shagadelic": an electric, lime green velveteen with a lacy cream jabot and a cameo broach.

I wore it to my first boy-girl party.

It was the last thing Grandma and I sewed together.

As dementia set in, my beloved grandmother started hiding perishable food in her closet. Began pounding on neighbours' doors in the dead of night. Bedridden after his car accident, my grandfather couldn't go after her. My grandma swore he was trying to kill her. After the first few calls to the police, when neighbours grew wise and started simply bringing her home, she told me she had a plan to get away from that "murdering monkey of a man." She assured me, "I'm crazy like a fox. I'm one wily vixen."

I understood only when I overheard my parents making hushed and hurried plans to put her in a home. My prim and proper Victorian grandmother, the woman who never wore pants, had visited a new neighbour, three blocks away. Through the snow she'd run, naked as a jaybird, wearing nothing but her boots. She faded away, then passed away in the summer of 1972.

I was seventeen. I still see her whenever I smell lavender.

I miss her less when I'm sewing.

I sewed non-stop in high school, because if I wanted anything other than hand-me-downs, I had to make them myself. In stylish self-defence, I'd order funky paisley material from the Eaton's catalogue, or jump on my bike, ride out to Fabricland and sew up a new blouse or skirt from a remnant for under a dollar. I made everything but my underwear, all from my babysitting money. I especially loved the most accomplished item in my closet: a brushed-suede peacoat, jade with bright brass buttons. My mother had glanced and shrugged. "It won't stand up in the rain." When I took it next door to show Mrs. MacCallum, the best home-sewer on our street, she gave me peanut butter cookies warm from her oven, praised my detailing and tailoring. When I proudly announced it cost only three dollars, including the buttons, she smiled.

"And how many hours of your life?"

I looked at her like she'd come from Alpha Centauri, not Tabusin-tac, New Brunswick.

"All the things you sew are lovely, Dorothy, but whenever you add up the cost, you should also figure in your time. That's valuable, too."

That was news to me. That anything about me was worth any-thing was news to me. I stretched pennies as part of the challenge, but also because I believed I didn't deserve anything new. My coming-home outfit was the only new clothing I'd ever owned. I was always the last owner of my cousins' hand-me-downs. Mother threw them in the trash and bought her daughter new clothes. Mother explained it: I smelled. I stank to high heaven. I reeked like cast cheese.

My feet were indisputably sweaty.

Even in socks, I left wet prints on her clean floor.

Sending me to the shower as often as twice a day no longer needed words. She'd lean into my face and hold her nose. My siblings did likewise. It's a crafty cruelty to tell an insecure teen with little sense of smell that she smells. Convinced I had the genetics of a skunk, I never wore any item of clothing twice. I washed everything by hand. Instead of being grateful I did my own laundry, Mother said, "Since you're using more than your fair share of detergent, Dorothy, you better start buying your own."

To kill the sinister stench of me, she bought me baby powder, Gold Bond Powder, foot spray after foot spray, then Mitchum's Extra-Strength Advanced Antiperspirant for Men.

"Dorothy, it doesn't say not to roll it on your feet. Smelly beggars can't be choosers."

Forty years later, I came across an Internet article with a medical explanation. It argued that to ensure humanity's survival in the close quarters of caves and hovels, blood relatives typically do not identify each other's body odour as offensive. It's the sweat of those not related to us that strikes us as smelly. This explains why adopted children are often told they smell.

But it wasn't just my teenage body that stank; it was my shoes. My siblings' canvas runners could be tossed in the wash; my Oxfords could not. Mother made me leave them on the porch. Now I had cold, smelly shoes that didn't work. Scarlet wings kept Herkimer aloft, but not Horatio. In a spectacular fall down a full flight of stairs at ACI, Horatio snapped his wing right off. Dr. Salter diagnosed the obvious: those wings won't fly. I needed custom-made shoes.

I didn't know until I got to his shop that this shoemaker made polio boots. He would make me a "boot baby." I refused to play nice. I refused to sit down. Only once he promised I wasn't getting calf-length "gimp boots" did I agree to let him make lasts of my feet. Mother kindly reminded me that the cost of custom shoes would shoe the whole family, so they better work. When my custom-made ankle boots appeared, when everyone ignored the fact I'd been lied to, when Horatio laughed and kept rolling, my mother did the math. Instead of ruining two hundred-dollar custom-made boots in two months, I could bloody well go back to wrecking fifty-dollar Oxfords once a month. She made it clear: I should cost her as little as possible.

Where was my father in all this, you ask? Good question.

He defied my mother only once and in secret.

On July 20, 1969, the night Apollo 11 landed on the moon.

Thanks to our daily cottage swims, I'd become a good swimmer. All winter, we walked the two blocks to the Alderwood pool. I passed all my Red Cross badges, but my strength came from my stroke. My ankles dislocated if I kicked, and holding my feet rigid proved as ineffective as chopsticks. Dad had tried all my life to find me flippers; none fit my fat little feet. That night, on a midnight swim off Grandpa's dock, Dad swam out to our rocky point and returned with a grin as bright as the moonlight. "Here, Pooch. Wanna try some moonboots?"

Years before pool shoes, he'd smuggled my custom boots out of the garbage. For the first time, I could kick. I could feel the power in my kick. We swam out to the point and back. We lazed on our backs, looking up at the Eagle on the moon, where another small step for man would soon be taken.

"I'm glad I lived to see it, Pooch. I hope you'll remember that you saw it with me."

At the end of our swim, I handed him my shoes and he re-hid them for next time. "I've been hiding stuff there since I was a boy," he whispered on our way up to the cottage. "But mum's the word. My mother and yours, they don't ever need to know."

We all have one summer enshrined in our memories as *the* summer. For me it's that summer, the summer of '69, between grades nine and ten, when I turned fourteen. The death of Judy Garland. A little blue Volkswagen driven off a Chappaquiddick dock. The Stonewall uprising protesting police brutality against "the gay community." Charles Manson's Helter Skelter. A man on the moon and four hundred thousand music lovers meeting up at Yasgur's farm for a little shindig known as Woodstock. I'm so grateful to have been the right age to appreciate that summer: a tuned-in but not yet cynical teen. Decades later, in tribute, I set my first novel, *When Fenelon Falls*, in those three iconic months of magic and loss.

I'm also thankful for this timely coincidence: my teen years saw the undisputed reign of elephant-ear bell-bottoms. Like a Harry Potter cloak of invisibility, mine fanned out over my feet and frayed on the floor. Except in gym. My gym teachers had no time for hokey-pokey me, and whenever I changed into my blue gym suit, there was no magic spell to counter the envy. When I saw the speed and ease with which thirty girls yanked off their street shoes and pulled on sneakers, I choked down tears. Except for my mother, my family members all had one pair of shoes. I didn't know normal teens could change shoes several times a day. I didn't know that girls would want to get an A in gym or could actually enjoy playing hard without pain.

Forget the Gold, Silver and Bronze Ableist Awards of Canada Fitness Testing.

In true high school athleticism, I'm both coach and athlete. It takes thirty minutes to convince Herkimer and Horatio to wear shoes. To stand, I must tie them as tightly as we can stand. "Come on, boys! Take one for the Gipper." I never stop training; I lace up, stand up and get back up from falling. Every day. All day. All without anyone seeing the sweat, the tears, the effort or the cost.

I made sure no one saw it.

In grade ten, I stayed silent because I'd seen what happened to young people exercising their right to protest. Forever backgrounded for me by the haunting voice of Neil Young, four unarmed students protesting the Vietnam War at Kent State, Ohio, were shot dead on May 4, 1970. The next year, in grade eleven, we studied a book I loved: *A Separate Peace*, by John Knowles. I made myself a pink shirt to match the one Phineas made to protest his war. But I didn't fight my own battle. When Miss Dewsnap assigned a debate, "Be it resolved that one of these conflicts is the hardest to fight: Man vs. Man, Man vs. Environment, and Man vs. Self," and put me in Man vs. Environment, I let my friends ramble on about shipwrecks and deserts. I didn't have the stones to explain what it meant to fight shoes and stairs.

In September of grade thirteen, my entire high school crammed in front of a tiny TV for the last game of the 1972 eight-game Summit Series between Canada and the Soviet Union. The real victory was missing math class, but when Paul Henderson scored the final goal, I roared as if hockey was the only game in town, in Canada, on planet Earth, in the known and foreseeable universe. By the end of grade thirteen, I came to a silent separate peace with my feet.

A pharmacy's worth of drugs had been prescribed and retried. Typical to the red-headed genome, pain meds regularly fail me. Most drugs work for about six months. I've been on every pain and arthritis medicine known to man, but I inevitably return to extra-strength aspirin. Cheap with few side effects, I can still hear Herkimer and

Horatio. It cuts the edge without making us dull. It makes me just flexible enough to do the nightly massage prescribed by an army of physiotherapists, although I can never rub deeply enough with my arthritic hands. I've been offered opiates multiple times and turned them down, fearing I'd get addicted to a drug that would, like all others, stop working. But disabled and chronically ill people should not be shamed; for many, opiates are the only pain management that works. We all have the right to choose whatever works.

As high school ended, I accepted my working truth: I'd never graduate from pain.

When you're in chronic pain, you can't end it, ignore it or beat it. You can only befriend it. Inventing my own self-care, long before I first heard the word *visualization*, to fall asleep I pictured the bones in my feet and, one by one, sang them a lullaby. They still love the Beatles' ninth album, known as the White Album. "Rocky Raccoon" does indeed soothe the savage named Herkimer. It cuts my pain from a seven to a four. Concentrating on TV, reading or knitting pushes it to a three. When I lose myself in writing, pain falls to a one. I first discovered this when I leapt from my bed, Christmas Eve, age nine, to pen: "Oh, where has the meaning of Christmas gone? Has it float-ed away on a breeze? Oh, where has the meaning of Christmas gone? The meaning no one sees." You don't need more of it, you really don't. But years of bad teenage poetry did give me a tentative voice. A private, fledgling courage for words.

Writing also unveiled another unexpected, pain-combating gift: I was funny. Almost as funny as Archie Bunker. His show, *All in the Family*, ran from 1971 to 1979. Its first two years were my last two in high school, the last years I lived at home. My parents wouldn't let my siblings watch. Like old times, it was just the three of us. With Archie, Edith, Meathead and Gloria, we munched tea and cookies, regularly snorting both out our noses. Ensconced in his neighbour-hood bar, Archie joked about all the topics we never dared: Vietnam, racism, religion, rape, miscarriage, breast cancer, abortion, swinging, sexism, homosexuality and homophobia. His working-class voice had poetic punch, a mash-up of mixed metaphors and malapropisms:

"Your Honour, may I encroach the bench?"

"You gotta grab the bull by the corns."

"I ain't no bigot. I'm the first guy to say it ain't your fault that youse are coloured."

And no team has ever had better comic chemistry and timing than Archie and Edith.

ARCHIE: If you're gonna have the change of life, you gotta do it right now! I'm gonna give you just thirty seconds. Now, come on, change!
EDITH: (*pause*) Can I finish my soup first?

The more I watched, the more a tiny voice said, "I can do that. I want to do that."

I began watching to see exactly *how* they did it. I saw Archie milk a line, wait, pull another face, then, still silent, milk it again. In Archie's battles with his liberal son-in-law, I saw newspaper headlines writ small. The genius of Norman Lear went beyond the "comic relief" Miss Dewsnap praised in Shakespeare. It was something new. Comedy that didn't relieve anyone, that raised uncomfortable truths. When I became an improv coach, I called it *comic release*: comedy that releases inhibitions, offers a safe laboratory to test out, weigh, measure, fail at, solve and resolve the most difficult of topics. That's what *All in the Family* did for my family. After each episode, my parents and I talked, really talked, voicing opinions we otherwise would never have shared. That occurred in living rooms across the planet. In the legacy of Swift and Moliere, and more recently, George Carlin, Richard Pryor and Hannah Gadsby, Archie married the political with the poignant, infused anger with power. He invited us to change.

Watching Gloria and Edith change, eventually refusing to obey Archie's commands to "Dummy up!" and "Stifle!" built my own courage. I asked Doctor Salter THE QUESTION:

"Why aren't my feet normal? Don't I have the right to know what happened to me?"

"You do, Princess. But –" I remember his shrug, large pink hands flopping against a stark white lab coat. "If I had to guess, and it is a guess, I'd say your feet are the product of cinching."

I knew what it meant. But I needed to hear him, someone, anyone, say it. At least once.

"Cinching, well, it means. . . . It means your mother pulled her belt too tight when she was pregnant. There wasn't enough room in her womb. Your feet paid the price. That's my best guess, but without the medical histories of both your birth parents, there's no way to be sure."

I see a "devastating dwarfish deformity," a creature cinched onto a skateboard with his father's belt. I do not ask these questions: Would my dad rather have picked a healthy red-haired baby? Would Mrs. Warren have cinched her baby to death if she'd known it was Billy?

I have to close my eyes to ask the good doctor what I had never said aloud.

"So, you can't be sure it isn't hereditary. I might pass it on, if I have children?"

He paused. "Yes. Possibly. I wish I had a better answer, Princess, but there isn't one."

I'm grateful. He gave me all the truth he could.

I'm grateful my birth mother didn't cinch my unborn head. When you're a belt notch away from being an abortion, when your mother tries for months to kill you, when two mothers don't care if you live or die, you welcome denial.

You cinch yourself silent. But you're still a monster.

You live your whole life expecting to give birth to one.

Exposing the Exit Door Through Which I Shoved My First Boyfriend

From the knees up, Gerald was the cutest boy I'd ever seen. California Surfer Boy cute. Blue eyes. Unruly blond hair a still-respectful tad too long. Muscular arms. Expressive hands. A slow, crooked smile. His family had a Muskoka cottage, he was president of his debate team and he had been to Paris, France. In 1971, when I was sixteen and he was eighteen, he lived up the hill from me in Alderwood. All the mothers loved him. Even mine. And she didn't love anybody.

When Gerald passed our front porch, when he stopped to chat up my mother, I glimpsed what my father must once have seen in her. She smiled and laughed, sounded smart and sassy. Gerald relaxed her in a way I never could. Watching him converse so effortlessly with the woman who seldom spoke to me felt like comfort food, like home should be.

But when Gerald smiled at me, I puked.

He was a "boot baby," a "feeb," a "polio retard." Teachers frowned on words like *wop* or *kike*, but all of Alderwood waved at Gerald with the same "joke": "Hey, Gimp Boy! Where's the circus?"

In September, the first time he knocked on my front door, I flushed the toilet, climbed out the bathroom window, vaulted a hedge and vamoosed through three back yards. I refused to be seen with him. I had to be seen as a normal teenage girl, had to believe I was one. You won't pass for normal if someone spots a gimp then stares at you. I'd prevent that scrutiny at any cost.

Bell-bottoms would always be in style.

I could hide my feet forever.

I'd never been teased in public; that was the barometer. I gave no credit to the fact my dad was one of leaders of the Alderwood's thriving Boy Scout troop, and held the badge and camping fate of my male classmates in his hands. I equally dismissed what was likely of greater deterrent: Mother had the most cutting tongue on the street and sharpened it there daily. Instead, I told myself only this: I walked to high school with my friends. I belonged.

To be a normal girl with every right to a normal boyfriend, I had to reject Gerald on principle. My feelings were complicated and shameful. I imagined burying my California boy waist-deep in the sand. Then, when others walked by, they'd look at me with envy. I fantasized miraculous healings, operations that sent Gerald running tanned and healthy into my arms.

But without a miracle cure, Gerald was as good as dead to me.

My parents' generation grew up with polio, had friends live with it and die from it. But I knew only Gerald. In 1952, using the now-famous HeLa cancer cells, stolen from a black woman named Henrietta Lacks, Dr. Jonas Salk developed the poliomyelitis vaccine. He released it in April 1955, two months before my birth. Thanks to the Canadian health care that paid for it, and a public wise enough to embrace it, the vaccine eradicated the disease. My experience of polio was limited to Franklin Roosevelt and those lovely blond children with slim silver braces tucked under their chairs, the angelic poster children for the March of Dimes.

Two years my senior, Gerald had not been so lucky.

He couldn't wear bell-bottoms. Two heavy black gimp boots entombed his feet and calves. Six leather straps and buckles cinched up his shins. Studded with metal knobs, his boots hooked into the metal braces that armoured both sides of each leg. A metal rung pierced under each boot. In summer, he used a crutch in his left hand; in winter, he needed one in both hands.

The second time Gerald came calling, he knocked on my side door. In what I believe to this day was a move calculated with geometric precision, he then backed off to the exact spot where he could see if I tried to escape out any back window, or the front door. My mother pushed me to the side door and made me open it. All three of us sat in the living room for one half hour. Then she stood up, shook his hand as if he were a charming Fuller Brush salesman and invited him back for Sunday lunch. After that lunch, I invited him back.

Gerald pitched me a woo that moved me as no man has ever done since.

Books. He brought me books. Not library books, not lenders. New books. Ones he'd bought for me. With his own money. He'd walked all the way up to W.H. Smith in our new mall, Sherway Gardens. In an extravagance I'd never been offered, he bought two copies. Ears turning scarlet, he asked me which book I might like to read together first.

I Know Why the Caged Bird Sings, by Maya Angelou.
The Crystal Cave, by Mary Stewart.
Look Homeward, Angel, by Thomas Wolfe.

The first two were novels I longed to read; the third was the book of my heart. The stone angel on its cover took wing. When I told Gerald I'd already read Wolfe, he promised to go home and read it that night if I'd agree to talk with him about it tomorrow. *Look Homeward, Angel* is five hundred pages of dense, lyrical, microprint. Discovering a coquettishness I didn't know I possessed, I said he could *only* come back *if* he'd read it by tomorrow.

I worried all night he might give up and want his books back.

He arrived with favourite passages meticulously underlined. Complete with marginalia.

By Thanksgiving, we'd shared books and I'd set our boundaries. From opposite corners of my basement, with twelve tanks of guppies waving their tails between us, we worshipped Dickens and despised *Moby Dick*. We marvelled at *Steal This Book* and *Fear and Loathing in Las Vegas*. Hot off the presses, we devoured *Lives of Girls and Women*, by Alice Munro. It's impossible to explain what a miracle that was, four decades ago: a book by a living Canadian writer, by a woman, a young woman in her thirties.

There's a moment in life when you first feel appreciated as an adult. You never forget it. If you're lucky, especially back in 1971, there's also a moment as a young woman when you know a young man respects you as his thinking equal, when together you glimpse a future you didn't dare admit you wanted. Gerald and Ms. Munro gave me both moments. I'm happy to finally thank them. He did it by saying something extraordinary about her book.

"I'm not a girl. I'll never be a woman. You're both, Dorothy. I'm here to listen."

I may have become an English teacher because of that moment, but Gerald was the kind of natural mentor I've never been. Patient. Empathetic. Encouraging. Empowering. He made me feel like a grown-up Nancy Drew cracking *The Mystery of the Tortured Teenager*. He loved ideas without needing to take credit for them. Disagreed without judgment or ego. Debated without needing to win. By example, by not even trying, he helped me see beyond myself.

There was scant kindness or generosity in my home, but I learned both from Gerald, along with hope. Just as his parents assumed he'd go to university, he assumed I would, too. When I said no one – no teacher, family member or friend – had ever suggested such an unspeakably impossible thing, and certainly no one I knew would ever pay for it, he brought me scholarship applications. His belief in me made me believe I could be both teacher and writer.

But I told him we couldn't leave the basement.

I insisted on a purely literary friendship, like Elizabeth Barrett and Robert Browning, before he got it into his silly head to scoop an invalid into his arms, blanket and all. As long as Gerald kept a blanket over his legs, I told myself I could agree to keep seeing him without having to be seen *with* him. By Remembrance Day, when it got dark by suppertime, I agreed to meet at his house, but we never went out together. Not to a movie. Not to Il Paesano, our local pizzeria. Thankfully his commuting father drove him back and forth downtown to private school, so Gerald never asked to walk me home from school. I'd have said no. By my decree, if we passed in the street, we kept moving. I said nothing to my girlfriends.

But I knew I was being courted by a real live boy. Slowly. Honestly. Irresistibly.

The boy who couldn't sing wrote funny new lyrics to my favourite Gordon Lightfoot songs and asked me to sing them to him. He gave me standing ovations, pulled himself to his feet when it clearly hurt his legs and pride to do so. When I let it slip that I disliked my frizzy red hair, longed for a yard of pin-straight blonde hair like Peggy Lipton on *Mod Squad*, long before Google, he found every ginger heroine in print and portrait and sang her curly praises. Best of all, he stopped talking to my mother beyond required pleasantries. He saved all his charm for me.

In December, telling myself my basement really was chilly, after the umpteenth invite to share his blanket, I did so. I wasn't really holding his hand if both hands were under said blanket. Eventually, I closed my eyes and let him kiss me. Inevitably, we kissed like a hot Jacuzzi. But it went no further because, for the first time, I was the mobile one. Fast enough to escape, strong enough to keep a boy from holding me down for a quick feel, or an exploratory grope.

That power was new to me. And I liked it.

Today, some half a century later, I wonder if that was the real reason all the mothers liked Gerald. If they looked at him and saw a safe, sexually neutered man-child. Saw his disability and escapability as double insurance that he could neither seduce nor overpower their able-bodied daughters. But if they saw him as a eunuch, that's certainly not how he saw himself.

On Christmas Eve, Gerald invited me over to trim his tree – hoping that more than the tree would get trimmed. But I couldn't be seen on his sidewalk, so I took an alternate route.

In 1971, Alderwood was a young suburb fed by factories. Few could afford fences. If I skulked through backyards like a furtive thing, I wasn't alone. There was this very cute boy named Leo I'd been waving at for years as he cut past my bedroom window on his way to Catholic school. He'd seen my nighties, my training bra and, sometimes on purpose, my birthday suit. That suited me fine because Leo did something no boy I knew ever did: he gawked. He whistled. He made me feel like a girl. When I posed at the window, he couldn't see my feet.

Lately, I'd seen the Leo on Gerald's face.

Appendages under our blanket had grown too hot for my basement. When my father kept coming downstairs, ostensibly to feed guppies that would have long died from gluttony, we decamped to Gerald's bedroom. But I kept pushing him off, before our rising action reached any kind of climax. He thought it was because I was a good girl. He was wrong. More than blood on the bedsheets, being called a slut by my mother, or even getting pregnant, I couldn't bear the idea of being humped by a boy in braces, braces that pumped into my ugly, little boy shoes. But that's not all the truth. What I truly feared was this: that he'd want to take both his braces and my socks off. That seeing each other naked below the knees would make one of us puke.

And, this time, it wouldn't be me.

So, I was already ambivalent as I pussyfooted into his backyard that Christmas Eve. It wasn't that I didn't like his parents. I liked them far better than mine. His dad was a lawyer; his mom, the only wife I knew who worked outside the home, had a glamorous literary job: typist for a parenting magazine. With a home full of art books, they introduced me to Tom Thomson, Emily Carr and Paul Cézanne. I admired their quipping affection, marvelled at their tenderness for their only child. They hugged him. Said they loved him. Having never heard or seen such things, I was to no end flattered when they asked me to please call them Dan and Denise.

Once the tree was trimmed, to escape Dan's off-key carolling, Denise got up to make cocoa. Being a dutiful girl-child, I followed her into her red and white kitchen and added the baby marshmallows. That's when she handed me two steaming Santa mugs, put her hand on my cheek, glanced down at my frayed, floor-scraping jeans and smiled. "I'm so glad your mother and I decided to put you and Gerald together. You're so well matched. Two peas in a pod."

Cocoa splattered like shit on her clean kitchen floor. I ran for my coat and the door.

I only stopped at my door because I didn't want him following me through it. Not that night. Not ever. I kept my back turned until his chugging boots reached me, then I turned on him.

"You only called on me because our mothers set it up? You agreed to that? And you never told me, not once, not in all this time. What am I, your pity friend?"

He tried to reach for my hand. I pulled away. He tried to explain.

"No. I wanted to get to know you. Right from the start. And –"

"The start? Who bought my books? Was that a set up, too?"

When he avoided that question, nothing else he said mattered.

"Forget that. Now it's more than that. You know it is. I'm glad you're my girlfriend."

"Your *girlfriend*?" I spat it out like the filthiest word I'd ever utter. "I'd *never* be that."

"Of course, you are. You know how I feel about you."

I slapped his hand away again. "What about how I feel about you? Do you think there's something wrong with *me*? There isn't. I'm not –" I paused but didn't stop, "I'm not a cripple."

He took a step backward. Love still in his eyes. Love I couldn't stand.

His face should have cracked my heart. Instead it hardened it. I saw only that I hadn't hurt him enough. That he'd leave my door, but be back tomorrow, or next week. He'd convince me I'd spoken in anger, say he could forgive and forget, that he knew I hadn't really meant it. He'd grin that lopsided grin and tell me I was a better person than I thought I was. And he'd mean it. And he'd be wrong. So, I did the only thing I could think of to keep it from happening.

I leaned forward, grabbed his crutches and kicked his boots out from under him.

I pushed him face-first into the snow. Then I did the worst thing possible – I laughed.

When I closed the door on him, he did not come after me. Not then. Not ever. I hear he married his law partner and had five children. I hope so. I like to think of him as a legal Merlin in his crystal cave, even if this caged bird remained as tethered as Wolfe's stone angel. It took two decades before I made him the smallest of apologies. It took *Forrest Gump*.

It took me that long to hear it: "Stupid is as stupid does."

In 1994, at age thirty-nine, for the first time, I went to a movie alone. I'd seen the trailer of a boy in braces, and couldn't go with anyone who might see me cry. As I watched, I realized this: in refusing to be the good girlfriend Jenny to Gerald's worthy Forrest, the blame wasn't all mine. At the nastiest moment of fairy-tale ableism, at the "Run, Forrest, run!" moment when he sheds his braces and discovers not just that he can walk, but run – instantly, painlessly and effortlessly, faster than boys on bicycles – I stood up and yelled, "Horseshit. Fuck that. Fuck you for making him think he had to run. Fuck all of you for making me run from him."

As the usher escorted me from the theatre, I glowed. For Forrest and for Gerald.

I hope Gerald has forgiven me. I'm working on that myself. I fully and freely confess I treated my first boyfriend like crap. I kept a boy in the basement. I pushed a young man who loved me to his knees and shoved him out of my life. Able to side with ableism, I did so. Like Vichy, the wartime French government who sold out to the Nazis, I collaborated for the same cowardly reason: to keep myself safe at another's expense.

Today, five decades later, I appreciate the karmic irony of losing both my bell-bottoms and my mobility. It does not absolve me in any way to add what I now also understand: the complexity of shared blame. I treated that lovely boy the way my world treated me. The so-called *Happy Days* of mid-century North America were never happy for all. Ableism threw so many under the bus. I didn't deserve Gerald, but none of us deserved the hatreds of our day.

They did more lasting damage than any teenage heartbreak.

Is Forrest's famous tag line in itself an ableist slur? Some mental health advocates argue it's the reclamation of a slur, a disabled man making it clear that he wasn't "stupid," but so-called "normal" people often acted that way. That would be me. On that long-ago Christmas Eve, after I pushed Gerald into the snow, I went straight to the basement and threw his dirty books and spoiled scholarship applications into the trash, proving sixteen really is as sixteen does.

Some two weeks later, when my mother correctly assessed sufficient time had passed for the onset of regret, three beloved books magically reappeared on my bed. She put the scholarship applications on my desk, with application fees and postage attached.

My mother didn't love anybody.

But there were times when she tried.

Fashion, Feminism and Fornication: Why Good Girls Go to University

In 1973, I was accepted to all my chosen universities, but the only one that mattered was the University of Western Ontario. They gave me several scholarships, one from the IODE: the Imperial Order Daughters of the Empire. I jumped on a bus to London to register before they caught their mistake. With a name like Palmer, with a Cambridge Divinity Graduate grandfather born to Church of England missionaries, on paper I looked as British as Sir Arthur Conan Doyle's epitaph: "Steel True. Blade Straight." I told myself that heritage was legally mine. But I couldn't shake the fear that this little bastard would be called out as an imposter.

I've coined a name for my anxiety: *Disabled Adoptee Imposter Syndrome.*

Imposter Syndrome is common to high-achieving people, especially women, who struggle to accept their worth and accomplishments, battling a constant fear of being exposed as a fraud. As an adoptee pretending to be abled, I feared I didn't deserve scholarships, felt I didn't deserve to walk in somebody else's shoes. But I had to attend Western. I didn't know why, I just had to. Partly because Alice Munro went there. Partly because none of my friends were going there. I longed for rebirth, to leave all who knew about my adoption and my feet behind.

After my last operation, Dr. Salter had confirmed what I already knew.

"Here's the final skivvy, Princess. Your surgeries were partially successful. You can be proud they produced new reconstruction techniques that helped others. My guarded prognosis is that you'll walk a decade longer than without surgery. Maybe into your forties." He grinned his Lurchy grin. "I know that seems impossibly old, but it isn't. It is long enough for medical advancement. Hopefully, by then, we'll be growing replacement cartilage in a petri dish."

This time I shrugged. "I'm not sure I want to be a guinea pig again."

He nodded. "Your choice. You've got years before your arthritis really kicks in."

He stepped in front of my mother, eclipsing her completely. "And think about this: One way to win a fight is to choose to stop fighting it. To move away and move on."

When I nodded, he smiled. "And hear this: a wheelchair isn't the worst fate in the world."

I smiled back, but for the first time, didn't believe him. I do believe the last words he gave me: "Princess, we make our own hope."

Unfortunately, my parents also expected me to make all my own money. In the spring of grade thirteen, when I showed them my Western acceptance letter, they congratulated me. I waited all summer for "the financial conversation." I thought they'd propose a loan. With interest. When they said nothing, I didn't ask. I worked all summer. Since turning fifteen – not sixteen, though Dad told them I was – I'd worked from the last day of school until the first, at the company he'd worked at for thirty years: First B-A Oil, then Gulf Canada, now Petro-Canada. On the night before I left for Western, my mother stood in the doorway of my room and sighed.

"When you came to live with us, Dorothy, you were a broken baby. Sick, sad, malnourished, afraid of people, unable to sleep and desperately unhappy. I poured every ounce of love I had into you. I'm sorry it wasn't enough."

I had no idea what to say to that, so I said nothing.

Mother filled the silence for me.

She informed me that since they'd gotten me a good summer job for years, since the choice to go away to university was mine, I could pay for it. I'd just turned eighteen. All my life, the age of majority had been twenty-one. My friends and I grew up expecting our parents would be responsible for us until then. The law only changed to eighteen in 1971. A mere two years earlier, if my parents had abandoned me with nothing at age eighteen, it would have been child abuse. It still felt like it to me. We weren't poor, even if my parents behaved in every second as if they could be made poor at any second. At restaurants we all had standing instructions to abscond with all the salt, pepper and sugar packages we could carry. Mother dumped whole bowls of them into her purse. Twice a year, she sat us kids at the kitchen table until we poured every package into her stainless-steel baking canisters. But the point is this: We went to restaurants. We had disposable income to spend, even on disposable me. When I reminded my mother how hurt she'd been when her parents wouldn't pay for her education she shrugged.

"It's not the same thing," she said, and left the room.

Beyond the odd five-dollar bill, mailed by my mother to guilt me into a thank-you note, my parents paid not one dime for all my years of education. But I never confronted them. I made excuses for them. I reminded myself I had several girlfriends who hadn't applied at all, knowing their fathers wouldn't pay for a girl. In what was probably the last decade it was possible to do so, many of my friends paid their own way via summer jobs. None of us left in new cars.

But I was the only one I knew who left with nothing.

When I returned home that Thanksgiving, my mother had given my brother my room. She gave me a cot in the laundry room. I'm definitely the only university student I've ever known who came home each summer to sleep with the washing machine, to be told I had to pay room and board to stay in my own home. How did my siblings and my father react, you might ask? My brother was a good boy. He never mentioned his adoption. Not once. After years of watching my mother's treatment of me, my siblings followed my father's example and toed the line for fear they'd be next. When I left, they were still little kids. I think my departure made them feel like they were the real family, and I was just their almost-sister. And I let them think it.

Why didn't I get angry?

I couldn't risk being told not to come home at all.

I got a job at the university information desk and ate cereal, often for all three meals. I piled relish on student cafeteria hot dogs, knowing I wouldn't see another vegetable that day. I accepted it as my due, internalized what my mother was really saying: After looking after lame, little bastard me for fifteen years, I'd been burden enough. Her charity ended at her home.

When I got to Western, in her very first letter my mother informed me I also had to buy my own shoes. I couldn't have afforded orthopedic Oxfords, even if I'd wanted them. So, I improvised. I passed as abled in shoes that passed as cool because, yet again, I benefited from a pivotal moment in fashion history.

The years bridging high school and university birthed disco, for which no human can be thankful, and platform shoes, for which I'm prodigiously grateful. Laugh all you want, but platforms are the only women's shoes I've ever been able to wear. Deep, wide, round-toed and flat-soled, platforms appeared at the exact moment I needed them. They took a not-quite five-foot girl and made her a "Little Woman." I walked tall, humming that 1969 million-selling hit by the very dreamy and also short Bobby Sherman. I knew that a fall from platforms risked serious damage. But all falls risked that. Better to fall like a woman then look like a boy. To accept my high school diploma, I crossed the stage in a flowing, floor-length, carrot-orange halter dress and equally stylish white platform shoes. I left for Western with three pairs: tan, black and a pair of blue suede platforms that made me feel like this little Elvis owned the building.

As platforms waned, I discovered the joy of unisex. Beyond paisley shirts, neckerchiefs and Nehru collars, unisex gave no lasting fashion freedom to men. It gave me denim overalls, painter pants and the best shoes ever made: little boys' workboots, circa 1975. Made to last, of the heaviest leather, I found them where working-class parents did: at Sayvette, a precursor of Woolco and Walmart. At $3.99, even on my budget, I could still buy two pairs. With a 1.5 and 2.5, I could wear one shoe from each pair on my differently sized feet. But in the legacy of my Scottish grandparents, I couldn't bring myself to throw the other two perfectly good shoes away.

Orphan shoes wailed in my closet.

I became a shoe hoarder. I told no one.

When even the toughest workboots proved no long-term match for Horatio, I developed the Secret Hidden Installation Technique:

1. Buy two pairs of boys' workboots or sturdy leather running shoes, extra wide.
2. Discard the foam insoles. The under-sole is hard, but this makes shoes deep enough.
3. Buy six metal nail files. Glue gun them together in two groups of three.
4. Glue them into the far edge of each shoe, pointy end up to the toes.

Now that's some good SHIT.

Metal is the one bone Horatio can't break. At least not immediately. If SHIT gives me blisters, if metal cuts me, it's a small price to pay. Shoe spines keep me upright, most of the time. But sleuthing for socks to wear with SHIT shoes requires the persistence of Sherlock Holmes.

I've always marvelled at the fluffy sports socks girls pull over their nylons to warm their tender tootsies. Not happening. I can't wear fuzzy socks, or adult socks, only skin-tight kids' socks. A lump can throw off negotiations and throw me to the ground. I need the thinnest of socks, and I need a pile of them. Treading on nail files, sometimes socks last a week. Sometimes a day. A veritable sock connoisseur, I scout endless dollar stores for cheap imports. I can tell at a glance if the cuffs will chafe my scars. When socks are the perfect thinness, I'll spend hours picking out the tiny threads of elastic in each cuff. I think of jumpsies with every snap.

When socks fit and last, I go back and buy every pair. I have some standards: I won't buy Thomas the Tank Engine socks. Given Ariel's red hair, I make exceptions for the Little Mermaid. But I refuse to be my martyred mother and darn bloody holes. Not once. Not ever.

All you smart women readers out there are probably thinking, "Why doesn't the silly girl just buy an enormous bag of nylon footies and be done with it?"

I've tried footies, but they irritate my scars. Repeated incisions in the same spot have carved a big smile from my arch to my ankle bone. The scar tissue adheres to the bone; the skin doesn't move. Footies tug on that smile. Herkimer's final operation severed nerves, leaving the far side of my left foot numb from baby toe to heel, so I can't feel the smile ripping. I don't see damage until I take off my shoe and see blood. So, no footies for me.

But thanks to SHIT in my shoes, at Western, I could wear workboots and still be seen as a girl. An edgy, artsy, fashionable girl. I felt the self-confidence of a woman strutting her stuff on planet Earth. I more than passed; I belonged. In a twist of karma that I'll eventually explain, I studied nineteenth century social history in the very home of my own history. When American student protesters of the '60s got their Ph.D.s in the '70s, my ultra-conservative alma mater was so delighted to hire Ivy League graduates they pretended not to see that they were draft dodgers with education deferments, escaping Vietnam a second time. Their lefty passions ignited ours and academia itself. History exploded into social history, women's history, feminist history, Marxist history and Marxist feminist history. One of these young profs, Craig M. Simpson, became my first mentor. His belief in me and his meticulous scholarship on Henry A. Wise, the man who hanged abolitionist John Brown for leading the raid to arm the slaves at Harpers Ferry, gave me both the confidence to think for myself and the life-lasting tools to examine my history.

Women were also busy changing history. In 1972, my last year of high school and also the year my Victorian grandmother died, I spotted a magazine with Wonder Woman on the cover. It was the first issue of *Ms.* magazine. That year, *Ms.* published the names and stories of women who'd had illegal abortions. A year later, 1973 made its own history in the passage of Roe v. Wade, making abortion legal. Young women began to say the word *sex*.

To have it openly. To celebrate it. And to study it.

At Western, I began collecting nineteenth century "woman's guides." They provided sex education when none was appropriate, when any violated obscenity laws. In an age unafraid of a long title, *A Light on Dark Corners: A Complete Sexual Science and Guide to Purity and Physical Manhood, Advice to Maiden, Wife, and Mother, Love, Courtship, And Marriage* railed against "self-abuse" and "dissipation" in all its forms: drinking, flirting and bad novels. The *Ladies' Guide in Health and Disease: Girlhood, Maidenhood, Wifehood, Motherhood,* by the esteemed Dr. John Harvey Kellogg, he of Battle Creek, Michigan, and cornflake fame, astoundingly contained fold-out diagrams of a uterus, one complete with an unborn baby.

Today's bookstores host entire sections on sexuality. Peggy Palmer's library, my high school library and the entire Alderwood Public

Library had not one word on sex, unless you count that weird splitting thing enjoyed by paramecium. In 1972, I saw my first modern sex manual, *The Joy of Sex*, followed a year later by what became our fledgling feminist bible, *Our Bodies, Ourselves*. My university girlfriends and I studied it with all the devotion I once gave Deuteronomy. It did more than describe plumbing. In a miraculous heresy, it preached the rapture of getting plumbed.

When I thought about sleeping with a boy, I also worried about the sleeping part.

To fall asleep and stay there, I must mummify myself in blankets. I can't roll over. I can sleep in only one position: on my left side with Horatio topping Herkimer. The nerve-dead space on Herkimer's scar is the only spot that can handle being pressed into a mattress. If I roll over, it dislocates my feet and I scream. I knew that wouldn't be the kind of scream any young man who might find himself in bed with me would be hoping for.

I further worried about not being able to fully embrace the vision of *Our Bodies, Ourselves*. My body belonged to myself only because no one else had ever wanted me. But I kept quiet about our new bible's missing parts. It said nothing about adopted disabled bodies, let alone how to make love in one – or to one. I told myself it must be because there were so few of us, that we were such unusual exceptions to the normal, able-bodied rule that we didn't matter.

I told myself I was eighteen and I liked it.

I took women's studies, cut my hair, stopped wearing makeup, threw all my skirts in the trash and treated all in earshot to why I rejected high heels.

"Like Chinese foot binding, they're a tool of patriarchy. They incapacitate, infantilize and sexualize. They're designed to make it impossible for a woman to run. She can neither get anywhere first nor escape an attacker. They disfigure a woman's spine and shorten her Achilles tendons, all for the male gaze." At a party, after a drink too many, I told a young man I'd just met, "High heels are instruments of sexual humiliation. Of torture. They hobble women to make us easier to ride. They reduce us to eager baboon asses."

Unfathomably, he did not decide to date me.

A number of young men I regaled on the subject also proved not to be plumber material. But I didn't care. If I scorned heels loudly and often enough, I figured I'd never be asked to wear them. If I trashed femininity with my stomping boots, I'd be safe.

Refusing to identify as disabled meant I had to embrace all it took to deny it. Today, I see my self-loathing as *internalized ableism*. I championed unisex by default, because my feet could never grow into any other kind of womanhood. In truth, unisex was just the best costume in my limited closet. In the '70s, I didn't have the right to choose. None of us did. Even with feminist friends, I had no choice but to play the expected, second-banana role in *The Girl Game*, a catty old movie still playing in reruns at a theatre near you.

"My goodness! What cute little feet you have, my dear!"

My line must be "Thank you." Not "The better to see you need glasses, my dear."

"You're so lucky! Your itsy-bitsy little feet are so feminine. Mine are such boats!"

I must nod at being "lucky." I must appear sorry for the self-proclaimed owner of boats. I must offer the footwear equivalent of "No, it doesn't make you look fat," and say, "No, your feet don't look like boats to me." But they do. And I'm drowning. In envy. A woman with boats for feet can set sail at a whim and float across planet Earth in all the ways I can't.

"How I wish I had dainty little feet like yours! You can wear kiddy socks!"

"You get the best prices on shoes! Lucky you, you don't even have to pay tax."

"Your feet are so damn cute. I bet lovers like to kiss your cute little baby toes."

I must smile and nod. I must never go off script and say what's actually in my head:

"Dainty? Use your fucking eyes. They're tiny because they're deformed."

"They have an early expiry date. They're rotting from the inside out. How lucky is that?"

This is the simmering back burner I must never let flame. It would burn my closet down.

These nasty thoughts did not, however, keep me from "doing the nasty." That's what we called sex in the '70s. It made the contradictions we felt as young women clear. We went to university to lose our virginity and decorated our outsides accordingly. But inside, we were still nice girls of the 1950s. After a few teensy drinks too many on a girls' night out, we often admitted we feared our mothers' disapproval. We felt conflicted, guilty, easily shamed.

Please be advised that the rest of this chapter carries a content warning for sexual abuse.

After my first experience, the young man I loved rolled off his futon looking annoyed. When I asked what was wrong, he didn't even try to play it cool. "That was obviously not your first time. Why did you lie to me?"

"What do you mean? Of course you're my first. I wouldn't lie about that."

"Really? Then how do you explain that there was no, no . . ." He groped for words like he groped for flesh: inadequately. He turned red for the second time in five minutes.

"No what? Tell me." I knew he didn't mean no orgasm; I was pretty sure he'd had one.

"No . . . resistance, no barrier." He narrowed his eyes. "No pain and no blood. There's no possible way you were a virgin for me. You're a liar. Admit it."

I couldn't convince him. He couldn't look at me as I got dressed. He let me leave. When I got home, I closed my door on my roommates and cried myself senseless. Just how senseless didn't hit me until the next morning: a nineteen-year-old boy with all the sexual savvy of a stud guppy knew more about my body than I did.

Jump back in time to me at nine. Before my first operation, Sick Kids kept me for a full week. I accepted mother's story of a schedule mix-up, but we lived under an hour away. Why didn't they send me home? Because they were sending me for daily chats with the nice lady with long red braids wrapped over her head like the girl on the can of Old Dutch Cleanser. She held my hand, "Sweetie, you can tell me anything. Why are you covered in cuts and bruises?"

I told her the truth. Because the day before admission, I had decided I would learn to ride my bike or die. I got my father's wrench, removed my training wheels, wheeled my bike to the schoolyard and spent the day falling off it until I could ride it home. No matter how often she asked, "What else hurts you, dear?" I answered, "My feet. Just my feet," every time.

Jump to me at twelve. When mother and I had "the talk," one she delayed until after my first period, she casually mentioned that first-time sex didn't always hurt. Some girls had already lost their virginity, she said, by falling off a bike or jumping off a dock. I remember thinking those explanations medically suspect. I said nothing.

Jump to me being attacked at thirteen. How I couldn't throw a punch, couldn't defend myself in any way. Could only lie still, frozen. Infantilized. Small. Waiting for it to be over. The very immobility of "fight, flight or freeze," that medical science now affirms often characterizes victims of sexual assault.

Jump to me at seventeen, to the alarm on my mother's face when I told her I'd bought my first tampons. She came right into the bathroom. "So, are you . . . okay?"

Clueless me, so deep in denial. "Guess I'm lucky. It went right in. Didn't hurt at all."

"Well," said my mother. "Yes, lucky indeed. No need to worry then. Good."

Jump to my mother again. On my eighteenth birthday, she actually sat down on my bed.

"I know you think I've never been sympathetic, Dorothy, but you're wrong. On my way home, after your first operation, I had to pull over on the 401. I was crying so hard I couldn't see the road. I've never been so sorry for anyone in my life. The way they hurt you . . . how they hurt you. . . . It's too much for me. I can't talk about it. But I am sorry. And I always have been."

I thought she meant my feet.

I thought she was the one hiding from my history.

Jump to me, all alone, the morning after losing the virginity that was no loss at all, when what should have hurt did not. When I finally faced the jeopardy of this question: "Why not?"

You may remember I said there were two reasons why I remembered my coming home outfit. The first was that I recalled it in living little-girl pink when photos were only black and white. The second is this: I have other memories, also in living colour. Of things that happened before I came to live with my parents. At least, I think they happened before I came to live with them. I hope to sweet baby Jesus they did. When you don't know, you have to accept the only thing you do: Anything is possible. You have to claim your body's history yourself.

I am a survivor of infant sexual abuse.

But how do you prove it when you have no words for where or when or who?

How do you prove it when you're adopted? When before you were three, you had seven different foster homes and three stints in the hospital, and all those records are sealed?

How do you investigate it, let alone prove it, when there's no one to ask or accuse?

You don't. You deny the memories and you doubt your sanity. You tell yourself you're an imposter. That it's nothing but a dream. Just ignore it. Just forget it. It never happened. Did something happen?

No, nothing at all. You perfect denial for years, and it works just fine until you are slapped in the face with the reality that a teenage boy didn't need to read *Our Bodies, Ourselves* to tell you that you don't have a hymen. And you have no explanation for its loss.

The lack of said hymen is confirmed a week later by the woman doctor at the university health clinic who gives you your first internal. When you finally ask, you get an answer.

"No recently broken membrane, but, yes, some old scarring. Evidence of past trauma."

Now new scars match those on your feet. But they aren't smiling. Yet again, scars make you dirty. Triggering is real. I'm doing it now. Rather than relive it, I hope you can forgive me for quoting my novel, *When Fenelon Falls*. It's both history and herstory:

You are maybe three years old. You have two sets of pyjamas. They stay the same, even when The House and The Family don't. When they're going to move you, they iron your yellow dress stiff, snap the silver locket around your neck and the silver lock on your red suitcase. For now it's empty, stashed under This Crib, and waiting for next time. Your pyjamas have lived here, safe in a drawer in This House, for more than seven sleeps: your soft green nightie with the bunny rabbit, your thick winter sleeper with snaps. It's yellow too. Tonight, you are wearing it. Good. Sometimes snaps confuse him. Smile at the bluebird. She's how you know you're not in the hospital. She's like This Crib, baby blue. Hospital cribs are metal. This one has a happy picture pasted on its wooden head. This Lady has made it herself, a birdie cut from a magazine, perched in apple blossoms, bursting pink. Happy notes come chirping out of her tiny beak. You know only the first line of her song, "Bluebird! Bluebird! Smile at me!" That's what This Lady sings as she drops off your bottle, "G'night, baby. Kiss, kiss! Now close those eyes." Bouncy brown curls all soft round her face, she pats your tummy, flicks light into night, and rap-tap-taps down the hall. You sit back up. You drink half your bottle. Never more. You crawl into the farthest corner. Press your back against the bars. Chant the alphabet – you know most of it. Just keep chanting. Hum. Sometimes when he

hears how good you are at ABCs, This Man changes his mind. There's the
slow crunch-thud, crunch-thud – his step in the hall. Sing louder. "A-B-
C-D . . ." There's the slower grind of doorknob. ". . . E-F-G." Can't you
see me? "L-M-N-O-P!" He looks right at you and lowers the bar. Such a
racket! Surely This Lady must hear it This Time? He yanks the bottle from
your hands. He grabs your feet and drags you to him by the ankles. It hurts
to kick him, but you try. A damp palm clamps your mouth, smothering
"W-X-and-Y and" – "Shut up, you lame little bastard!" He smiles.

I still have no words for what he did next.

For how many times he did it.

Or the things he did it with.

But I can make my own hope. I can reframe the jeopardy by asking new questions.

What did my mother know? How much of my history did she
choose to keep under unspoken lock and key? Did fear explain her
distance? What had Children's Aid told her?

It was 1958. What had well-meaning doctors told Children's Aid
in the first place?

Perhaps it was something mother noticed while changing my
diapers? Or something caught by the good Doctor Ridley, when I
kept wetting the bed into my teens? The truth might be sealed in my
adoption file. What had all those trips to the hospital really been for?
My NII said cystic fibrosis. But I also heard my mother's words to Dr.
Salter: "failure to thrive."

Did they not know, or all tell themselves their silence was in everyone's best interests?

I'll never know. Here's what I do know: After three years of women's
history, I went to a feminist therapist. She was the first human being
I trusted with my dreams. I expected, in truth I hoped, she would af-
firm them. She didn't. In 1975, when you used the *r* word, you meant
grown women. No one discussed child rape. As for the rape of tiny
infants, that horror simply did not exist. I assumed myself freakishly
alien, inhumanly alone. Apparently, so did she.

"Was it real, Dorothy? The physical scars suggest it, as does the anecdotal evidence. The details about your bottle and the alphabet both seem so specific, too personal, to be anything but real memories. What worries me, however, are your comments about how during the alleged events, the man hurt your feet." She shrugged. She stood up, although our time wasn't over.

"I really can't imagine how any little girl experiencing... this kind of ... of violation, would be worrying about her feet. I'm sorry, but that makes the whole thing seem more like a later-in-life invention to me. Like something standing in for something else. Maybe it's sublimated anger from losing your real mother? We can talk about that at our next session."

I never went back. I told no one I'd been.

It has since occurred me that most people can't imagine any of my life, let alone help me with it. That able-bodied therapists, even if they're feminist therapists, may not be the best judge of how a disabled infant might react to being probed by adults who may or may not be aliens.

Today, I am so very thankful for all who speak up as survivors of rape. Knowing they'll be disbelieved. Knowing it can ruin their lives. They speak for those of us who cannot. Literally cannot – we were babies. Too young to name a stranger. Too young to name the act. Too little to know the words we needed. Too tiny to ever possibly be believed. It took half a century and the courage of countless survivors before I could say this out loud to another living soul:

"When I say a rapist hurt my feet, I'm not a lying, lame little bastard after all."

Gladly, the Gimp Gets Pregnant

After Western, I did what everyone in their twenties wanted to do as the 1970s became the 1980s: I moved out to Canada's reasonable facsimile of San Francisco, Vancouver. I longed to join an edgy, artsy, lefty culture. I desperately wanted a winter without snow.

In 1979, I met my husband in the heady world of left-wing Vancouver politics. I wanted to learn how political theorists I'd read – Marx, Lenin, Trotsky, Gramsci, Goldman, Althusser, Arendt, Adorno, Chomsky, Foucault, Marcuse, Firestone, Ehrenreich – applied to real life. I wanted to find a family of feminists. Learning all the words to every Ferron song, I began hanging out in lefty cafes along Commercial Drive. Picketing in solidarity with striking clerical workers at Simon Fraser University, I nearly got arrested on the AUCE picket line. In what seems quaint today, I picketed purveyors of porn, shouting, "Red Hot Video. Shut it down!" I helped organize the tour of the first feminist dissident exiled from the Soviet Union, poet, journalist and artist Tatyana Mamonova. With ex-members of the Waffle, the radical wing of the New Democratic Party, I pushed the NDP to honour its socialist roots. I rallied to free the arrested young urban guerrillas of Direct Action, known as the Squamish Five. I joined the Revolutionary Workers League – the RWL – the Canadian branch of the Fourth International, carrying their *Women's Liberation and the Socialist Revolution* (Pathfinder Press, 1979) around in my purse, convinced I'd see both.

To be ready leaders of imminent revolution, the RWL voted to seek unionized jobs. To increase my chances of getting hired, I got my St. John Ambulance first aid ticket and became a First Aid Attendant on the bacon assembly line at Fletcher's Fine Foods. Sliding doors behind a tightly trussed receptionist opened to dripping, gutted pigs dangling from the ceiling. They laid me off, with all the other Christmas workers, one day before the end of our probation. At AEL Microtel, I proudly joined my first union: IBEW, the International Brotherhood of Electrical Workers. Clad in scrubs, wielding a tiny soldering iron, I built circuit boards.

Unfortunately, generation after generation, the left really does eat its own. Our "Turn to Industry" narrowed into sectarian zealotry. Some comrades, unsurprisingly the bossiest, most able white men, devolved into chest-beating workerism, embracing the macho lie of nineteenth century capitalism: sweaty, manly labour matters most. This faction, which scorned public sector unions and worshipped the International Woodworkers of America as the only "real" union, took over the RWL. Many feminists quit, myself among them. Of course, history proved the chest-beaters dead wrong. Public sector unions led change, the IWA shrunk and the RWL collapsed. The bullies slunk off into obscurity, consoled by comfortable incomes in computers.

Not my women comrades.

We rallied and roared. We became lifelong activists.

I have such respect for, and so many warm memories of, the extraordinary women who lived in or dropped into our big sky-blue house on Bute Street: abortion activist Judy Rebick; Orange Prize novelist Linda Grant; lesbian artist Dr. Sara Diamond, who became president of OCAD; and my lifelong friends Pam Singer, who drove for the

London tube and trained shop stewards, and Dr. Heather McLeod, a professor of Arts Education at Memorial University. As practising feminists blending theory and praxis, ours was a lived struggle. It remained so.

It was at Bute Street that I first met Audre Lorde. Sweet housemates, I thank you.

I was well versed in first-wave feminists: Elizabeth Cady Stanton, Susan B. Anthony, Lucretia Mott, Lucy Stone, Julia Ward Howe, Victoria Woodhull, Margaret Sanger; however, except for Harriet Tubman, Sojourner Truth and Ida B. Wells I'd studied no women of colour at Western. None of my history courses even mentioned Indigenous history, let alone Indigenous women. Beyond admiring Angela Davis and the Black Panthers, my knowledge of second-wave feminism – Betty Friedan, Gloria Steinem, Shulamith Firestone, Barbara Ehrenreich, the National Organization for Women and the Equal Rights Amendment – was also largely white. No one heard the term *third-wave feminism*, a call for a more inclusive movement, until a 1992 *Ms.* article by Rebecca Walker. Before Bute Street, I'd read Maya Angelou, Octavia Butler, Zora Neale Hurston, Alice Childress and Alice Walker, but nothing prepared me for the visionary, working-class, black, disabled, lesbian poet Audre Lorde.

She said I should speak *because* I was afraid. *Because* I was not meant to survive.

I cried for days at that insight, published in *The Black Unicorn* in 1978. Eventually, I read her every word: *From a Land Where Other People Live* to *Coal*. I'd never read an activist writer who embraced disability. After her mastectomy, Lorde refused a prosthesis: "Either I love my body one-breasted now, or remain forever alien to myself." With advanced myopia, Lorde was legally blind. But her vision of women as warriors, her desire to examine all her intersections as a black, disabled, working-class, aging lesbian living with cancer, her need to fuse social justice with righteous anger, have made her a personal role model for the last forty years.

I had no way of knowing that the social history I studied, the way I was taught to critique it, the literature, politics and feminism of Bute Street would someday birth a disability activist. If you'd asked me in my twenties, I would have been horrified at the very idea I might become one. I wanted to be a "normal" leftie. I wanted no one to guess how hard I had to work to be one. In my Vancouver years, 1978 to 1983, I grew up, but my feet remained children. Petulant. Willful. Self-centred. To defy their power, I did an entirely logical thing: I got pregnant.

I wanted to have children early. Wanted to be able to push their strollers. Longed to still be walking at their high school graduations. Although we were living together, and rejected the institution of marriage, my partner and I got married. I would not repeat my childhood wound. I refused to give birth to a bastard. I would not give my child a lifetime of almost and second best.

When we visited a geneticist, of course that's exactly what I got. All she could do was take my husband's extensive medical history, look at my empty half of the equation and shrug. All my doctors have been forced to repeat the error so reviled by Sherlock Holmes: to hypothesize from insufficient data. Guesses as to whether my feet were hereditary or caused by cinching range from "almost certain" it was the former to "nearly positive" it was the latter. When I got pregnant in the summer of 1980, guessing itself became insufficient. I phoned Dr. Salter's office, expecting to have to beg his red-nailed secretary for a photocopy of my records.

"Hello, Princess. What's the skivvy? How's tricks?"

Forty years later, I'm still stunned by the immediacy. By his memory. By the reputation that preceded him and followed me. "*The* Dr. Salter?" star-stuck doctors still ask wherever I go. They grip my feet as if shaking hands with the great man himself. His name adorns their textbooks. One full wall of his office holds a giant world map, confidently thick with marking pins, pinprick incisions of operations in deserts, mountains, rainforests and tundra, but he answers me without hesitation.

"Try not to worry, Princess. I really do think it was likely cinching. There is every reason to hope that your baby will be just fine."

He was the specialist. Who was I to question him?

In the textbooks, I'm Patient #617, Female Child.

On his map, I'm a pinhead.

I thanked him for remembering me. I all but genuflected. But when I hung up, I was only two months pregnant and the world quickly became a more fearful place. Clifford Robert Olson began his spree, kidnapping and murdering eleven children in BC's lower mainland. Terry Fox ended his Marathon of Hope in Thunder Bay, diagnosed with cancer. When ultrasounds could not properly see my baby's feet, Dr. Salter's suturing failed; I became completely unlaced.

I remember the flop of large pink hands shrugging at heredity.

Such luxury, such privilege, to be able to shrug at heredity.

At four months, the only thing related to me began to kick.

I began sleepwalking. Twice a week. Every night. My husband installed another sliding chain lock I couldn't reach. He slept like the dead, so no one came after me. I found myself alone at the open door, awakened by the clang, clang, clang of a very-pregnant Jacob Marley yanking on yet another chain. But I preferred it to sleeping, where another nightmare defiled my dreams.

One I know for a fact is no fantasy. It's the story of the It-Girl Edwina. She had to be an It-Girl, a thing, a circus freak. She could not be a real girl like me.

It was my third operation at Sick Kids. I owned the place, wheeling ward to ward, needing no passport but the blue wristband confirming I was Dr. Salter's patient. I went to visit Brandy, in for an eye operation. And I found Edwina. Added to the room, added to a young girl's life at the only fair moment, when her eyes were bandaged. Mine weren't.

I saw Edwina Elephantiasis. Her left foot jumped out from her ankle longer and thicker than her thigh. Three grapefruit toes with grey toenails like baby TV screens. Her left arm ended at the elbow. I didn't want to think about what they removed that was better replaced by a hook. Her right-arm-thing lay still. It crushed the pillow, smeared the pillow, a heavy yard long, an infected lobster claw. Red, cracked and crusty, it had two clucking pincers, no fingers.

"Hi, there," says Brandy. "You'll have to introduce yourself to my new roommate, Edwina. She doesn't talk much." Edwina turns. Edwina Squashed Nose. Edwina Idiot Face.

I ran. That's what you'd call it, even in a wheelchair. Cursing my seeing eyes, convinced in that moment and ever after that Edwina was there to get her other arm cut off, that Dr. Salter would display it still sporting its blue wristband, in some noxious-smelling, aquarium-sized vat, floating like a prized pickled egg with pimply student fingers pointing, "Freak. Freak. Freak."

For all my pregnancy, I gave birth to Edwinas.

I'd prod my belly and count three legs. Then two legs, but no feet. Then two feet, with twenty-six perfectly countable bones, sticking out of its bum like flippers. I was Princess Dorothy of Freak. I carried a monster.

If anybody could fail childbirth, it would be my body. My water didn't break, it leaked. After three days in hospital, they gave me an enema, to "move things along." I made a respectable deposit, told the teenage candystriper I was done then realized I was so very wrong. She thrust a bedpan beneath my bum an instant too late, at just the wrong angle. My shit tsunami deflected off the bedpan, up her uniform, into her face, up the walls and onto the ceiling.

I will never forget her quiet Irish voice.

"Jesus fucking Mary and Joseph. Blessed St. Brigid, take me now."

I just googled *St. Brigid*, discovering that not only is she a patron saint of Ireland, she's also the patron saint of babies, abused children and bastards. What kind of karma is that?

At least I finally went into labour. When the bloody bundle arrived, it was a difficult birth. Pity in the crease between their eyes, they apologized. After the epidural, I felt nothing from the waist down. For the first time in my life I was entirely pain free, and they apologized.

A glance at my newborn son revealed the appropriate number of waving appendages.

His feet looked fine. I told the nurses to take him away. I told my husband to fuck off. He said I'm only supposed to swear during birth. I replied, "Exactly. This is birth. Now get out."

I'm still bitter. It still hurts me: This is how normal people live. This is what they take for granted. In charge. Running with words, able to gallop thought ta-da thought. Without Herkimer's whine, or Horatio's sigh. Without waiting for bone to snap. This is all my mother wanted for me. Not much. Normal. Everything. It lasted sixty-two minutes. No one apologized.

When I'm out of the hospital, friends come to see the baby. These pain-free, adoption-free, freak-free, bundle admirers all tell me the pain of worrying must have been far worse than any physical pain. Must have been. For their sakes.

Five years later, as badly as I wanted another child, as much as I longed for a daughter, what I really wanted was a second epidural. Another episiotomy scar was a small price to pay for a pain-free hour. My feisty daughter arrived so quickly, I didn't get one. Pink and perfect, she got outta Womb Dodge in under an hour. Her feet are still miracles. Thin, strong and dainty.

When my children were born "normal," I was relieved – and resentful.

I tried to hide it. I stood to bathe, diaper and dress my squirming babies. I even played tag. But when they asked why I limped, I said I was tired. When my daughter asked why I never wore dresses, I said, "to disenfranchise the male gaze." An answer I'm sure satisfied a little girl with a bedroom full of Barbies. Just as I'd refused to let my son own toy guns, I originally wouldn't let her have Barbies. When my sister thought it funny to buy her one anyway, we played Barbie the Doctor, Barbie the Construction Worker and Barbie the Archeologist, but my daughter still refused to wear anything but her "chewies dress." Resplendent in her pink cherries, I'll never forget her furious little face at the age of four, when she threw all her pants in the garbage, declaring, "I am a woman. I wear dresses."

In further recursive karma, once I gave birth to babies who weren't bastards, my dad became one. We'd always known Grandpa Palmer was older than Grandma. We'd always known they went by their middle names. Photos of my reverend grandfather showed a handsome man with an exuberant Edwardian mustache and my father's wavy auburn hair A pince-nez made him look professional; the grin did not. A photo of my grandmother at nineteen captured her in a Gibson girl blouse, smiling straight at the camera with my father's dusky eyes. As enshrined in family lore, their story was a love story: they met in church, in Leicester, England, fell in love, married and came to Canada.

Both were long dead when a letter arrived from South Africa exposing their sex scandal. Four decades later, I confirmed its details when fact-checking this book.

My grandfather Robert Cecil Palmer born in 1870 to missionary parents in Ningbo, China, did graduate Cambridge as an Anglican minister in 1894. But my grandma wasn't his first wife. My father and his three siblings weren't his first children. In 1897, he married Caroline Dudley Wilson. He was twenty-seven; she was nineteen. They had three children: Robert, 1898; Catherine, 1901; and Valentine, 1909. After becoming the vicar of All Saints, Wigston Magna, in Leicester in 1901, in the spring of 1912 my minister grandfather became a thief. He stole all the money in the church poor box and jumped on the first ship to Canada. A few weeks later, he was joined in Montreal by his Sunday school teacher, Florence Agnes Pawley.

Born in July 1891, she had just turned twenty.

He was forty-two, more than twice her age, twenty-one years her senior.

To get to Canada, to get off scot-free, they lied about their names, ages and occupations. A year earlier, in the 1911 census, Florence is correctly listed as nineteen, living in Leicester with her widowed mother, four siblings, her widowed brother-in-law and his two children, aged two and four. In this nine-person household, her brother-in-law was a butcher; her mother and sisters toiled in a hosiery factory. Florence was a "Teacher's Assistant." Her passenger record on the *Corsican*, on which she arrived alone on June 9, 1912, documents a well-planned deception. She incorrectly listed herself as legal age, twenty-one. She listed her occupation as "painter," and under reason for coming to Canada wrote, "to be married to Cecil Palmer, farmer."

She posed as Mrs. Reverend Cecil Palmer from the second she got off the boat.

My pious Aunt Muriel was born exactly nine months later in 1913. Then Harold in 1915, Jessie in 1920 and my dad in 1922. The letter said Caroline Dudley Palmer had never divorced. It told my father his minister father was a thief, an adulterer and a bigamist. It told my father and all his siblings that they were illegitimate. They went to their graves believing this true.

You can imagine my surprise when, in 2017, I found court records that had been under mandatory one-hundred-year seal since 1916. They told the story of how Caroline Dudley Palmer, abandoned in scandal with three children – fourteen, eleven and three – was forced out of the vicarage, her home for over a decade. She had to sell all her worldly goods to pay her husband's debt to the church. Then she divorced him. Her 1916 petition was granted on the grounds of his desertion and adultery with Florence Pawley, adultery proved by the birth of a bastard baby in Canada. In absentia, Reverend Palmer was ordered to pay the full costs of this divorce: sixty-seven pounds, eleven shillings and one pence.

There is no record of payment. Caroline never remarried. She lost a son in each of the world wars. Living another thirty-two years without child or spousal support, she died in poverty at age seventy, in 1948. Some of her family moved to South Africa to escape the shame.

I can find no proof my grandparents ever married or knew of the divorce. In cheerful bigamy, they may have married illegally in Canada under new middle names. The 1921 census lists Grandpa as "40," when he was fifty-one. He's "married" in Toronto with three children and "wife," Agnes, correctly listed as "29." He is a "clergyman and teacher" at the prestigious St. Andrew's College for boys. My grandfather earned an excellent income teaching boys to become men, but this stud guppy in a clerical collar paid no child support and never saw his three British children again. Every Sunday, he mounted his pulpit to preach about living a godly life.

Did he fear being caught? Apparently not.

Did he get caught? Apparently not.

If the church knew he'd committed theft, adultery, "living in sin" or bigamy, he'd have been defrocked. Or maybe not. Powerful men always wink at each other's transgressions. But it may explain why he was buried alone up north. Anglican bishops might keep silent for a Cambridge graduate, but might draw a sanctimonious line against burying him on sacred ground.

What did my grandma think and feel about all this? What passions drove her at twenty? Was it true love? Or the desperation to escape a grinding working-class life? Perhaps both?

When she had children, did she finally feel the enormity of what she'd done to another mother of young children? Did she eventually feel karmic judgment? After she left with the husband of a forty-two-year-old woman with three children, the same man left her a widow with four children at age forty-three. Was it worth it? We'll never know. I saw only the minister's wife who read her Bible every day. Everything she ever thought died with her. She told no one.

My mother told everyone. When she read the letter, she crowed. She said the Palmers always thought they were better than everybody else and it would do them good to be knocked down a peg or two. In a quiet moment alone with my dad, he cried. For the father he'd now truly lost. For siblings he would never meet. For parents who lied. For a love story that wasn't one.

I said, "It's okay, Dad. Now you and I get to be little red-headed bastards together."

Holding the Door Like Hodor

As a teacher for twenty-four years, for every second of every teaching day, I had to work to hold my closet door closed. I had to pretend to be something, and someone, I wasn't.

After my son was born in 1981, I did my teacher training at Simon Fraser University. In the bandwagon, buzzword of the day – *multicultural education* – we discussed race, sex and class as practising feminists. We began to critique the celebratory "I see no colour" approach of multiculturalism, realizing we could celebrate food and holidays all day long but racialized kids still got bullied and beat up at school. We listened to educators of colour and supported their call for anti-racist education, an approach that directly opposes racist power and privilege.

When I graduated in 1983, the newly elected right-wing Social Credit government had laid off hundreds of teachers. I got a job, but had to leave BC to do so. My husband and I, two socialist atheists, packed up our two-year-old and drove a rickety old van to La Crete, Alberta, a Mennonite colony on the border of the Northwest Territories. Farm kids, most without TV or radio, my grade fives were the healthiest children I've ever seen. They spoke Plattdeutsch at home, English at school. The colony had split into several churches with varying degrees of orthodoxy, wearing everything from home-sewn bonnets to blue jeans. The girls did PE in their dresses, infinitely better than I did. Some parents resented the intrusion of "English" heathens. My shopping cart got rammed at the Betsy Bee by infuriated Old Colony women calling me names I thankfully didn't understand. But my first class was a dream, without a single discipline problem. There wasn't a single fist fight in the school in my entire year at La Crete.

The students in my second job, in a four-room school outside Olds, Alberta, home of Holocaust-denier Jim Keegstra, were also fit, but far more competitive. For contrast, we next moved to Calgary, where I worked in an adult high school. Next to a prison, some students got escorted to their seats in chains. After the birth of our daughter in 1986, we returned to Ontario in 1987. Between university, BC and Alberta, I'd been away fourteen years. My siblings had grown up without me. My parents had grown old and moved to Pickering.

We settled ten minutes away, in Whitby. I taught for the next twenty years for the Durham District School Board (DDSB). I moved from Parkside Elementary to Ajax High School and then to O'Neill Collegiate in Oshawa. When I arrived at their Performing Arts program, I discovered the major production had already been chosen – *A Christmas Carol: The Musical*. When I cast a young woman as Scrooge, it raised some over-plucked eyebrows. But beyond that small rebellion, I designed the set, directed the play, costumed it, sang along, applauded and said nothing. Tiny Tim limped on a different foot in each scene. Needing some better tiny actors, my son played A Boy Called Ignorance; my daughter played A Girl Called Want.

For all my Durham years, I joined Ontario Secondary Schools Teachers' Federation (OSSTF) initiatives and committees, including one anciently called the Status of Women Committee, after the 1967 *Royal Commission on the Status of Women*. For the last fifteen years of my career, from 1993 to 2007, I taught in a brand new, highly diverse Pickering high school: Pine Ridge Secondary School. Affectionately called "the Ridge," and pejoratively "Pine Box," it had multi-subject workrooms to encourage "teaching across the curriculum." Unfortunately for my very right-wing school board, large open workrooms also empowered union solidarity.

In the 1990s, when I served as elected Branch President, we earned our reputation as one of the most radical schools. During the attacks of the Mike Harris Conservative Government to dismantle public education, I wore two hats as both Branch President and Picket Captain. I stuck my head into oncoming cars, trying to convince drivers not to cross our line. I've been insulted, sworn at, spat at, threatened by irate parents and hit by a wooden stake ripped from a picket sign. I gave up any chance of promotion in my anti-union board. At Maple Leaf Gardens, I joined twenty-four thousand teachers to protest Harris' Bill 160. It is the proudest achievement of my life to have helped lead the largest work stoppage in the history of North America. On October 27, 1997, 126,000 teachers shut down every school in Ontario. In three provinces, I've walked a picket line for three months of my life. I've lost three months' wages defending other people's children.

I fought all my life for everyone except my disabled self.

By 2001, my limp was unconcealable. Years of pulling my ankles upright had inevitably worn out my knees. No medication could mask my pain. My new orthopedic surgeon had the rubicund cheeks of a British schoolboy freshly returned from chasing a spring kite. After a requisite worshipping at the feet of Dr. Salter, he frowned at my X-rays and echoed him.

"Well, Ms. Palmer, as you can hear and feel, your knees are down to bone on bone. I could do a double knee replacement now. That's really what you need. But here's the catch: at age forty-six, you'd be looking at two double knee replacements in your lifetime. Thanks to baby boomers, however, knee replacement is improving rapidly. I recommend arthroscopic surgery now. It lasts five years. By then, if you're lucky, you'll only need one double replacement."

I thought I could handle hearing the word *operation* again. What I couldn't handle was hearing it applied to another part of my body.

Like my favourite new TV show, *Survivor*: just when you think you've managed to "Outwit, Outplay, Outlast," you get voted off the island.

"Wouldn't it make sense to do the double replacement now, to walk as long as possible?"

"You're free to get a second opinion on how your feet factor in, but any doctor will be guessing. You've already defied the odds the Great Man Himself gave you." Then he shrugged.

It came out of my mouth before I could stop it – anger I'd long stifled in silence.

"Why do doctors all shrug? Do they teach it like some bloody Mason handshake?"

Thankfully, he took it stride.

As those with a healthy stride have the luxury to do.

Yet again, I had a choice that wasn't one. I opted for arthroscopic surgery and informed Herkimer he'd be going first again. His answer was unprintable. Swear words I didn't know I knew. My new surgeon consulted multiple specialists to ensure he wouldn't ruin the fragile cooperation that kept my feet and me on the same script and performing in concert. Multiple X-rays got shot. No technician called my feet "piggy hooves," but I heard it just the same.

If anybody could fail simple day surgery, it would be my body.

Herkimer and Horatio were outraged I'd rewritten our script so late in the show. Wooden armpit crutches I hadn't used since my teens fit right back in hand, but I fell non-stop. On a good day, I could cross a room. On bad days, I hit the floor at step three. When you fall on armpit crutches, it bruises your arms and blackens your breasts. I tried not to panic. I switched to metal crutches with forearm cuffs. But the five of us – Belinda, Beau, Herkimer, Horatio and I – never bonded. No matter how I begged my feet, something fundamental in the way we walked had changed. Something in my body or brain or both had stopped cooperating.

By not speaking when I walked, by concentrating like a Zen master, I'd managed to script three voices. But a cast of five produced the incomprehensible chatter of the Tower of Babel and I came tumbling down. One of Horatio's bones cracked like my mother's china doll.

It pains me still.

Throughout my recovery, I had more than one kind soul tell me how their dad, distant cousin or dog catcher was instantly healed by arthroscopic surgery, praise Jesus, and played tennis the very next day. Some eyed me with suspicion, as if I were malingering or lying. As if I wanted to be on crutches for half a year. As if it was all a clever plan to deplete my earned bank of sick days and my retirement gratuity. As if I sought attention and pity. As if I were faking it.

The physiotherapist I liked the least helped me the most when she caught me crying.

"I'm sorry," I told her. "Not being able to walk makes me sad."

She leaned into my face. All three hundred pounds of "No Bullshit Need Apply."

"You're not sad, Missy, you're pissed. You been angry a long time coming. And you got a right to be so. You got two shitty choices. Give up now, go get a wheelchair. Or, stop fighting the pain. Let it win. Forget how you used to walk. It's gone. You gotta start all over again."

She was right. I had to take "baby steps," real ones, not those of ableist metaphor. Using only Beau, I unlearned, then relearned. I re-auditioned each of my extraordinary bones, rewrote stage directions for all of us. Seven months after surgery, the three of us returned to teaching.

I'm ashamed to admit that I didn't start hearing the nasty ableism in everyday language until I returned to Pine Ridge in 2001, crutch in hand. As the only one on a crutch in a school of two thousand pairs of feet, I heard things I once would have missed. On the first week back in my workroom, I heard a pair of fit, young feminist teachers smugly decide that "lazy women use food as a crutch," concluding, "It's so lame. They just need to grow up and step up."

"So lame," indeed. All I had to do was get taller and step up? Thank you so very much.

Their meaning was clear. A crutch was an excuse. A fake prop. Used only by the weak in character. A poor substitute for health or maturity. This was my introduction to one of the worst myths about disability: That we're all faking it. Exaggerating. Lazy. In it for the sympathy. That our crutches are nothing but "crutches." I knocked Beau over to see if the metal clang of a real crutch hitting terrazzo might give my judgmental colleagues cause for pause. It did not.

I remember pulling into my accessible parking spot on one of my first days back in September 2001, when my radio declared that a plane had hit the World Trade Center. My son was in New York. His story is proof of the power of the arts. Like his dad, when he was little my son struggled to move his eyes from left to right. He saw print and numbers upside down and backwards. At age five, his verbal skills tested at the high school level, but his grade one teacher, all of twenty-four in her first year of teaching, kindly told us he would never graduate high school. His teachers thought it was dyslexia, then dysgraphia, then auditory processing disorder. To strengthen his hands, he began playing piano in grade three, and then in grade seven picked up the flute because it fit in his backpack. I believe the five horizontal lines in music notation grounded his eyes. After Tosha, his springer spaniel, the flute became the love of his life. I had to yell at him to get him to take it out of his mouth to eat. In grade eleven, he earned a seat in the Toronto Symphony Youth Orchestra. In grade twelve, in a very rare honour for a Canadian, he won a full scholarship to a prestigious conservatory school, the Manhattan School of Music in New York City.

On that terrifying day in 2001, it took all day to reach him. One I spent with my ableist imagination on steroids, fearing he was dead, or worse: burned, left with hands too maimed to play. Could I convince him to want to live anyway? Thankfully, I found him safe and sound.

It is only now that I'm retired that I can see how my teaching years injured me.

In my three decades of teaching, I never taught a book with a disabled hero.

I never taught a book about a disabled woman, or by a disabled woman. I taught plenty of books and plays with disabled villains, all of them male, all of them damaged, all of them damaging to me. But I said nothing. As teachers of literature, we work hard to find books that represent our diverse students. No one ever talks about the fact that diverse teachers suffer the same erasure and silencing. We can spend our entire professional lives teaching a curriculum that misrepresents and excludes us. We may never see our authentic selves in what we teach.

Can we teach beyond the stereotype of Tiny Tim?

I never managed to do so.

Teaching excellence has two unalterable criteria: We must be indefatigably abled and unfailingly cheerful. Arriving on time each time, we must race around a large, crowded building all day, lugging lessons, audiovisual equipment, assignments and teaching texts to multiple rooms. We must be able to stand all day at the blackboard and reach over our heads to write on it. We must be "on" and on call to meet the educational, social and personal needs of some eighty teenagers at a time. After arriving at 8:00 a.m., I gave up my lunch for improv practice. After school, I might have a union meeting or play rehearsal. After supper, I prepared lessons and marked endless *Macbeth* essays, sometimes until well past midnight. Like all good mother martyrs, teachers are expected to work while sick, to never let pain or illness affect "our kids." We must deny any stress or strain on our mental health. We must deal with committees, colleagues, parents and administration with unflagging energy and good cheer.

The very philosophy of education is ableist to its core: It praises "a healthy mind" in "a healthy body." It assumes at every moment that both are "normal," available to all and merely a matter of will. To be this "healthy," "good" teacher, I doped and denied my pain. So many other closets got proudly thrown open during a career that spanned three decades, but not mine.

When I began teaching in 1983, there were no openly gay or lesbian teachers. Coming out would have cost them their jobs. Over time, we elected LGBTQ union reps, welcomed gay and lesbian department heads, administrators and consultants. Schools had openly dating gay and lesbian couples. I attended the wedding of lesbian kindergarten teachers, held in their school library. Similarly, as a beginning teacher, I had no openly gay or lesbian students. Coming out would have cost them their teeth. In the 1990s, a few brave students came out in grade thirteen. Some got bullied and beaten. By the time I retired, many students were more safely out, often when they walked in the door in grade nine. We had joint staff and student Pride Committees.

In 1983, school leadership was uniformly all-white and all-male. The only employees of colour were custodians. My career saw initiatives such as STAR: Students and Teachers Against Racism and students of colour elected as student council presidents. By my retirement from Pine Ridge, half my colleagues were women, many in leadership roles. We were led by my board's first black woman principal. But in a school that identified as one-third black, one-third brown and one-third white, we had few teachers of colour. A needed change that's still evolving.

But the change that blossomed for other marginalized groups never took root for mine.

I had no openly disabled colleagues. Off probation, many colleagues divulged invisible disabilities, but begged me not to tell. My union, OSSTF, negotiated contractual improvements to fairly transition those who became disabled mid-career out of teaching and into long-term disability. We had no initiatives to hire disabled teachers into teaching. The rule of athletic boys on the playground normalizes the continued rule of abled men in every level of education. In a collusion of inaccessible schools, affinity bias and racism, white, abled,

English-as-a-first-language, middle-class male principals still prefer teachers who look and sound like them.

Rejecting that cookie-cutter mentality, my LGBTQ and neuro-divergent students often sought out the alternatives of goth, tech, emo and nerd culture. Some joined a fandom or started live action role-playing (LARPing). Having fallen in love with improvisation at Loose Moose Theatre in Calgary, I helped them build another refuge: the only two-year, two-credit improv program in Canada. Thanks to standing-room-only at our Friday lunchtime shows, my improvisors earned the status of football stars. Our winning teams competed nationally in the Canadian Improv Games.

Of course, in the first week of improv class, even the nerdiest boys tried to run the show. My teaching years saw male comics rise to celebrity status: George Carlin, Eddie Murphy, Tom Hanks, Robin Williams and Scarborough's own Mike Myers. They made it possible for boys, even jocks, to choose improv without anyone questioning their masculinity. In predictable art-imitates-life, boys assigned themselves high-status roles and made the girls their second bananas: he was the doctor/boss, she was the nurse/secretary; he was the man hiring her, firing her, trying to kiss her, lie to her or kill her. He was always in charge. Some girls raged. Some clammed up. Some reached for the 1950s shtick of Phyllis Diller and Joan Rivers: in self-deprecating, self-victimizing bimbo humour, they made themselves the target of their own jokes. When the girls ceded the stage to boys hogging the show, the boys not only didn't see a problem, they loved it.

If I'd taken an "I see no colour or gender" approach, nothing would have changed. Instead, I did the math.

At the end of the first week, I read out tabulations of airtime, gender, race and role status – stats my class hadn't known I was taking. Year after year, I can still see their shocked faces, ranging from a desire to do better, to denial, to fury. Inevitably, the most infuriated were the popular, funny white boys. They had the most airtime to lose, didn't like being told they'd stolen it from girls and students of colour. My job was to help my class build an inclusive democracy, to build their confidence as they explored how to best share joy.

I began with a personal motto: "Learning is also about unlearning. To put something new on the stage, first you have to clear the stage." I announced that second-language accents, verbal zingers, violence, guns and victim humour were lazy, cliché and hurtful. Because we were funnier without them, they were hereby banned from the stage.

I always got the same reaction: "But there's nothing funny left!"

It took a whole period to discuss why racist or sexist "jokes," why Apu on *The Simpsons*, were all victim humour. It took longer to convince high-status white teens for whom ridicule was a staple of success. My students of colour schooled us all on this far better than I ever could. The class began to keep their own stats, began to see that improv wasn't about being individually funny but collectively and reflectively alive. Their grade came from the generosity they put into building troupe mentality, what I called "the symbiosis of sharing." I taught them the forced fit, a central tool of improv and a motif of my life: take two incongruous things and "marry them together," so that "working against, with and through each other" they "deepen the drama."

I'm most proud of my improv girls. Today, we all see Melissa McCarthy, Leslie Jones and Kate McKinnon as top-tier comics. When I began teaching, with few role models, girls in my troupes had to teach each other what few believed back then: girls are just as funny as boys. Sometimes funnier. Today, I can also admit that the comedy was always something of a front.

Behind closed doors, my theatre was the home of my political practice. In my drama training, I fell in love with Teacher-in-Role, a long form improv developed by Dorothy Heathcote where both the teacher and the whole class stayed in role the entire time. In role, Heathcote would create a problem in another time and place and the class would work with her in role to solve it. I got my Drama Specialist certification in London, England, with celebrated lefty dramatists

Jonothan Neelands, Tony Goode and Warwick Dobson, who developed Whole Group Drama by deepening Heathcote's techniques. When I took my students on tour to other schools, I added the Forum Theatre of Augusto Boal. Without a script or props, Boal used Forum Theatre to build expressly political problems into his work. An improv became a "forum" when improvisors invited the audience to take on roles inside the improv to address the problem.

For both staff and students, I created anti-oppression Whole Group Drama workshops that seem sadly prescient today: an immigration drama where the country of Candidia faces the choice to build incarceration camps and the arrival in an idyllic small town of witchfinder Matthew Parris, who asks villagers to save themselves by building pyres and burning women.

My students and I toured our board with audience participation improv workshops on bullying, sexism, racism, homophobia and sexual harassment. Teaching one hundred and fifty students a year, times twenty-four years, totals to thirty-six hundred teenagers. They taught me that the ceding and sharing of space can be done with collective joy. Together, we built reflective, inclusive, activist classrooms. As I told my every class and still believe, "Improv doesn't just make better performers. It makes better people."

Thanks to the joy of improv, I had less regret about not being a writer. In retrospect, I also see that improv taught me how to be a better writer. To always say "yes" to the drama. To scene build quickly. To endow and enhance character. To raise the stakes. To never settle for an easy laugh. To disrupt status relationships. Above all, to listen. As I hope you read here, improv teaches us to cultivate recursion, to "look, look and look again." To plant an idea and keep returning to it, until we've sprouted every single seed of learning. And then, to say thank you.

But did I share this equity and personal growth with my disabled students? No. I did not.

The only disabled comic I'd ever seen was Geri Jewell, who did stand-up about living with cerebral palsy. She was the first disabled actor in a primetime series, *The Facts of Life*. But it ran from 1980 to 1984 – none of my students had ever heard of her. Each September, when I asked my classes to name a disabled comic, actor or writer, none ever could. But it wasn't their fault. You can't read or watch disabled artists if none are cast or published. School librarians made sincere efforts to include women and racially diverse authors. I had class sets of *The Color Purple* and *The Handmaid's Tale*. Although disabilities are truly intersectional, are found in every marginalized group, there were no disabled authors in my high school curriculum.

I want to make it incandescently clear that teachers are not to blame for this.

When teachers aren't already worked to the bone, when we don't have intolerable class sizes and marking loads, it's a pleasure to spend our personal time seeking out, reading, pondering, researching and planning lessons for a month-long unit on a new novel. But you can't teach books by disabled authors if none are published. You can't buy any new books without a budget. We barely had funds to repair books, let alone buy new ones. Getting diverse books into schools has never been about convincing teachers; it's about money. It requires dedicated, government-checked funds that principals can't siphon off to the football team. To get new books, my colleagues and I often pulled out our purses. On my own dime, I staged Ntozake Shange's Tony-nominated play, *for colored girls who have considered suicide / when the rainbow is enuf*. Learning from that cast of seven amazing young black women remains one of the best experiences of my career.

But I went my whole life, as student and teacher, longing for books with people who looked like me. Longing to teach them. Longing to read them. To my students, my children and myself. In my English and Drama curriculum, disability had no presence except a negative one. I could not counter the fairy tale or the free-floating bile, all the carrot and stick messages of ableism: beautiful people are deserving and good; disabled people are ugly and crippled at heart.

Traditional English pedagogy fed my students the poison of eugenics, told the same lies that led to Hitler's disabled cleansing. With a hidden, breaking heart, I explained that in "great" literature a damaged body was predisposed, if not predetermined, to harbour a monstrous soul. A disabled body might house a brilliant mind, but never a kind human heart. Shakespeare enshrined the evil cripple Richard III. From Long John Silver to Captain Hook, amputation of the body decreed an amputation of the soul. It fuelled Frankenstein's monster's hate, an envy that disfigured monsters inevitably took out on the abled world. "A broken body," I can still hear myself forced to explain, "dictates a broken moral compass and a broken mind."

Although the term *inspiration porn* hadn't yet been coined by Stella Young, I heard many students spouting it. When I showed *The Elephant Man*, they found it inspiring to see a disabled man doing ordinary things, like being seen in the street. They all agreed that Joseph Merrick was "gross," but he "deserved to live because he was nice to people." This casual acceptance of euthanasia reoccurred with *The Chrysalids*, with students defending the idea that after a nuclear holocaust of course anyone with disabilities, or even slight differences like six toes, would have to be killed or sent to the Fringes, "so that the real people could survive." Few students had read *A Christmas Carol*, but thanks to the Muppets, Disney or Jim Carrey, they all knew Tiny Tim. They accepted the spectre of his angelic death, just as they accepted that the first to die in *Lord of the Flies* was the boy with the mulberry birthmark. Both deaths make perfect sense in the ableist hierarchy we all absorb from childhood. Be a good little Tiny Tim and we'll pat you on your inspiring head until you die. Speak up, complain or name the beast and we'll kill you.

Mulberry Blemish Boy, we won't even bother to learn your name.

Beyond the classroom, I earned a role as a red-headed feminist rebel. Refusing to dress "professionally," needing warmth and a full range of movement, my teaching wardrobe consisted of track pants and knit tops. Denouncing Casual Fridays as "a classist, sexist attempt to police what we wore Monday to Thursday," I claimed Casual Every Day, insisting that students needed to see that professional women didn't have to look like Barbie dolls. If my colleagues wondered why a woman who quilted, who loved fabric and colour showed up each day in little boy's running shoes, few asked. If I only wore loose, untucked tops, if I've never been able to wear a belt, if cinching one around my waist makes me panic and start to cry, no one ever knew why.

But wear a costume long enough and it isn't one – it's your wardrobe. Only my sensitive, Harry Potter–loving daughter saw it for what it was: my cloak of invisibility. She said, "Mom, wear a dress with your running shoes. You'll look like a real bad ass, a total punk rock queen."

I appreciated, but could not take, her advice.

I literally had no words to do so.

I didn't hear the word *ableism* until after I retired. I certainly didn't know that the shame I carried about my limp, my running shoes and my every fall was the product of internalized ableism. Without language, I did what I could. I told my students no slapstick, for safety reasons. I didn't understand what is so clear now: it's both victim humour and ableism to laugh at falling, at the temporary humiliation and demotion to incapacitation. Today, I unfriend anyone who sends me "funny" links of people falling. When my students laughed at slapstick, I felt sick but told myself my over-sensitivity was my problem, not theirs.

I absorbed every drop of shame. I played a good little Tiny Tim.

Nobody knew that silencing better than my disabled students. To this day, I wish I'd served them better. Built in 1992 to new accessibility standards, Pine Ridge was the first, and at that time the only, high school with ramps and an elevator. Disabled students from all over Durham County got bused in. Full of hand-picked young teachers, Pine Ridge developed many progressive initiatives, but no one questioned the way we stereotyped "the wheelchair kids." Defining them by their chairs kept them at a distance. I don't know if other teachers saw what I did: that other than "buddies" assigned to them by Guidance for the first week of grade nine, the wheelchair kids had no abled friends. They studied alone. They ate alone. While teachers knew better than to ever suggest our students of colour "segregated themselves" in the cafeteria, that phrasing went unchallenged for disabled students. Progressive, caring teachers saw no ableism to fight. I remained an outspoken critic of "I see no colour," but I collaborated with and was totally complicit in perpetuating "I see no disability."

In private, I pried my closet door open just enough for a disabled student to peek in, admitting my years with crutches and wheelchairs. They'd never seen such a teacher creature. I encouraged my disabled students to audition for school plays and the improv team. I wasn't surprised when they did neither. I didn't ask twice. When I learned they all had to go every day to the office to ask for an elevator key, one they had to give back each night, the notion of a school patting itself on the back as accessible, but making disabled students beg each day for a key, infuriated me. I copied my key and gave one to every disabled student I saw. When our school evacuation plan left our disabled students grouped on display in the foyer to be shot at or burned, I refused to leave the principal's office until that got changed.

But my solidarity went no further. I couldn't yet imagine a disabled community; it never occurred to me we could be one. No one ever reached out to disabled students collectively. No one encouraged them to use their combined voices to speak up, and out, about their lives. I still struggle to explain why I couldn't do better. I'm ashamed of the answer: I benefited from my silence. I'd worked hard for my abled privilege; I couldn't give it up. Without role models, without curriculum, without allies, without language, I couldn't side with the wheelchair kids.

Everyone, including me, smiled at them in the hall and kept walking.

Invalid is Not Invalid

In 1993, my first year at Pine Ridge, I made the difficult decision to leave my husband. Some thought it was because I'd found a younger man. In truth, I'd met someone who, the first time I explained it, instantly apologized for using the words *bastard* and *lame* and vowed never to use them again. That was one promise he kept. He took Herkimer and Horatio in his hands, and asked me to teach him how to massage my feet. He volunteered to do so, every night, for all our nineteen years together. Ask any physiotherapist: passive movement builds strength and stamina. It battles pain. JP is one reason I walked for as long as I did. I give him full credit for it.

In 1996, we moved into a small, dilapidated, pre-Confederation house north of Uxbridge in the hamlet of Leaskdale, two doors down from the manse of *Anne of Green Gables* author, Lucy Maud Montgomery. Like most old house virgins who underestimate the time and money renovation requires, we spent ten years thinking we'd be done next year. But, for a time, we were obliviously happy. In a dawning century, I found new hope. I reconnected with my parents. My dad taught my kids to swim in Balsam Lake. My mother and I struck another separate peace. Together, we gave her grandchildren Christmases to remember.

In Leaskdale, I began having another reoccurring childhood dream, a good one.

I'm Ensign Palmer, star-hopping with Captain James T. Kirk in the USS *Enterprise*. Unfortunately, when we land on the unexplored Zephyria, I'm wearing a red shirt. When I fall off a cliff, I'm saved by Zephyrians, but Captain Kirk finds no green alien to kiss. Zephyrians are shimmering silver spheres, like flying soap bubbles the size of bowling balls. They can hover, rest on ground or water, zip effortlessly though both and through each other. They meant it as a greeting when they zipped through fallen me. Faced with a life like the burnt-up *Star Trek* Captain in a Box, Christopher Pike, who despite living in the future remained disabled, I chose another option. The Zephyrians transferred my human consciousness into a brand-new sphere. I bade goodbye to my star-faring comrades and my human life. I found happiness.

Zephyrian dreams seem to last forever. I never sleepwalk during them. In Zephyria, I fly. I dance. I scurry up trees with the gravity-defying grace of Earth squirrels. Zephyrians zip faster than dragonflies and stop on a dime. It isn't just the absence of pain, although that is a wonder. It's the quality and equality of communal life. The unity and belonging. I live with others interested only in my heart and my brain, beings with no concept of prettier, taller or skinnier. They have no conflict, no weapons and no war. They view all kinds of competition as a sad waste of time, as proof of an immature and inferior species. They share. Each Zephyrian has a voice, a musical thrumming with which they can commune with one or several or all, regardless of distance. Each has meaningful work: they build, they make art, they ponder philosophy and science, all by projecting holograms from deep inside themselves. In total wish fulfillment, my subconscious designed the most equitable and deeply satisfying life I could imagine.

I also note, only in retrospect, that my fantasy world erased disabled people.

It looked suspiciously like my real world. In 1993, in my first autumn at Pine Ridge, I was a thirty-eight-year-old mother of a twelve-year-old. On October 24, on a canola farm in Wilkie, Saskatchewan, forty-year-old Robert Latimer murdered his twelve-year-old daughter, Tracy. Born with cerebral palsy, Tracy was six months older than my son when her father rigged up his truck and put her in it to die of carbon monoxide poisoning. Claiming he had acted out of love, he insisted he wanted only to put his child out of her misery. Many friends and colleagues expressed open sympathy for a parent burdened by such a daughter. Some argued that he acted out of true love and compassion. Some said mercy killing should be legal. But the heart of any such debate isn't love; it's hate. If killing a disabled child isn't murder, it means that disabled children aren't really human. I knew and felt this but let the debate rage around me, saying little or nothing. I still could not defend Tracy, for fear people would see the Tracy in me.

It was increasingly clear to me that disabled people and teachers were both disposable.

In 1997, the Conservative government ordered protesting teachers back to work and raised our teaching load from three classes of some ninety students to four classes of 120 students per day. Our employers increased our workload by 25 percent, but still expected "good teachers" to do a stellar job without complaint. Teachers were demoralized – we were run ragged. Many developed health problems and depression. One day, I said something I'd never in my life said to a child: "Please ask somebody else. I'm too tired to help you."

At the end of one such day, when I got on the elevator, another teacher entered with me, one of the most organized and decisive teachers in the school. The doors closed. We waited. When the elevator didn't move, we panicked. This was before cell phones. It didn't occur to either of us to use the elevator phone. We were trapped. For the night. Our children would go hungry. We both started to cry. Then we realized that neither one of us had pushed the button.

That exhaustion, that inability to think and help like teachers, is what Mike Harris' Conservatives gave the children of Ontario. I believe future Conservative governments will happily do worse.

I began to see how capitalism colludes with the "survival of the fittest" to divide us.

For years, I'd taught that nasty hierarchy of Renaissance Christianity, the Great Chain of Being. It ranks all forms of life, from God through angels, stars, kings, nobility, commoners, animals and vegetation, right down to stones. My students needed it to understand *Macbeth*, to see how Shakespeare was telling Elizabethan audiences that Macbeth was justly punished for violating the natural, God-given order of the Chain by killing the king. One year, I asked myself a new question: Why aren't there any disabled people in this supposedly Christian world view?

Over time, I created my own nasty Great Ableist Chain of Being, careful to include the stones. Gold-medal Olympic athletes are gods. Dead athletes are angels. Living athletes are stars. Young, male, highly paid players of hockey, basketball, soccer or football are kings. The ultra-fit and sporty are nobility. Abled folks are commoners. Fat people are the giant apes that sit between humans and monkeys, who can choose to be human again if they lose weight. People with invisible disabilities are lovable monkeys. People with visible disabilities are also monkeys, but they aren't cute. Non-mobile disabled people are plants that need to be confined to their beds and sometimes given a good spraying. Non-verbal and non-mobile disabled people, they're as useless as stones. Throwing them into the desert to die would be no loss to anyone.

Is this world view offensive? Damn straight it is. That's the point.

It's the perfect world view for competitive, colonial capitalism. Bolstering racism and sexism, in each level of the Great Ableist Chain of Being, young, white, cis, straight, upper-class, good-looking, legitimately sired men top their group. This hierarchy enshrines competition as normal, natural, desirable and inevitable. Each group stands on the backs of those below and looks only up, to their perceived betters, in admiration and supplication. They never look down, except in disdain, pity or charity. It's a world without solidarity. Without unions. Without empathy. Where euthanasia could easily be, and historically has been, rationalized. A world, to quote Audre Lorde, where people like me were not meant to survive.

In another forced fit irony of my life, when I rejected the Chain, my daughter climbed it. She became a nationally ranked synchronized swimmer with Olympic aspirations. Blending her athleticism with feminine grace, I wish my father could have seen her swim. I tried to hide the ambivalence with which I watched her. I tried to hide my jealousy. I drove her to practice six days a week. I paid synchro fees totalling thousands of dollars a year. I designed her team costumes. I cheered and applauded and brought her roses. But watching her excel at a sport made me furious and ashamed of my fury. I told no one this: my own child made me feel profoundly proud and impossibly inferior.

After April 20, 1999, everyone who walked back into a high school after the Columbine massacre knew another fearful fury: that the lack of gun control, the lack of mental health services for young people and the toxic, entitled anger of young men would continue to cost student and teacher lives. No wonder I longed for an escape from the real world.

When I finally told JP about Zephyria, he rolled his eyes. "Leave it to you to design a world without sex. How do these bowling balls get it on? How do they make little Zephyrians?"

"They don't. Zephyrians don't need children because they don't die. If their sphere gets damaged, they repair it themselves. They don't need to reproduce because they're immortal."

He sighed. "So, this is your utopia, a world without physical love, without intimacy?"

"No, they love. They touch. They spin up next to each other and share colours."

He laughed. "No thanks. I'm quite happy to have a penis, thank you very much."

That should have been my first warning.

By 2007, at age fifty-two, I'd walked longer than anyone ever guessed I would, but thinking on your feet is definitely the privilege of those who don't need to sit down. When I tried to think and walk at the same time, my brain couldn't function through pain soup. Beau dumped me multiple times a day. In crowded school hallways, he let rushing student feet kick us both flying. By the final bell, I was dead on my feet. I'd taught many students in wheelchairs, but I couldn't imagine how to be a good teacher in one. I'd long accepted I could never take another job in my board; no other school had a ramp to the stage and an elevator. But how could I direct, or do improv, in a wheelchair? I'd never seen anyone do it. I was too proud of all I'd done to do what I feared would be an almost second-class job. I reached the point where I couldn't teach, or grade, with a clear mind. Pain had won. My role in the walking world was coming to an end.

I was beyond grateful when JP encouraged me to retire early.

In Ontario, teachers have successfully negotiated the eligibility to retire when we reach the eighty-five factor: a total of age plus years of service. If you have taught for thirty years, since age twenty-five, you can retire with full pension at age fifty-five. But because teacher pensions are end-loaded, and I didn't start teaching until age twenty-eight, my early retirement at age fifty-two left me with a pension of only nineteen thousand dollars a year instead of a full pension of fifty-three thousand dollars. JP assured me it wasn't an issue. I'd supported him for years as a self-employed artist and an underemployed taxi driver and bookstore clerk. In the last two years he had become a senior vice president in a video game distribution company. His salary had rocketed to $250,000 a year. We could live well. I could get off my feet. I could book the knee replacements I'd deferred for seven years. JP promised me I could finally, three decades deferred, embrace my dream to write.

I began my novel. Writing bliss lasted exactly eleven months. The full story is easily another book; it's also not this book.

In May 2008, as documented in official court record by the Superior Court of Justice Family Court in file FC-10-234, after nineteen years together, right before my double-knee surgery, JP took a business trip to Buenos Aires, went to a sex club called Madahos and bought himself a twenty-year-old girl. He dumped me to continue to purchase her. He spent all his RRSPs, all our savings, on her. With independent legal representation, we negotiated a legal separation agreement using the government's *Spousal Support Advisory Guidelines*. We signed it December 6, on a cold anniversary: the day of the Montreal massacre when fourteen women engineering students were murdered at Montreal's École Polytechnique.

As per the court record, for two years, JP took his "girlfriend" on holidays to Scotland and Mexico, paying all her expenses and her two-hundred-dollar nightly fee. To keep paying her, he stopped paying spousal support. He dragged court proceedings out for over a year, but lost his case. He was imputed income and fined for "disingenuous disclosure." The judge set up permanent, court-ordered spousal support. JP paid it for ten months. In June of 2013, he quit his job and disappeared. On June 22, 2014, after he failed to show for multiple court appearances, the Ontario Court of Justice issued an arrest warrant for Jean-Paul Bernard Rehr.

Still on the run from the law and in default of over $160,000, he has paid nothing since 2012. But in a perfect example of law made by men for men, defaulting on child or spousal support isn't "a criminal offence" in Canada. Accordingly, the police won't do anything to find him, or bring him to justice. They claim it's too expensive.

In 2016, at Christmas, I found him. In the south of France. In grad school. On my dime and my back. Taking the M.A. and Ph.D. in history I could never afford. Publishing and presenting around the world, he's become an expert in "the history of heresy." I imagine he quite likes that more palatable euphemism digital humanities experts have coined, so he doesn't have to admit to being an expert in burning women. Canadian authorities still won't pay to have him arrested and returned. They expect this disabled old witch to burn for the rest of her life in the precarity of financial jeopardy, while yet another abandoning man gets off scot-free.

When you're dumped by a crutch and a crook, a Beau and a beau, you forgive neither.

"Someday, I'll take *Despicable He* for every cent he owes me, Alex."

"Just Be a Sec, Hon," and Other Jolly Justifications for Stealing My Space

I love driving and will cherish it as long as I am able. An open country road in autumn, a summer night speeding under stars, a portal to portal drive into Toronto, all give me the mobility and the freedom walking cannot. Until forced to sell it, I had my dream car: a Volkswagen Beetle Convertible named Bessie Blue.

Behind the wheel, I look like any other woman. Until I park.

I've had my Handicapped Parking Permit for thirty years. That's what it was called when I first put it in my window. I think changing the name to Accessible Parking was a mistake. Given my need to park as close to the door as possible, especially in winter, my disability is a handicap: a restriction, impediment, constraint, hindrance or obstacle. Let's name that clearly. I want the world to respect my extra difficulty. The term *accessible parking* erases my difficulty. It enables a fundamental moral shift.

Simply put: when my spots were called Handicapped Parking fewer people stole them. Decent people consider it extra shameful to steal from a handicapped person. Call it Accessible Parking and the theft of it doesn't sound so bad. The spots are *accessible*. Able-bodied people can *access* them. So, they do so. In droves.

The newer, pink "baby carriage" spots only encourage further thievery. They're the gateway drug. Everyone knows they're a courtesy, not a legality. Once you've stolen from a baby, once you've driven right over a pink baby carriage, it's easy to drive over a blue wheel-chair. Twenty years ago, I almost never saw a permit-less car in one of my spots.

Today, the theft of my disabled parking is getting worse, not better.

Before you roll your eyes and label this a mere inconvenience, a micro-micro-incursion, let me be clear: My car is a mobility device. It's as necessary and important to my life as a crutch or a wheelchair. Stealing my disabled parking is a HULK SMASH attack on my person. It is not a "victimless crime." Indulge me for a moment. Let's start at the beginning.

Why does anyone have an Accessible Parking permit?

Where did they get it from?

Assuming it wasn't stolen and sold online, a driver has one because they and their doctor both signed legal government forms certifying the applicant as having a visible – or invisible – disability, illness or condition. It's none of our business. A doctor has decided that their patient should not risk extra distance over pavement that can be uneven, wet, icy, too far, too cold or too hot. It's hard to qualify for a perma-nent permit. Many are only temporary. When it's permanent, it's for damn good reason.

Beyond the medical, moral and legal imperative, accessible park-ing is also a social justice issue. It represents the world we're building. One with, or without, inclusion. One with, or without, the casually ableist brutality of stealing my safe spaces. Because as the theft gets worse, so do I. On good days, I'm lucky to take the thousand steps able-bodied people take before noon. I hoard every step. Because my steps are literally numbered, I cannot, I will not waste even one.

On a crutch, this is how I buy gas:

I drive ten minutes from home. Not because gas is cheaper; it's more expensive. But because after months of scouting, I found a gas station with pumps that sit on a very low, narrow island. If you didn't know pumps have raised islands, let alone at different heights and widths, that's because you've been looking at them all your life and not needed to see them. They're no barrier to you; they didn't used to bar me. But now that it takes two arthritic hands to lift the hose, I can't use my crutch. I have to leave it in the car. At gas stations with tall, wide islands, I can't reach hose or buttons unless I step up on to the island. I could lean one hand on my car to mount the island, but then I'd be marooned with hands full of hose and no way to get down.

At my station with its narrow island, I can reach both buttons and hose from the ground. I wait for pump C, where squeegee and garbage sit on my path at the fourth of nine steps I must take anyway to get to the pump. I can dump coffee cups and clean my windows, all without a single extra step. I can keep a grounding hand on my car, for a fighting chance to stay upright. It takes nine steps to pay. Then three to the hose, three to return it and nine steps back. Twenty-four steps. If I want to clean my windows, it's fifteen steps down the sides and seven across the front and back. Should I take these forty-four steps, or live with dirty windows? There are always other things I'd like to try and do that day. More necessary, or more pleasurable things, for which I could really use those extra forty-four steps. Because, know this: my steps never last a full day.

This is the meticulous devotion I must bring to every step of my life.

Whenever I'm forced to take another twenty, or two hundred steps past a permit-less car that has stolen my spot, I fear one of those extra steps will be my last. The one where I fall for the last time, fall on the waiting spot on the planet that has my broken-hip name on it. Then, I really won't get up. It makes me livid. I start to hyperventilate. Because of some selfish, jerkface, thieving pig, I might have to take the one extra step that ends my walking life forever. If you get only one thing about my disabled life, please get this: it's expensive.

Pain exacts a toll. Fatigue doubles it. Fear triples it.

Every single day, day after day, I'm handed the cumulative cost of that bill. You can either help lower my costs, or make me pay more dearly. Each extra step makes me that bit more tired; raises the risk that I'll fall, possibly alone in my apartment, where no one will find me for days.

But it's not just my life you're risking. If that one more step adds one more moment of pain, so I see the child running into the road but can't lift an aching Horatio to the brake in time, I won't just hurt myself; I'll kill someone's baby.

The thieves who steal my spots never have to think about any of this. Centring their abled entitled selves, they "Just Do It." Emboldened by the pervasive prejudice that disabled people are few in number, lazy and faking in the first place, many do it repeatedly without guilt or shame. That obliviousness is ableist privilege in action. So, what can I do to stop them? Before judging my final decision, please know I spent decades trying everything else I could think of first.

For fifteen years, my Denial Phase, I did nothing. Like Mary, I pondered it in my heart. In my ten-year Pollyanna Phase, I sometimes, ever so sweetly, asked drivers without a permit if they had one. A rare few re-parked. Most shrugged. Many swore. Or both. In my five-year Passive-Aggressive Phase, I put hundreds of cards on offending windshields: *You stole my Handicapped Parking spot. I took a photo of your car and sent it to the police. Expect your $400.00 fine in the mail. If you do it again, expect to get caught again.* In my short-lived Occupy Phase, I blocked a thieving car, cut my engine and called the cops. When they arrived, they gave the thief a caution. They apologized to him and berated me.

Of course, nothing I did worked. That's how entitlement works. That's how abled folks take care of each other and defend the world made to their convenience. Permit-less drivers of all persuasions, teens and taxi drivers, housewives and horticulturalists, hippies and high rollers, all keep cutting me off and stealing my spot. They jump out of cars singing, "Just be a sec, hon."

Or the more anatomically honest, "Fuck you, freak."

Hence, my Anarchist Phase, begun in the snowy winter of 2012. When Beau kept dumping me and my ex did likewise, I superglued a big brass button to my crutch. If asked, I planned to tell half the truth: this retrofit was medically advised to keep my arthritic hand from sliding off the handle. I did not plan to add that after using my trusty nail file to trim the button's edge, with apologies to Bryan Adams, it cuts like a knife. If, in my uneven winter gait, it accidently slits zigzag scars along the sides of permit-less cars, if paint scraped from the cars of thieves tats the breast of the new fallen snow, well what can I say but oooopsie!

At fifty-three, in 2008, I survived my first Christmas alone in thirty years, while a man exercised his white, male, ableist, racist, upper-middle-class privilege to be a stud guppy, to keep buying and keep screwing a beautifully abled young woman from an impoverished country. His twenty-year-old squeeze, like my twenty-year-old grandmother, clearly cared nothing about the spouse and children she hurt. By 2012, the man I loved added illegal impoverishment to injury. Was it projection? Did every parking spot thief stand for his thievery? Absolutely. Vengeance put the rum-pa-pum-pum back in my Christmas.

Do I regret it? No. Not one single scratch of it. I've finally found a sport I can believe in.

To paraphrase a slogan from the '60s: "Think globally. Vandalize locally."

Keesters and Kybos: Why the Matter of Bathrooms Never Stays Flushed

In the twenty-first century, facing escalating fascism and global warming that spells planetary suicide, we're debating bathrooms. Right-wingers want to dictate who can use them, to fear-monger about what they claim will happen in them. The transgender community and the disabled community are waging parallel, but sadly separate, defence campaigns.

How can we best offer solidarity to each other?

Let's start here: We all have the right to use a public bathroom of choice. Period.

And separate is never equal. This means the transgender community and the disabled community, which of course includes the disabled transgender community, have the right to use their bathroom of choice. For disabled people, our only possible choice is an accessible bathroom. A *wheelchair accessible bathroom* is one not barred by stairs, with a stall large enough for a walker, wheelchair or scooter. With grab bars and a door we can open, shut and lock. Where we can reach tap, soap and paper towel or dryer. Without being humiliated or infantilized. Without having to ask for help. *A fully accessible bathroom* would meet a much higher standard of care, including an adult change table, call button and Braille signage.

I'm asking all those supporting the right to put a keester on a kybo of choice to support the right of the disabled community to do likewise. It's critical. Control my bathroom, and you control my dignity and my day. Please don't steal my safe place to pee. My ass is literally on the line. If you note a change of tone here, you're right. I'm embarrassed. I find this topic so painful, so intrusive, so goddamn insultingly obvious that I have to write about it from a distance. As full-blown satire, as the butt of a joke that isn't one.

"At great cost to my pride, Alex, I'll take us all to *A Winter's Tale of My Tail*."

'Twas the night before Christmas, when I left the house. Every creature was stirring their festive beverages, when I had this double-double epiphany in Tim Hortons: when you get old, pee is your first priority and poo is a pressing number two. So, whether it's an itty-bitty bloom in your jeggings – the premature ejaculation of a giggle or sneeze – or a geyser spouting up your belly into a giant soggy map of Australia, you might as well turn a spritzing tail into a comic tale.

My shit hit the floor on that almost Holy Night because my car phone charger died.

For anyone, it's an inconvenience. For me, it's terrifying. Imagination explodes. I'm alone. I can't call for help when my crutch throws me into traffic, over a bridge, under a Mack truck or this grandma gets run over by a reindeer. You get the picture. I needed a new charger. Now. On Christmas Eve. At closing time. Fortunately, a phone store sits two blocks away. Unfortunately, it's a retrofit in an old mom-and-pop. I trust by now you know it's an ableist privilege to be able to use the nearest store? It's a luxury I don't have. Instead, just as Sherlock had to keep a map of London in his head, I have to store this kind of accessibility information:

1. The strip mall in question has only six parking spots. No accessible spot.
2. The store has a narrow concrete doorstep, easily an unlawful foot high.
3. It's got a heavy wooden door from hell, determined to knock me down.
4. It's got a high-set, hard-to-turn doorknob – no e-button, no push bar.
5. Said door opens the wrong way, out into the street.
6. Lifting Herkimer to the stoop, I have to balance Horatio and my crutch back on the ice.
7. Then I have to twist the knob, step back down and backwards, to pull the door open.
8. I have to hold it open, regain the step and slide my weight along the door.
9. When the door shoves me into the store, I have to take its push without falling.
10. When I leave, I get to do it all over again, like Ginger Rogers, backwards.

Try it sometime. If abled folks had to do this, it would headline the Winter Olympics.

I'd like to "buy local," but I'm tired of Able-Bodied Bullshit Bullying Advice. That's ABBBA (apologies to ABBA), my term for any suggestion that rules made by and for the able-bodied apply to me. They don't. I can't take transit. To buy local, I need locale parking.

I pull into Walmart and brace myself for the Christmas carols.

After a decade in choir, if I hear even one, I start thinking in lyrics. The pain doesn't show signs of stopping. I've got some corns a' popping. But when I try to park in the snow, greedy thieves, they won't let me do so. I can't have myself a merry little Christmas when shiny horsepowered sleighs go dashing through the snow to steal my accessible parking. Then, of course, a Christmas-dispirited millennial elf rolls her Magic Marker eyes at ancient me.

"Of course, we're like, outta chargers. Whatdidcha expect? Everybody knows they're the best, like, stocking stuffer. Like, right?"

In true, like, miracle, I scale the Matterhorn of my local store and buy a charger seconds before closing. The clerk is a meticulously groomed young man in a crisp white shirt and thin black tie. I watch to see if my, like, bill gets stapled to, like, the *Watchtower*. I cannot watch my tongue when Mr. Millennial deigns to show me, button by button, how to use my debit card.

"Young man, you can explain this to me after I teach you how to tie your shoes."

"What? Of course, I know how to do that."

"So, it would be condescending and insulting of me to stereotype you by your age?"

He looks at me like he wishes I were an old Xbox. At least then he'd know how to play me. And my crusty, retro qualities could be considered charming. Instead, fearing I might pull a glowering of cats from my purse, he grabs my arm to joystick me out the door. To prevent a fall, I lean my butt full weight on the old wooden door frame, hoping to slide down against it.

And I get stuck. Really stuck. Christ-on-the-cross stuck.

How is that even possible?

The proud head of an old screw speared the butt cheek of my track pants. Suspended off the stoop by my elastic waistband, it's the one time I can't fall at jumpsies. I'm as helpless as the Scarecrow in *The Wizard of Oz*. In homage to *The Princess Bride*, I'd yell, "Inconceivable!" but while that does apply to the fathering of baby J, it does not apply to my own limp dangling.

A passing weekend warrior in a Maple Leafs jersey skates right up to me. He grabs me, almost appropriately, yanks me down and rips me a new asshole.

Now that's an episiotomy no one can love. An Oh Holy Fright sound made worse by the fact I can feel the newborn breeze, but not see just how big the rip that birthed it might be. Mr. Millennial has a bird's-eye view. His face betrays a conflicted forced fit: a "Ha ha" straight outta *The Simpsons,* and *Monty Python's* advice to the nauseated, "Better get a bucket." I reach 'round my rear to source his discomfort and mine. Where pants should be, I see pink old lady flesh.

From the top of my crack to the top of my thigh, my new asshole is triangular.

Mr. Millennial, like, giggles. Mr. Hockey, with good sportsmanship drilled into his athletic head, tries not to laugh. He fails. It comes snorting out his nose.

Back in my car, Jack Frost is nipping at more than my nose. The jingle hop has begun. I have to pee. I also have to poo. I lack a partridge in a pear tree, but do have a poking turtle head. Home is close but – it's Canada – Tim Hortons is closer. I blame all that happened next on this: I had to take another fifty steps. My accessible spots had all been accessed by thieves.

Thumpety-thump-thump, thumpety-thump-thump, look at Gimpy go!

All I want for Christmas is my two front feet to be held up by my third, but as I pull on Timmy's heavy glass door, Beau slips on a patch of unsalted ice. He goes flying. I'm lifted up by a young family, stared at by the youngest who sniffs, frowns and slowly hands me my crutch.

"Mommy, is it Tiny Tim?"

Her mother, intending kindness, smiles. "Yes, dear. It's just another Tiny Tim."

And heaven and nature sing. There it is. I'm an "It."

It is everything and all they see.

The accessible stall reads "Out of Order," but I can't use it anyway. The same six-foot-four man who sets "eye-level" peepholes sets the height of accessible toilets. As bereft of the tools I need as Hermey the wannabe dentist on the Island of Misfit Toys, I cannot bring a pole vault to a toilet. I must leap up and down without one. Unsafe and unsanitary: when your feet don't reach the floor, you can bounce your teeth off the bathroom floor. Been there, done that, got the not-Hermey-but-a-real-dentist's bill. I know the abled world finds slapstick funny, as long as it sticks someone else. But it's no joke when you're the one snot-bleeding on a floor that could grow penicillin, when you're the one watching snickering feet go by. So, I cram into the "normal" stall, hang up my coat and pull down my pants only to be greeted by the baby-shit brown milkshake with which the infant messiah anointed his swaddling clothes.

This is what no one tells you about getting old: it soils everything.

I can't bend my arthritic spine. Gone are the days when I could do the Medically Advised Arse-Wipe for Women, away from the vagina, front to back. Instead, I have to spread my knees and bend at the hips until my face is level with the toilet. But this day, just as Mary had no room at the inn, I've got no room next to the sanitary bin. I can't spread open. I cannot wipe my bum.

Someone is going to make themselves filthy rich – pardon the puerile pun – inventing a portable bum-wiper. I don't understand why no one has cottoned on to this and done so already. I've drawn possible prototypes in my head but can't decide what to call it. I waver back and forth between *Crack Attack, Poo-Be-Gone, Tush Tickler* and *Palmer's Ass-Wipe Whisperer*. Without one, I have to do what I have done more times than I should ever admit even once.

Pulling my underpants up, I mount the toilet rim and commence not-quite dry humping it for dear life. Of course, it's disgusting. My no-longer-tighty-whities become the Wonder Bread upon which I energetically spread as much homemade, organic butt butter as possible.

Once my ass is merry and bright, I don't want to pull gooey granny pants over my shoes. So, I reach into my purse for my Shit Emergency Scissors. I cut up both leg holes through to the waistband.

Now I can pull the mess of it off me, shoes unsullied. To clean myself up, I raise a supplicating, shit-spackled hand, only to discover there is no toilet paper.

Inconceivably, as I stand up, I rebirth Mr. Turtle who has been hiding in my pants. A gymnastically-gifted reptile, he tumbles down my shins and backflips into a headstand on my left shoe. When I flinch, he somersaults off my no-longer-white runner, and I step on him.

What a holly jolly Christmas! Poo bedecks my limbs, my shoe, the toilet and the floor. I'm out of Kleenex and swaddling clothes. My high blood pressure joins the party, shooting a scarlet ribbon of blood out my nose. No, it is not possible to hang both ass and nose over a toilet.

This is not an inconvenience; it's a Christmas Carrel Cluster Fuck.

When another carrel seeker arrives, I explain there's no toilet paper and ask for paper towel. A kind Scottish burr replies, "There isna any, dearie. Only onna them air dryer thingies."

I consider trying to stuff my naked butt into it.

It makes me sore afraid.

But then, *zip*, in a whiff of lavender and a flash of blue hair, under the locked door of the accessible stall, a wise woman at least a decade my senior slides on her back with a bound. She thrusts her gift into my stall: a full roll of butt wad. "Happy Hogmanay, hon!"

I clean all I can reach. I can't bend down to reach the floor, so I "wax on, wax off" with toilet paper under my shoes. Conscious of how long I've made her wait and how much I smell like a manger, I dip a last bit of paper in a freshly flushed bowl to clean my hands, grab Beau and open the door. Too mortified for words, I bypass the sink and head out the door.

My Glaswegian wise woman flies after me. "Dearie, you'll be needin' this."

She ties my coat quickly around my waist. But she's too late.

Right at eye level at the table beside the washroom, sits the saintly First Family.

The littlest one yells, "Look! It's Tiny Tim! And I see his bum!"

The kids laugh. And their parents try not to, but fail. My Glaswegian angel snorts, and we both laugh. Then and only then do I see we've been treading unwisely in my footsteps where the poo lay dinted. Forget frankincense and myrrh; we wise women bear shit on our shoes.

Any hope of Gloria exits my Deo. I giggle. I dribble. I pee.

Piss sprays the floor and my wise woman's feet. I try to step back, but, of course, Beau slips. In preservation reflex, I reach for my wise woman's coat, latch onto a button and take her down with me. I'm apologizing to her, the First Family and All Amused Bystanders when the mop girl comes running. She slips. She skates. She doesn't score. Attempting an Elvis Stojko, she drops like Josée Chouinard. On top of us. How festive. How special.

We're Tim Hortons' freshest Christmas doughnut.

Complete with sprinkles.

Enough. Let's make my disabled midnight clear: it ruined my Christmas.

It felt like payback karma for a long-ago eve, when I pushed my Tiny Tim into the snow. I'm an atheist. I don't believe in divine retribution, but I'm still a minister's granddaughter. The next morning, in my coat pocket, I find a wise woman's second gift: a glowing brass button.

I figure my epiphany about how to use it came straight from the newborn baby J himself.

Lancing the Lingering Legacy of One Little Lame Liar

With each passing winter on my crutch, I grow more like Ebenezer Scrooge: all I want is to be left alone. After a day bent over my books, I don my nightshirt, remove my pinching shoes and stretch my toes out to my electric heater. I spoon my own gruel, aka instant chicken noodle soup.

All my suppers must be fast and cheap. On a good day, I can stand for the three minutes it takes to scramble eggs. On bad days, I can take twenty steps to the cupboard for a granola bar. I have to really want a cup of tea to stand back up for the endless sixty seconds it takes water to boil and attempting any more complicated kind of cooking with Beau is an exhausting farce. Wherever I lean him in the kitchen, he falls. He often trips me, as the spaghetti sauce on my walls and ceiling attests. After picking him up for the umpteenth time, dizzy to the point of nausea, I throw my half-cut salad in the trash and call the Supper Santa: Pizza Pizza.

As my life shrinks like Scrooge's skinflint heart, when I close my eyes, it isn't Jacob Marley's face that haunts me. It's the ghost of the girl that was me. A girl who jumped back up when she fell, quick to offer the chipper lie: "I'm just clumsy. Don't worry, I'm fine."

Like Marley, I still wear "the chains I forged in life"; I'm bound by denial.

In *A Christmas Carol*, his sentimental Victorian morality play famously set in Scrooge's mansion and that little house in Camden Town, Dickens casts Tiny Tim as the tragic hero. He's not. He's an unrealistic and unattainable standard of disabled perfection. But to speak out against him feels disloyal, like I'm disrespecting the almost-able tiny girl that was me. I need to find a way to denounce Timothy Cratchit without erasing either of us. I'm encouraged by the last line of Dickens' tale: "nothing ever happened on this globe, for good, at which some people did not have their fill of laughter at the outset." And by Archie Bunker: "When I get my hands on that phony-baloney, little, lame meathead, I'm gonna smack his cheeky, wrinkled ass!"

It's true. I long to spank the sanctimonious crap out of Timothy Cratchit.

History has long since debunked other vile stereotypes. Today, Uncle Tom, Little Black Sambo, Tonto, Shylock, the thieving gypsy, the pidgin English Yellow Chinaman and the silent, dutiful wife with slippers are all rightly rejected as offensive. It's only disabled people who are still stuck with a role model from the 1843 heydays of Queen Victoria. Tiny Tim sweetens abled childhoods, not mine. Otherwise woke, Disney-critical adults flock to *A Christmas Carol* as if being read for "charity" by Patrick Stewart or Neil Gaiman changes its ableist messaging. Adults who'd never listen to *The Story of Little Black Sambo* get all teary over little lame Tim. Like baby Jesus, Tim's primary role is to face death obligingly. Dickens liked to kill poor children: Little Nell, Jo, Smike and Paul Dombey. They lived just long enough to tug at readers' heartstrings.

Why do modern audiences still fall for a sickly sweet boy with uncritical hook, line and sentimental sinker? What does the youngest child of the long-suffering Bob Cratchit and the unnamed Mrs. Cratchit "stand" for?

He's the good cripple. Compliant. Non-threatening.

Above all, he's "inspiring."

Tiny Tim is ableism's Prime Image Poster Boy, the penultimate role model for all on a crutch. His parents represent "the good, deserving poor": non-analytical and non-complaining. Their tiny son is "the good, deserving cripple." Heartwarming. Humble. Kind. Patient. Passive. Optimistic. Unquestioning. Uplifting. Angelic. Equally non-analytical and non-complaining about the poverty that's killing him. He's ennobled by pain, reconciled to early death and incessantly, unstintingly cheerful. As Scrooge's character foil and saviour, in glowing innocence, his role is twofold: to make Scrooge look heartless and to magically heal his heart.

Tiny Tim is so wholesome, so ready to burst into song, he could be a Disney princess.

And he's an undying haunt, as unkillable as Sherlock Holmes.

From radio to stage and screen, from steampunk to scholarship, the sweet silver bell that is Tiny Tim keeps on a-ring-a-linging. Famous Scrooges include Alastair Sim, Laurence Olivier, Orson Welles, Basil Rathbone, Henry Winkler, Jim Carrey, Michael Caine, Bill Murray, Susan Lucci, Barbie and a Klingon. Countless TV shows and cartoons paid homage: *The Bugs Bunny Show*, *The Smurfs*, *The Jetsons*, *The Flintstones*, *Beavis and Butt-Head*, *Mr. Magoo* and *The Muppets*. Like that Mariah mall carol, Tiny Tim is a zeitgeist earworm. But he's always the second banana, always the prop. How many Tiny Tim actors can you name? I'm guessing none.

My Tiny Tim isn't angelic; he's a pernicious little shit. He's play-acting. He's Eddie Haskell on a crutch, the suck-up from *Leave It to Beaver* who tells adults what they want to hear. He's as believable as P.T. Barnum's Feejee Mermaid. He totally snows his poor father who deifies his tiny boy: "He hoped the people saw him in the church because he was a cripple, and it might be pleasant to them to remember upon Christmas Day, he who made lame beggars walk, and blind men see." When Bob Cratchit hoists his angelic son to his shoulder, he's as light as a feather and no burden at all. In the real world, as my mother never let me forget, beyond the financial burden, raising a real disabled child is not a spiritual experience. It's often chore and drudgery, as enjoyable as the endless re-mending of bloody leotards.

Conveniently omitted from every version since the original, Dickens' Tiny Tim is more Borg than boy. He "had his limbs supported by an iron frame." He lived in a cage. Real children in cages, as we have seen so painfully on America's southern border, feel trapped, defeated, frightened, despairing and angry. Tim's total denial of his cage is either insincerity or illness – a Christ-on-a-Crutch Complex. Regardless of Dickens' intent, here's the impact: "You better watch out, better not cry. Better shut up. Tell the Tiny Tim lie." For two centuries, thanks to the fictional Tiny Tim, no real disabled people can complain without feeling shame and guilt.

Tiny Tim has stolen our right to be angry.

His hagiography shrinks and silences us.

His beatitude scars us all.

Here's the true moral of his tale: the abled world wants to keep disabled people tiny, both in our numbers and in our voices. Saint Tim keeps himself so tiny, he's no trouble at all. As long as disabled people follow his example, we'll never complain. We won't demand awareness, accessibility, funding, housing, education, employment or good medical and community care. We won't see ableism at all. I should know; I spent decades being a good little Tiny Tim.

But that's not all of the skivvy.

Here's what the "look, look and look again" of improv tells me.

Like the misanthropic Scrooge, I spent my life distancing myself from my community. I gave disabled people the same cold shoulder he gave the gentlemen calling for charity. I scoffed at the nightmare of my disabled self as "an undigested bit of beef, a blot of mustard, a crumb of cheese, a fragment of an underdone potato." My disdain echoed his famous declaration about the poor: "If they would rather die, they had better do it, and decrease the surplus population." In the ghostly warning of his own death, Scrooge is a man so hated by his fellows they sell his bed curtains. When they visit Camden Town, the Cratchits are grieving the death of Tiny Tim. It portends a bleak future: "This boy is Ignorance. This girl is Want. Beware them both . . . but most of all, beware this boy." But the very notion that Scrooge can change history, heal himself and his world, simply by "discovering Christmas in his heart" is a truly dangerous lie.

Let's first consider the possibility that Ebenezer has an invisible disability, one his age, gender and the Victorian class system made easy to hide. What changes when we see Eb as a depressed senior? Isolated, too proud to ask for help, grieving the loss of his sister and only friend. His facade of superiority hides the fact he's lonely, eating poorly and in pain. Given his shy, geeky childhood, an inability to return affection, a compulsion to reduce life to numbers, he may also be neurodivergent. In short, there is serious disinforming danger in the very idea that Scrooge could be "scared straight." When he leaps out of bed, instantly spry and no longer needing his cane, he embodies the ableist trope that disability can be cured by a good attitude.

Real disabled people are not cured by ghosts.

Or by overnight attitude adjustments.

Scrooge and Tiny Tim are both constructs of Dickens' deeply imperialist, colonial mind: one that can see poverty and disability, but beyond the cure of capitalist kindness, has no strategy to change them. As long as disabled people and the poor are seen as needy children, Ignorance and Want will prevail. As long as disabled people are "burdens," we're weights that abled society can choose whether or not to shoulder. This deep-seated belief that our human rights are both charity and a choice underpins and perpetuates abled privilege. As long as we're "Christian burdens," the filling of poor and disabled glasses depends on "Christmas spirit" and "goodwill."

Valorizing the rich as saviours is the second reason Scrooge's story is dangerous.

For years, I thought the gentlemen calling for charity were the good guys. I was wrong. They forge the chains between classism and ableism, preaching: "Like the poor, disabled people will always be with us. We should help these poor souls at our good-hearted convenience, if and when they move us to do so." These "do-gooders" siphon off just enough guilt to make healthy, wealthy folks feel good about themselves while they keep poverty and ableism in place. They see no irony or insult in championing abled-only fundraisers, "silent auctions" and "fun runs." They graciously "spend a day in a wheelchair" with other abled people, ensuring they keep a safe, insulated distance from real disabled people. Abled do-gooders aren't kidding when they say, "The disabled kids I volunteer with give me more than I give them." It's true. They get feel-good affirmation of their top ranking on the Great Ableist Chain of Being.

They get to walk back out into the abled world, superiority affirmed and ego stroked.

And they stay comfortable, never having to address how they benefit from ableism.

Today, I see Dickens do-gooders walking straight out of the nineteenth century and into arts fundraisers. Intelligent lefty artists and arts supporters see no problem with fundraising to include disabled people. When you announce an event then fundraise for accessibility, when you raise money to move an event to an accessible building, or to hire ASL interpreters, or CART, here's what you're saying: "We'll invite all the abled people first. We'll budget to ensure those who look like us can attend. But if disabled people want to attend, sorry, there's no money left. We'll try fundraising. If abled people are generous and kind enough to pay extra, and if you disabled people agree to donate to pay extra for yourselves, then, hey, you can come, too."

If anyone ever announced that the inclusion of any other marginalized group would be contingent on fundraising, the arts community and general public would rightly be outraged. But it's still perfectly acceptable to fundraise so disabled people can attend because the inclusion of those few, rare disabled people out there is seen as a charitable, optional extra. It's no accident that the belief that disabled people are charity cases benefits those rich enough to patronize the arts, the same capitalists who have historically also run money-making charities. Why should disabled people ever have to rely on the capricious largess of guilty liberals and rich people?

Being dependent on goodwill and charity affects disabled people far beyond the arts.

It's the rationale behind all uses of the word *special*: from special needs camps, to the Special Olympics, special education, Special Housing and special living allowances like the Ontario Disability Support Program. As long as we are "special charity cases," we aren't equal citizens. As long as our welfare is optional, and not the collective, permanent, human rights responsibility of all, disabled people remain at risk. It's the very structure of "charity" that is the problem, the notion that beneficent, abled rich people can stoop down to help us "poor benighted souls." Or choose not to do so. We've all fallen for the most successful con job of ableist colonial capitalism: that no other way to organize life on Earth will ever work. We've been so expertly brainwashed that artists of all kinds endlessly reimagine the end of the world, but can't envision an alternative way to live without all the oppressions that plague this one.

How would a truly woke *Christmas Carol* change the narrative?

Scrooge and Tiny Tim would be visited by the ghost of Tommy Douglas, bringing free, quality medical care. When we all woke up, we'd ask Timothy and Ebenezer what they wanted, for themselves and from the rest of us. We'd listen. We'd organize Camden Town to feed, clothe, educate and love all our children. We'd never call them Ignorance and Want. We'd ask and use their real names. Together, we'd sing out our own ending: "We bless us. Everyone!"

My Mother Tongue Walks Like a Man

I often wonder what that was like for me, to have to give up my name and accept another. To answer to a stranger's name, after almost three years of answering to mine. I don't remember being angry or crying. I do remember my mother repeatedly handing me the first doll she bought me and saying, "No, you aren't Susie. This doll is Susie. Your name is Dorothy."

The first time I heard the word *crip*, I cringed.

By 2012, I knew I didn't want to be a Tiny Tim, but neither did I want to rhyme with *trip* and *drip*. Conflicted about turning the word *crippled* into any kind of endearment, I questioned the wisdom of rehabilitating ableist language. If slurs lose their venom, are we erasing the historic oppression they wielded? How do we explain how vile those words once were if we normalize them as everyday speech today? I've certainly seen the word *bastard* lose its historical insult, to everyone except bastards like me. I further worried that *crip* wasn't an inclusive term. Mad and Deaf/deaf people do not identify as crippled. In deeper resistance, as someone who had not come to grips with her own internalized ableism, *crip* still carried unpleasant associations for me. It felt damaged, inferior, slow and unworthy. I worried that we could reclaim *crip* for our bodies, ourselves, but it would always have negative connotations in the abled world.

If you haven't guessed it already, after falling, overthinking is my other true gift.

Of course, I was wrong. It just took time for me to see it.

Language is power. Words don't simply relate experience; they shape and value it. New words smash and recast power. Reclaiming language gives us the tools and the courage to reclaim ourselves. Today, I'm happy to discuss how crips can crip history, how both abled and crip readers need crip lit, how we will all benefit from crip-designed workplaces, buildings and cities, and I fully support #CriptheVote. As I gained respect for my crip identity and community, I stopped being a cringing crip and began cripping my own language.

I'm still learning. It's flat out impossible to expose all the ways ableism shapes and values language. It governs all discourse, spoken and written, every genre, all age levels. It slips out by accident, ambushes and strong-arms us (like this) even when we know better and are trying to do better. And sometimes, people don't really want to do better.

I take full credit for convincing hundreds of teens to stop saying, "That's so gay!"

I'm a total failure at convincing anyone to stop saying, "That's so lame!"

Year after year, my abled students watched me limp and told me *lame* wasn't an insult. They looked at me on my crutch, and told me there was nothing wrong with using the word *lame* to mean what it also means to all my otherwise politically correct, well-educated friends when they so casually use it: Wrong. Inadequate. Invalid. A pathetic second best. Half-hearted. Lazy. A laughable almost. A fake. Yep, that's me. I'm so lame, I let the world use me as a slur.

When I challenge friends for using *lame*, they utter a knee-jerk apology and use it again the next day. I cut my students some slack when I discovered that many, particularly my ESL students, didn't know *lame* had any meaning beyond slang. I had to use an example they knew.

"It means physically disabled, like Tiny Tim. He's lame. A lame boy on a crutch."

They always laughed, "Okay, so lame really is lame. What's the problem?"

Educated adults have no such excuse. And neither do I. Because I too often ignore it. I hear friends use it, wince and say nothing. If I challenge it, I feel guilty, petty and small. Then I tell myself, that's self-silencing. If I've learned anything from Audre Lorde, it's that silence is something I must never practice or empower. If I've learned anything from decades of anti-sexist, anti-racist, anti-homophobic work with teens, it's this: the foundation of any privilege is not having to see it, being able to assume your world view is normal, universal and always right. Abled privilege works the same way. People don't intend to sound like assholes when they call something lame, but they certainly sound assholian. When I asked one of my oldest colleagues to at least stop saying, "that's so lame" in front of me, he said, "You may have a disability, Dorothy. I'll acknowledge that much. But, hey, disability doesn't have you!"

Utter crap. My disability rules my every breathing moment. It has had me all along. We need to hear from, and listen to, those impacted by the words we use.

When friends tell me, "Amy's husband screwed their babysitter. That bastard can't keep his prick in his pants!" They don't apologize. They don't even realize they've said it. The word *bastard* is entirely normal and non-hurtful to them. So, they use it. Ableist language has similar power. When I was able-bodied, I didn't hear it. You don't feel the sting of it. It never crosses your mind that it might sting. It was only when I heard it with Beau beside me that I began to realize how pervasive and hurtful a hold it has on our tongues. Even then, I perpetuated it. I used ableist language to reject ableist language. I told myself people were "tone deaf," "blind to" being "tone deaf" and too "dumb" to "see" they were "morons." I told myself to grow a pair, put on my big girl pants, suck it up, roll with the punches, shrug it off and walk on by. But when I said nothing, I hated myself for not being able to stand tall, stand firm or stand up for myself.

It's one of the most problematic words for me: *stand*.

First and foremost, *stand* has an ableist denotation: the act of an able body rising to its feet. All its connotations are positive. *Stand* normalizes, values and praises able-bodied action. When you stand by your man, stand up at a wedding, stand up for your rights, stand firm or stand proud, you're standing strong. Standing in solidary at union meetings, standing by your word or behind the stand of your chosen political candidate, you stand tall. Conversely, when we can't stand liars, drunk drivers, sexual abusers, racism, homophobia, transphobia, white supremacy and all things Alt-Right, we refuse to stand with them, or by them. We stand against them.

A friend once tried to tell me *stand* didn't reference standing, that it simply meant "to support with your mind and heart." I suggested he try telling that to the next army captain who ordered his soldiers to stand. Simply put, the reason *stand* has so many positive connotations is precisely because it is based on the respected and respectful abled act of standing up. When we give up, we stand down. Cowards never take a stand. In short, disabled people are sent non-stop messaging that we are lower, less worthy, almost-humans precisely because we can't stand.

Can we crip the word *stand*?

Can we reclaim it, or should we stop using it?

In 2014, when the story of celebrity Jian Ghomeshi broke, when thousands online supported the women who accused him of sexual abuse and harassment, I tweeted #IStandwithLucy, but was also one of the disabled voices asking that it be changed to #IBelieveLucy. Sadly, that lesson was instantly lost. Everyone went right back to using *stand*.

But it helped me grow my own courage.

And to evaluate how to use it.

I often post an almost-joking tweet to activists and causes, saying, "Like many disabled people, I can't stand with you, but I do support you." Sometimes it makes me feel proud. Sometimes I feel small and petty; makes me worry I'm inserting myself inappropriately. I check my privilege. Straight/cis/white people like me need to shut up and listen to marginalized groups. White feminists especially need to listen to BIPOC voices, meaning those who are black or Indigenous or people of colour. Sadly, here's the dilemma for disabled activists: few abled members of any group of any kind ever pass the mic to disabled members of their own communities. Disabled folks of every identity too often have to take the mic from abled hands, assuming they can get to, and into, the space and place where the mic is being used.

It is also important to note that the disability movement itself desperately needs diversity.

As black disabled activist Vilissa Thompson so accurately campaigned on Twitter: #DisabilityTooWhite. As a white disability activist, I am acutely aware that I have, and unfairly benefit from, white privilege. White activists like me also need to pass the mic and to listen when we do so. We all need to seek out, read, follow, hire, respect and amplify disabled voices that are not male, straight, cis, university educated, middle-class and white.

The disability movement is also far too young. Two out of every three disabled people on the planet are seniors. Disability activists must reach out and recruit seniors, especially seniors of all marginalized identities. I once mentioned this to a leading disability activist and was shocked by the ageism and ableism of their reply: "I guess we need to go into nursing homes?" No, only 7 percent of seniors in Canada live in care homes. In our home communities, disabled people of all identities and ages need to build true intersectionality, to stand together in true diversity.

In crip solidarity, I wish I knew a good alternative to *stand*. Vilissa Thompson uses "I wheel/sit with you." But none of "I endorse," "I support" or "I'm with" pack the same punch. Sigh. As I lose my ability to stand, it's increasingly clear: we must reject or reclaim ableist language because whoever controls words controls both the meaning of experience and its value.

"I'll take *Dis in the Dictionary* for the rest of my life, Alex."

Consider the collective negative weight of these words, keeping in mind that this is only a distillate of the *dis* words we use every day: *disagreeable, disappointed, disbelieved, discarded, disconnected, discounted, discouraged, discourteous, disembowelled, disgraced, disgruntled, disgusted, disheartened, dishonoured, disliked, disloyal, dismissed, disowned, disparaged, dispensable, dispirited, displeased, disproven, disqualified, disrespected, distasteful, distrusted.*

All this negativity makes it so difficult for people to believe disability is not a bad thing.

I fall victim to this myself. Whenever someone says, "Don't you dis me! I won't be dissed by you!" of course I hear *disrespect* and *disrespected*, but I also hear this: "Don't you dare disable me! I'm not gonna get disabled by you, not by anybody!"

How do we begin to change this? Do we take baby steps – sorry. Strike beyond? Hunt down? Initiate alternatives? The very words we use to unpack and dismantle ableist language reinforce it. It's an endless fall down a bottomless rabbit hole. It unmasks just how much of our language, virtually all our language, is based on the body – specifically on one kind of body: Ableism's Prime Image Default Body; colonial capitalism's ideal working body; one with the fitness, nutrition, health, vision, hearing, mobility, strength, stamina, physical and mental productivity of a robust, abled, young, cis, straight, middle-class white male.

Today, we're all discovering this ableism in what passed for centuries as innocuous daily language, such as: "turn a blind eye," "crippled with loss" and "tone deaf." The disability community is clear: please don't use any disability to describe the temporary state of abled people. A scream is not "deafening." Debt is not "crippling." The commercial that claims we go "nose blind" to smelly pets isn't funny. Sighted people who judge contests with anonymous entrants are not "blind judges." Your sighted date is not a "blind date" and your car does not have a "blind spot"; it's a car. A truly blind eye would not need to be turned in any direction.

The disabled community especially asks us not to use disability to describe the negative behaviours and choices of human beings. Abled people are not "deaf to" or "blind to" anything. They are "purposefully ignorant" or "willfully dismissive." While countering the ubiquitous slurs of "crazy" and "insane," the disability community daily also has to endlessly ask abled social media to stop calling President Trump a "crazy fucktard," a "deranged dotard," a "senile sociopath" or a "racist retard." It is profoundly ableist to conflate mental health and hatred.

Colonial capitalism has done an excellent job stoking all kinds of hatred in the language of daily life. The deeply entrenched capitalist belief that *abled* is the valued, productive norm explains how hard it is to reclaim the word *disabled*. It likewise explains how hard abled people have fought to stay in control of language about disability.

Person-first language – calling us *a person with a disability* – began in the 1980s, when abled politicians, educators, academics, medical and human resources personnel invented any number of terms to avoid using the word *disabled*. In typical ableist paternalism, they did so without consulting the disabled community. These euphemisms all do two things: they give narrative control to abled people; they minimize and erase ableism.

If you call me *physically or mentally challenged*, it's my job to "overcome" the challenge. If I'm *differently abled*, we're all differently abled so there's no need to fund or legislate equity. If you emphasize *ability*, as in dis/ability or disAbility, you de-emphasize and erase the barriers of systemic ableism. If you call me *handicapable*, I'm obviously neither and a joke. As for the newer, vomit-inducing *diffabled,* and *alt-abled,* both erase ableism and create a false equivalency. Like being tall or blue-eyed, they miscast disability as an equitable "difference," not as being disempowered and discriminated against.

Don't call me diffabled unless you'd like me to diffable your teeth.

Abled people defend person-first language by claiming they want to assure disabled people we are persons. We know that, thank you. Calling me a person with a disability implies that disability is separate from my personhood. It suggests that, like a burden, or a suitcase, I could simply decide to put disability down and be a person without one. And, ironically, person with a disability implies that the norm of the word *person* is abled, then qualifies that a not-the-norm, abnormal, less-than-normal person is a person with a disability.

Proponents of person-first also claim they "see a person," but they "don't see disability." Not seeing disability is ableist privilege in action. If society willfully dismisses disability, then there is no need for accessibility in education, housing, employment or the world at large. There is no need for universal design in buildings and urban planning. No need to address the higher rates of poverty, unemployment, elder abuse, assault, sexual assault, police violence, incarceration and early death for disabled people. If you say you don't see disability, what you are really saying is you refuse to acknowledge it because you don't want to do anything about it.

Please see me. I'm not "a person with femaleness" or "a person of age." I'm a disabled senior woman, a package deal. My disability is integral to my identity. I claim the word *disabled* with crip pride. I claim it because it honours my disabled community. Since 2016, disabled activists on Twitter have been asking everyone to #SayTheWord.

What's in a name? Everything.

A rose by any other name isn't a rose.

Just as I respect a person's preferred pronouns, I will call an individual by any term they choose. But words for our community should be chosen by the community, by those who have read, written, followed, consulted, shared, done the work and built community. Autistic activists roundly reject "person with autism." In poll after poll on social media, physically disabled people overwhelmingly prefer the word *disabled*. No one appreciates the several times a day an abled tourist leaps into our feeds to chastise us for using the word *disabled*, smugly certain that they know better than we do what we should be calling ourselves.

I've witnessed and championed language change; I know it's possible. When "that's sick," and "it's the bomb" first hit my high school, they came out of every adolescent mouth within hours. I remember the courage it took in the 1970s to correct those who called me "Mrs." or "Miss," to explain I preferred "Ms." I got everything from instant support, to incomprehension, to snide commentary, to full-on attack. A decade later, we all used it. I hope the world accepts preferred pronouns more quickly. Unfortunately, I expect rewording and reclaiming ableist language will take decades.

I hoped to write a book free of ableist language and know I haven't succeeded.

I still make lots of mistakes. To my great shame, slurs from my childhood sometimes leave my mouth before I can stop them. I struggle with *able-bodied* and *abled*, often incorrectly interchanging them. *Abled* is all-encompassing; it's having an able body, a neurotypical mind and a socially normative personal presentation. I use *abled*, not *non-disabled*, because I want to draw the clear connection that it is abled people who have abled privilege because they benefit from ableism. I use *able-bodied* to counterpoint my body, but a person with an invisible disability may appear able-bodied and still be disabled. Crip language needs to reflect this diversity. But I sure don't envy all us poor bastards who have to keep asking for change that falls on deaf ears, to which most abled folks shrug and turn a blind eye.

What do abled people gain when they shape and control language about disability?

It keeps disabled people othered and tiny. It maintains their deeply convicted belief that disabled people are not a marginalized community, but only a tiny, statistically irrelevant bunch of lazy individuals, most of whom are likely faking it. And it saves abled people buckets of money. We don't need, or deserve the enforcement of accessibility policies if we're all imposters. After the March 2019 College Admissions Scandal, where wealthy parents paid to have their kids falsely diagnosed as disabled to secure more time in SAT testing, this teacher expects a resurgence of this belief, accompanied by backlash making it harder for disabled students to get the legal accommodations they deserve.

Abled people have always taken it upon themselves to control the language that defines and devalues disabled lives. Abled governments set disability legislation, deciding who deserves disability tax credits, benefits, care, housing and pensions. Abled charities set funding policies, ensuring we don't get to speak for ourselves. Sadly, even well-meaning abled friends, even lefty, intersectional feminists, seem to think they get a vote about what words I can use about myself.

Here's the nasty, self-serving heart of it: Abled people want to control the words they will agree to use about disabled people because it dictates their need to respond or not. When their chosen words erase ableism, when it is our personal, individual job as a person with a disability to "overcome and defeat" said disability, then abled people get off scot-free.

But here's the good news: a living language can always be reborn.

When I despair, I think of the little girl I saw at Halloween dressed in her Star Wars costume, brandishing her lightsaber crutch, festooned with pink glow sticks. She proudly told me her name: "Princess Leia the Lame and the Lovely; Leader of Men, Wookies and Robots."

I don't need to explain to you what it means to me to see a child choose her own name.

She is every word that matters. She is cripping the future.

No Place Like Home

I didn't meet another living soul related to me until I gave birth. Then, at fifty-five, I found my birth mother. I'd looked for her all my life, in vain. Canadian adoption files were closed by law, controlled by a male church and state to ease their consciences and their wallets. Inconvenient little bastards like me have been taken from young, poor, disabled, Indigenous and racialized unwed mothers for centuries. We weren't orphans. We all had living relatives. Sealed birth records have long ensured that abandoning men can't ever be held accountable.

I lived over half a century with my family in a government file I couldn't read.

Since turning eighteen in 1973, I'd joined several adoption search groups, like Parent Finders, but couldn't legally get any information. Pre-Internet, looking for a birth parent was like searching for a forbidden needle in uncountable haystacks. I had something many adoptees didn't have: my birth name, Susan Gail Johnston. But in the 1950s, a baby born to a married mother legally had to bear her husband's last name. My birth name is only almost mine: Johnston is the surname of the man my mother married before my birth, but he is not my father.

Finding my mother took historic change: a global feminist movement, decades of adoptee activism, a relaxing morality and new legislation. In 2010, on the first day I could legally do so, I applied for my "Statement of Live Birth" and learned my mother's name: Florence Ada Mclean. I hired a private detective specializing in adoption reunions, who found her in October of 2010. I wrote her a letter and drove it to the airport. She called me the next day.

We met in 2011, when she was eighty-three.

We met just once before she died.

She gave me so many answers. She has my daughter's eyes. All three of us share the same tiny hands. She made the same joke I do referring to a word we couldn't pronounce as kids, because we'd only seen it in books, and thus "put the em-PHA-sis on the wrong sy-LAB-le."

Her favourite book as a child was *Anne of Green Gables*.

I have a half-brother and a half-sister. My half-sister refuses to contact me. Her name is Susan. I can only imagine her shock in discovering she was not the first Susan. When my half-brother and I met, in a gatekeeping, pre-screening before I could meet my mother, he withheld another treasure I couldn't read: my mother's memoir, *Memories from Canada to California*. I was allowed to read about her family history and childhood only. All adult pages were barred by giant paper clips. He said, "Look at it as baby steps. It's all we're comfortable with."

For all my life, others have decided what is "good enough" for me and it's never enough.

It never includes all the things they want for themselves and those they love.

Of course, when my birth mother wrote her life story, she omitted the shame of me entirely. But I have often wondered, in the short time we were together, if she whispered some of her history. If it got imprinted in my psyche. Or, in a question so outlandish to me I never thought I'd ask it: Am I living testament to the theory of genetic memory? Now that this historian can finally research half of my family tree, the links to my life make my head spin.

Back in 1973, my need felt primal: I simply *had* to attend Western. I didn't know why.

As improbable as it sounds, to study history, I moved a stone's throw from my own history. My birth mother, Florence Ada Mclean, was born on the Western campus in University Hospital. A half-hour away, straight down the old carriage route of Longwoods Road, is the still-standing Mclean family farm. In 1819, in the second brutal wave of Scotland's Highland Clearances, my first Canadian ancestor, Duncan Alexander McLean, left the tiny coastal parish of Kilcalmonell, Argyll. Age sixteen. Eight younger siblings in tow, all abandoned. No parents in sight. Six generations of hardscrabble farmers, the Mcleans of Mayfair, lived and died on the family farm. Their once-thriving town is now a ghost town.

I come from a long line of survivors of forced relocation and abandonment.

I studied history in the home of my history and didn't know it was mine. I cannot properly explain what it felt like, thirty years later, to sit in a familiar seat at the D.B. Weldon Library, my family history spread out before me, with kind librarians hunting down more of it, eager to make up for the thought crime of keeping it from me. Land documents, diaries, letters, wills – all the primary resources historians love, lists of the farms and families Mclean, right down to their milch cows. For all the years I was a fees-paying history major, my birthright sat inches away, but I wasn't allowed to touch it. I could have researched my family in youthful, student leisure, rather than in rushed forays into London that today I can't easily access or afford.

But finally knowing my past brings its own head-shaking joy.

It feels like the past was always present, as if my history picked my friends.

Western is a huge university and I was a Toronto girl. Why did all my friends come from local small towns and farms? None of these people knew each other, but I somehow befriended them all. One of my closest friends, Peter Gubbels, lived on a farm just down Longwoods

Road. To attend Catholic school, he quite literally drove right past the Mclean farm every day. Another friend, Tim Platts, came from Glencoe, five minutes down Longwoods in the other direction. My best friend from first-year, Ann Campbell, came from a farm near Melbourne, the tiny four-corner town literally three minutes from the Mclean farm. In all of Western, I can't imagine anyone lived closer than these people, and somehow, I found them all. There are Campbells in my Mclean family tree; Ann and I may be related. When I went to her boyfriend's hockey games in Rodney, Strathroy, Dutton and Delaware, I was visiting towns full of my Mclean kin. I was quite likely related to some of those farm boy hockey players.

No one in my adoptive family is either a teacher or artsy, but my birth mother's Witty family is nothing but. Her mother was named Evelyn Corona Witty because she was born in 1902, when King Edward was crowned. A graduate of the Ontario College of Art, this grandma really was a painter. My birth mother gave me one of her works, a bold winter scene reminiscent of Tom Thomson. This grandmother taught English, French and art at a high school near Rodney. When her children were little, she took a journalism course and wrote stories and poems. Most touching to me, she put an ad in the *Toronto Star*, hoping to start a writers' group.

Her father, Edward Witty, was a teacher and high school principal from St. George. His family farm is three miles from the homestead of Harry Nixon, a place I visited for a paper on the 1919 progressive provincial government of his party: "The United Farmers of Ontario and the Cultivation of Canadian Protest." Five minutes down Highway 5 sits the memorial home of Adelaide Hunter Hoodless, founder of the Women's Institute and subject of another of my local history essays: "Milk, Motherhood and Misbehaving Women." In St. George, the tiny library I'd visited for research purposes more than once sits across from the graveyard of my Witty ancestors. My great-grandfather Robert Witty was an accused thief, dismissed from his job as a servant in Middleton, Yorkshire. It appears he chose exile to Canada over jail.

Recursive coincidences continue through my great-grandmother Florence Yarwood Witty, who wrote for the Methodist Church magazine, and her mother, Ursula Eveline Terrell. On his second scholarship, my son attended Yale, in New Haven, Connecticut. We are directly descended from several Puritan families who crossed the pond both on, and immediately after, the *Mayflower*. In 1630, John Winthrop's fleet of eleven ships brought a thousand settlers to build his "city on the hill." They founded multiple colonies, including New Haven. Given the colonial importance of these early Puritans, their full genealogies are meticulously documented.

My ancestor, Roger Terrell, helped found New Milford, Connecticut. His descendants taught at West Point, fought with Washington and captained Union armies. When I memorized Henry David Thoreau, Edgar Allan Poe, Helen Keller and Emily Dickinson, they were all my distant relatives. I'm equally delighted to call humorists Mark Twain, Lucille Ball, Steve Allen and Stephen Colbert my distant cousins. When I discovered Robin Williams and I share a five times great-grandmother, I grinned and cried all day. Being distantly, ever-so distantly related to Mitt Romney, Sarah Palin and two old gumpers named Bush is somewhat less delightful.

My Western friend and mentor Craig Simpson would have been astounded to learn that while he wrote the book on the hanging of John Brown, he had me, a descendant of John Brown, right there, breathing in his class. Professor Simpson also supervised my junior thesis on Mary Baker Eddy, the founder of Christian Science. She is my sixth cousin, five times removed. I still own my *Woman's Guide,* by John Harvey Kellogg, made even more special by the discovery that he is my sixth cousin, six times removed. Let me be clear: I'm an atheist. But I shiver at the realization that at Western, it's almost as if the Ghost of Christmas Past led me home.

My mother and my birth mother both gave the same name to two different daughters.

I have a grandmother named Florence and a birth mother also named Florence.

They are both named after their grandmothers named Florence.

I have two abandoning, red-headed grandfathers who may have been bigamists. Charles Edward Mclean, named after Bonnie Prince Charlie, was a horse dealer who married my teacher grandmother, Evelyn Corona Witty, in 1929. They had two daughters, my mother in 1930 and her sister in 1931. Five years later, like the Reverend Palmer, Charlie changed his name and vamoosed. He worked at the Calgary Stampede, blocks from my job at the Alberta Vocational Centre, then became a respected livestock dealer. He had three more children, never paid a cent of support to his first family and died in 1959 at sixty-four, at a train crossing in Medicine Hat.

From my mother's memoir, I was surprised to learn she had a Toronto childhood similar to mine. When Charlie left, Evelyn moved her daughters into the city. They lived a one-room, penny-pinching life, highlighted by rare trips to Niagara Falls, Casa Loma, the Christmas windows at Eaton's and the Santa Claus Parade. Each summer, she got a week at camp thanks to a local charity. We both had Sunday school picnics on Centre Island. She sang in a church choir and put on little concerts with her sister. She specifically mentions performing as king and page in *Good King Wenceslas*. My birth mother and my mother both lived near, and loved, Sunnyside Amusement Park. In another astounding bit of synchronicity, they attended the same elementary school, Swansea Public, albeit ten years apart. Coping respectively with single-parent poverty, an abandoning father, the Depression and a dead baby brother, neither had a happy childhood.

Whether family histories uncover pain or privilege, we must acknowledge both.

In the wake of Bonnie Prince Charlie's defeat at the Battle of Culloden in 1746, my ancestors lived as second-class citizens in their own occupied country. Theirs was a Scotland where the speaking of Gaelic and the wearing of tartans were forbidden by English coloniz-ers. In 1819, in the second wave of brutal Highland Clearances, whole glens were thrown off their land by English aristocracy. It will forever be a wonder to me that I can now claim that Scotland as my legacy. My sixth cousin six times removed, Sir Walter Scott, put it best: "Breathes there the man with soul so dead, / Who never to himself hath said, / This is my own, my native land!"

Scottish farmers got their land stolen, got shipped overseas like cattle, then got used again by the British to steal Indigenous land. Like all settlers, my ancestors accepted land without question. They were both used and complicit. The Mclean farm sits next to the Chippewas of the Thames First Nation Reserve. My grandmother Witty taught two years at an Indigenous school. My Puritan ancestors include the *Mayflower*'s John Alden. He's commemorated in Longfellow's poem, "The Courtship of Miles Standish," but his Plymouth Colony should rightly be remembered for the vicious, duplicitous treatment of the Indigenous people who saved their lives. Here and always, I apologize for my ancestors' greed and collusion. I won't sanitize it. After spend-ing my life trying to find my history, I acknowledge it and openly apologize for it.

I will always be thankful for the one weekend and the calls and let-ters Florence and I shared. I'm still proud of this: When I met my birth mother, I walked up to her on my own two feet. At fifty-five, I could periodically go without my crutch, but that door was quickly closing. Hastened by the stress of court battles and the ongoing trauma that the man I loved would repeat the harm of my grandfathers, would skip town and evade arrest to avoid paying court-ordered spousal support, I needed my crutch full time by 2012, when I was fifty-seven.

Beau's support proved likewise conditional. With him in my right hand, I leaned disproportionately on Horatio. When Horatio rebelled, Beau sometimes caught me, but he caused as many falls as he caught. His rubber tip was useless in rain and treacherous in snow.

He slid sideways on stairs. I had to micromanage his every move, but the attention pie is finite. Herkimer and Horatio resented the fact that the more attention I gave Beau, the less I had for them. Worst of all, Beau infantilized me. Flatly refusing to open doors, he forced me to ask for help. I had to pretend not to see the reactions: the kindness, the impatience, the smug superiority, the winces of pity and flashes of disgust. I had to pretend not to be hurt, yet again, by the erasure of my history.

In the 1970s, during my coming of age as a feminist, doors were today's toilets: cultural flashpoints and battlegrounds. One of the ways you proved yourself as a feminist was to refuse to go through a door held by a man, but instead, to hold it open for him. This seems quaint today, but back then, it had tangible political impact. Although we didn't yet have this word, men's reactions proved they knew their insistence on door-opening was a *microaggression*: a power play cloaked in manners designed to keep women in our grateful place. When tiny, twentysomething me opened a door for a big, strong man, I got everything from bemused thanks, to confusion, to alarm, to vicious insult. Many chanted "age before beauty," going through only if they "complimented" me first. Some grabbed the door out of my hands. I got called a "stupid broad," a "dumpy dyke" and once "a dirty commie cunt." While I don't believe that particular part of my anatomy is capable of expressing a political preference, it was the first time I ever heard the *C* word. In 1976, it hit this nice girl like a punch to the heart.

My point is this: it was always about more than a door.

It was never only about sexism; it was also about ableism. About keeping the able-bodied male in his rightful place in the Great Ableist Chain of Being: On top. Ruling the roost. Extending kindness or hate, entirely as he saw fit. When women opened our own doors, we claimed our bodies for ourselves. This became incandescently clear to me decades later, visiting my son in small-town Ohio. As a teenage boy bore down on me like a linebacker while I leaned on Beau to load groceries in my car, I admit to a flash of sitting-duck fear. If I was about to be mugged, neither fight nor flight were possible. Instead, he grabbed groceries and grinned.

"Well now, it ain't every day you get to help a little old lady Tiny Tim."

I swear to God, it's one of those rare times I thought there might actually be one. Jehovah must be a nine-year-old boy who finds it hilarious to kick a dead horse just one more time. Like men opening doors, this well-meaning young man meant no insult. If I'd tried to say his "help" was ageist and ableist, that he joked about someone who in his country would die from being too poor to afford health care, he wouldn't have heard me. He couldn't see the harm in his charity.

Do you understand how hard it is for me, coming from my generation of feminists, to struggle to open my own doors, and to often fall doing so? In archetypal Canadian politeness, bystanders help me up and brush me off. They see my fall as an unfortunate single accident, as my own, overweight, careless fault. They never see that in a fuller history, the fault is also theirs. That unsafe doors exist precisely because as abled citizens and taxpayers, they permit them to exist. Because it has never been their priority, or the priority of the abled folks they elect, to insist that doors reflect the e-button, or electronic eye, technology of the twentieth century.

Rushing to get a door for a disabled person, no matter how kindly you feel, is an ableist microaggression. Like "gentlemen calling for charity," you want to help on your terms. You don't see us in our numbers, struggling with every door across the land. You'd rather be a lone Good Samaritan than do the difficult work of confronting and correcting your collective ableism. Instead, please ask us if we want help. Consultation and consent make all the difference.

Consultation was likewise never Beau's forte. By fifty-nine, our differences were irreconcilable. He'd become abusive, hurting my hand, wrist, spine and hip. Aggravating my arthritis, he made my shoulder grind like the *Fargo* wood chipper. It's the irony of *iatrogenic pain*: pain caused by a medical remedy for pain. My fingers went numb, causing my hand to slip and my body to follow. In February 2014, I fell on a shard of ice that slit my left cheek open.

Yes, this time I actually do mean the cheek on my face.

As a supportive partner, pretty-boy Beau sucked the big one. But I fought the end of our relationship because I feared life without him. In permanently raised anxiety, I accepted the many times a day I could feel my blood pressure spiking. I could live channelling Il Papa and kissing the ground twice a week. But twice a day, that's just dirty. To avoid falling, I began to avoid walking. Began stuffing my phone in my bra, reasoning that when I broke my hip, I could call an ambulance and not die slowly, cold and alone on my bathroom floor.

I began having panic attacks.

My conscious brain had spent sixty years overriding the primal directive to escape pain. Eventually, the reptilian part of my brain reasserted itself. If I didn't have the common sense to sit down, it would shut me down. If I walked for over a minute, I got shaky, sweaty and nauseous. I began hyperventilating. Some of it was pain. Some of it was ill health, the wheezing and puffing of an obese, old woman. For some six months, I put up with embarrassing and health-threatening panic attacks, complete with gasping for air and some decidedly ugly crying.

All because I knew my next step was a walker, and I refused to take it.

But when Beau dumped me off a downtown curb, face first into an oncoming streetcar, when a quick-thinking little girl saved my life by yanking me sideways, I had no choice. I had to admit our relationship was a dead-end street, or risk dying in the street.

And still I fought it. I visited yet another orthopedic surgeon, hoping advancements Dr. Salter predicted had come to pass. Of course, my new doctor ordered new X-rays. I will say this for "hard scientific evidence": unlike so many disabled people, especially older, disabled women, I am always believed. Doctors take one look at my X-rays and instantly agree with anything I say about pain. They don't debate me, talk over me or tell me it's all in my head. They offer me every pill under the sun, shrug and shake their learned, bewildered heads. This doctor quoted *Inspector Gadget*: "Wowzah! There's a freaky little deformity you don't see every day."

He barely looked up from my X-rays. He did not see a Princess.

"No. There is no further surgical option available. You're going to need a walker."

I smiled. "Right, a decade from now. When I'm a really cute little old lady."

"No, today, so you don't fall and break a hip, or your back. Then maybe you'll get to live to be a little old lady. Period."

I knew he was right, but I needed him to be wrong. Internalized ageism can be as shaming as internalized ableism. To my silly, proud self, a crutch had dignity. A walker had none. It meant words I couldn't stomach: *Frail. Old. Decrepit.* It meant being seen at every moment of every day as 100 percent disabled.

Because Dr. Gadget failed to tell me about the 75 percent rebate program for walkers prescribed by occupational therapists, I made the incorrect Scottish assumption I had to buy the cheapest one available. I drove past Walmart three times. I sat in the parking lot for half an hour. Once inside, I tried to browse inconspicuously, but got accosted by one of those permanently perky, ponytail clerks who run marathons without spilling a drop of their kale smoothies.

"Can I help you, dear? Don't tell me you're ready for a walker?"

It might be reverse psychology; it is perverse psychology. Why say anything to hinder the purchase of life-saving medical equipment? But I knew exactly how to play that girl game. I lied.

"You're right. I'm looking for a walker, but not for me. For my much-older sister."

Ms. Perky-Kale-Smoothie didn't bat a fake eyelash.

"Well, assuming she's your height and weight, let me suggest this one."

When I got home, there wasn't enough ice cream in the world. An unopened box glared at me from my closet. A week later, telling myself assembling it wasn't using it, I dumped it out, screwed it up and cried until I threw up. All I could hear was my mother's voice telling me I was a "devastating dwarfish deformity." I stuffed my shameful newborn back in my closet.

I refused to give that lame little bastard a name.

On Original Numbers and Odds in Our Favour

I've never been a numbers person. When I started to notice disability statistics, I was surprised by how much they comforted me. I began collecting them, holding them close, like the treasures in my grandparents' basement. When you've always felt freakishly alone, the discovery of your numbers is exponentially liberating. This almost-able almost-daughter who never belonged now belongs to two of the largest human families on planet Earth: disabled people and seniors.

I don't share our numbers to advocate their competitive use. I reject all notion of ranking marginalized groups by size. I count to tally the missing, to make our under-representation clear. I count to be seen, to refuse and refute invisibility. On elevators, at Walmart, at literary events, I find ways to ask this question: "What percentage of the planet do you think is disabled?"

Please answer this in your head, now.

The most common answer is "I don't know. Maybe 10 percent?"

It's important to note three things: Everyone admits they don't know but supplies an answer anyway, and their guesses are always low. No one ever guesses more than 15 percent. This holds true of the general public and progressive political friends who confidently tell me Indigenous people are 6 percent, black people are 4 percent, transgender people are 0.5 percent, the total reported LGBTQQIP2SAA community is 4 percent, people of colour total 22 percent and 14 percent of Canadians live below the poverty line. So why does everyone consistently underestimate the number of disabled people?

Let's do the math. It's time to see gimpy old people.

If you google "What percentage of people are disabled?" you'll get a wide range of answers. Statistics vary country to country, study to study, depending on who is counting, how they count, if they're counting anonymously and, most tellingly, what does or does not get counted. When I began my research, I quoted UN stats: "About 20 percent of the planet is disabled." People rolled their eyes, convinced I was exaggerating. Today, I know 20 percent is also an underestimation. As every teacher knows, the answer you get depends on the question you ask. When studies use a more inclusive definition, when they give neurodivergent people and people living with mental health challenges the opportunity to self-identify as disabled, it generates more inclusive, more accurate numbers.

In 2018, the US Centers for Disease Control and Prevention (CDC) designed such a study, surveying only adults, as children tend to be healthier and skew the results. It defined disability as life-impacting difficulty in any of six areas: Mobility, Cognitive, Vision, Hearing, Independent Living and Self-Care. By this definition, a full 25 percent of adults are disabled. In true intersectionality, the CDC found that disability increased as income decreased: "disability is more common among women, non-Hispanic American Indian/Alaska Natives, adults with lower income, and living in the South." Mobility disabilities were "five times more common among adults living below the poverty line as opposed to those with income twice the poverty line."

They found an army that marches like me. The largest group of disabled people are those with mobility disabilities. We are one in every seven adults. We are 14 percent of the population.

Canadian statistics reinforce these numbers. The 2017 Canadian Survey on Disability states that 24 percent of women aged fifteen and over are disabled, as are 20 percent of men.

I've come to see the consistent underestimation of our disabled numbers as one of the most successful mind-control tricks of ableism. If you didn't grow up seeing disabled people, if there aren't any of us at your work, your kid's school or your favourite bar, it's not because your inaccessible world keeps us out; it's because there are so few of us in the first place. This belief is not your fault. We've all been groomed by history to expect disabled absence. The capitalism of the nineteenth century, which created big-business health care, moved disabled people into income-generating group homes, freeing abled family caregivers to earn and spend wages. Shame and stigma sealed the deal.

Capitalism remains crafty; today, inaccessibility is incarceration without the asylum. Housebound or bound in homes, disabled people get locked up either way. That's one reason why you stare at us. You believe us to be rare, exotic, statistically insignificant creatures. This is advantageous to you. It means you get to see our absence as "no big deal." If the world is only missing a tiny minority, "a few old folks on canes" or "a couple of wheelchairs," your ableist privilege is easier to shrug off. You can steal our parking spots because you don't think one of us rare or antique cars will show up to need it.

What changes when we acknowledge the enormity of the missing?

I'll offer a personal answer first. The inclusion of my two missing communities would have quantitative and qualitative impact on my life as a drama teacher and writer. I'd love it if everyone stopped helping themselves to our spots. If the industry of Canadian Literature we call CanLit truly represented Canada, one of every four authors, agents, editors, judges, readers and panelists would be disabled. When I went to readings, festivals and conferences, one of every seven presenters and attendees would have a mobility disability. There'd be canes, crutches, scooters and walkers galore.

Instead, I rarely see anyone like me. American, Australian and UK statistics concur: disabled writers represent at best some 3 percent of publication.

Does this mean no one wants to read about disabilities?

The opposite is true.

Books and movies about disabled people have made big box office and big bucks for decades – all written by abled writers. Disabled people are always expected to cede the mic to abled doctors, caregivers, medical organizations, fundraisers, politicians, parents, siblings, spouses and academics. These ableds get called experts, but they're actually tourists. The media would much rather interview abled tourists than get too close to real disabled people. Abled audiences prefer imposters, meaning abled authors, like abled actors, make their reputations telling stories about us, without us. Abled authors control how we are seen. Rohinton Mistry's *A Fine Balance*, featuring disabled beggars, wins the Giller Prize, while Canada leaves real disabled people begging to be heard. *Precious Cargo*, a book centring on what an abled author learned driving a school bus of disabled kids for a year, wins a prestigious spot on the nationally televised *Canada Reads*. When disabled people object to being called cargo, when we ask to tell our stories, ourselves, we are ignored.

Disabled people are not a culture. It would be wrong to call the appropriation of our lives *cultural appropriation*. It is *ableist appropriation* when abled writers steal disabled history, voice, experience, expertise, employment, role-modelling, vision, analysis, community, joy, pain and our disabled future. When abled tourists steal our stories, it's theft inside and outside the book. They spin our stories as they please, masquerading as experts. Then they go on tour, attend writing retreats, appear in readings and at literary festivals. They take our spots with their abled bodies ensuring that no one will have to employ or accommodate disabled bodies.

This ableist appropriation is both theft and big bucks. Blockbuster movies like *The Phantom of the Opera*, *Rain Man*, *What's Eating*

Gilbert Grape, I Am Sam, Me Before You and *The Theory of Everything* bring abled actors fame and fortune. It's a stereotype because it's true: the best ticket to an Academy Award is a disabled role. It's called "cripping up," or "disabled mimicry." Today, 95 percent of disabled characters in film and TV are cripped up, played by abled actors. Disabled actors don't even get cast in bit parts as neighbour or friend. Worse, we can't play ourselves. Can't represent our community. Can't be employed as ourselves. Can't be our own role models. Artie on *Glee,* Chirrut in *Rogue One* and the little boy in *Wonder* are all imposters. When the 2016 Academy Awards were correctly challenged for their lack of racial equity at #HollywoodSoWhite, black disabled activists also protested their double erasure.

Canada is the only country with a disabled superstar still famous three decades after his death. Athlete Terry Fox, who lost a leg to cancer, had to quit his awareness-raising cross-country run in 1980, exactly when I got pregnant. He died in 1981, a month after my son was born. Elementary schools still hold Terry Fox Runs to honour the young man who couldn't finish his. The iconic image of Terry running through small towns, pushing his prosthetic leg into a gait somewhere between a long limp and a jump, is seared into our national consciousness. In 2016, when Drayton Entertainment staged *Marathon of Hope: The Musical,* they hired an able-bodied actor to play Terry. They used an icon of hope to tell disabled people we must not hope to play ourselves onstage. When they posted photos showing how they had attached a fake prosthetic leg in front of the actor's healthy leg, one that didn't quite touch the ground, so this magically healed Terry Fox could sing and dance, I admit it: I saw red. I posted and tweeted non-stop.

From cast and company, I got excuses. They actually said they "couldn't find a disabled actor who could sing." They assured me they'd be "sensitive." Wanted to "dialogue." When I said there was no discussion needed, that cripping up was wrong on its face, they invited me to the play to see how well they'd done it. When I said I'd never attend and no one else should, they blocked me and mocking trolls attacked me. But I wasn't alone. In my first Twitter protest, the online disabled community rallied. Their support made it possible to fight imposters together.

My second profession, in the world of Canadian Literature, has been rocked more than once by accusations that a writer has falsely claimed membership in a marginalized group to gain unfair advantage. Self-identification depends entirely on the honesty and integrity of the identifier. I believe we're on the threshold of recognizing the disabled community as a vital component of diversity; that we'll see increasing space, platform, employment and funding dedicated to all kinds of disabled artists. Will some abled con artist out there try to cash in? Will the pervasive belief that there are so few of us and we're really no more disabled than Scrooge someday lead an abled imposter to decide they aren't really doing anything wrong if they fake it, too?

It could easily be done. With some good research, with some disabled people willing to mentor you, with a cane as a prop, an abled con could walk the walk. Especially if you were charming, good looking and well spoken – a chirpy, palatable, Tiny Tim supercrip, one who never said the word *ableism*. If you were unchallenging of the status quo, you wouldn't be challenged. If you kept your story individual and personal, if you expressed no crip solidarity with our numbers, if you never asked for ASL or captioning, if you attended inaccessible events because you could get up the stairs, if you never asked anyone to relocate inaccessible events, if you never asked who else is missing from the arts, or who can't afford to attend, or who is ignored, talked over and erased, Canada would embrace you to their abled bosoms. Because when a disabled person stands uncomplaining and alone, it "inspires" them.

What would my disabled activist community do if a disabled celebrity artist role model suddenly stood up from their wheelchair and said, "Ha ha, I could walk all along"? If their podcasts were proven plagiarized from Helen Keller? If they earned fame and fortune, took funding and space by holding themselves up as the new Terry Fox? Then we discovered they'd stuck a fake prosthetic leg to their shin so they could sing and dance the life out of the rest of us? I'm pretty sure we'd all be aiming our Bruce Cockburn rocket launchers at that Marathon of Nope. We'd ask for a return of ill-gotten gains via large donations to organizations run by and for disabled people. We'd demand accountability: No other artist should appear with them, buy their art or promote them on social media, until a full apology and restitution is made. All those who made big bucks from a fraud would be asked to contribute to that restitution.

Because let's be clear: fame, awards and buckets of money are all at stake.

In 2018, this became embodied in the unlikely persons of Scarlett Johansson, Dwayne "The Rock" Johnson and Kevin Hart. After criticism for playing an Asian manga hero in *Ghost in the Shell*, Johansson signed on to play a transgender man in *Rub & Tug*. Facing righteous push back from the transgender community and its allies, she stepped down. For the first time in history, it was made clear to an actor that taking a marginalized role might cost, not make, fame and fortune. Mere days later, the super-abled Dwayne Johnson hit the screen impersonating an FBI agent with a prosthetic leg. When criticized for taking a disabled actor's role, he did the push back, insisting that his work was "a tribute" to disabled people. When homophobic comments surfaced on social media, Kevin Hart lost his spot as host of the Oscars. Days later, when he opened co-starring in *The Upside*, uttering ableist "jokes" non-stop as the aide to Bryan Cranston's cripped up role as a paraplegic man, their movie outsold *Aquaman*. The outrage of the disabled community is always ignored by the media and the general public. Abled audiences look at *The Shape of Water* and see romance. We see a disabled woman left so isolated and lonely that she believes she can be loved only by a monster.

As for disabled seniors, we don't even get to be misrepresented.

We're simply erased.

"I'll take *Simplifying the 2016 Census for Thirty-Six Million*, Alex."

In a county of 36 million, our 5.9 million seniors are 16.1 percent of the nation.

When the 2.3 million citizens over sixty are included, we're a whopping 22.3 percent.

But to grasp the scale of senior's under-representation in the arts, just as the CDC did, we must remove children; they don't work as artists and so skew the results. Canada has thirty million adults age nineteen and over. There are 8.2 million adults over sixty, meaning these seniors are 26 percent of the adult population. If we were represented in our numbers, one of every four works of art in Canada would be by an artist over sixty. One of every four authors reviewed in every newspaper, journal and blog, one of every four at every literary event and one of every four nominated for, and winning, literary awards, would all be over sixty. And our numbers would be growing. By 2036, seniors over sixty will be a full 29 percent of the adult population. Yes, that is essentially one-third, or one out of every three people in Canada.

But when I did a head count of fiction released in 2017, writers over sixty were as rare as hen's dentures – a paltry 4 percent. I suspect youthful CanLit looks at the handful of writers in their fifties and thinks "old folks" are well represented. It's important to note that the writers in their fifties I found were already established with multiple publications, beginning in their youth.

Where are our first-time writers over sixty?

How many can you name?

The generation that first asked, "Whose voice gets heard?" isn't being heard.

The most telling proof that seniors have been erased is that we have no concept of age appropriation in the arts. Back in 1964, when she was in her mid-thirties, Margaret Laurence published *The Stone Angel*, the story of ninety-year-old Hagar Shipley. Half a century later, this novel by a young woman is still considered the definitive Canadian classic on aging. Today, if you want to make a book, poem, play or piece of art about your grandma? Great! You're thirtysomething and you want to write in her voice as an eighty-year-old woman? Go for it. How kind of you to speak for her. You must really love your granny to pay tribute to her that way. This is how we all fall for erasure and theft, because it passes itself off as sentimental kindness. If you really love granny, pass her the damn microphone. Publish her stories, poems and artwork. Start seeing and fixing the under-representation of her community. Start supporting and funding projects for the grandparents out there to make art in their own voices, for and about themselves, fulfilling lifelong creative dreams and putting income in impoverished senior pockets.

Don't you dare think we're too old and frail to write. Seniors retire from many occupations, but storytelling isn't one of them. Our absence is a double insult because seniors keep the arts solvent. We are one of the largest book-buying demographics and attend the most live theatre. As the senior-fuelled ZOOMER media empire attests, we want stories about ourselves. Theoretically, an army of senior storytellers rich with life experience, finally free from the constraints of employment and parenting, should be flooding the market as first-time writers.

Where are the initiatives, funding and contests for under-represented senior artists?

We offer endless initiatives, contests, workshops, events and prizes for emerging artists. But *emerging* does not have to mean "emerging from puberty." It should denote the stage of an artist's career, regardless of age. Our 4.5 million youth between twenty and twenty-nine are 13.7 percent of the nation. My 2017 head count puts them at 9 percent of publication, suggesting close to numerical representation. Seniors tally twice the numbers of youth at 26 percent. Where are the workshops, contests, events, retreats and prizes for senior artists? In representational fairness, there should be twice as many initiatives for seniors as for youth. I know of none in Canada and one in the

US: the Off the Grid Prize for poets over sixty. Why is the gross under-representation of seniors not even on our radar? Because ageism and ableism collaborate to support the central lie of capitalism: that only young, healthy bodies count enough to count.

In the '70s, feminists asked: "Why should women pay for men's culture?"

Today, I'm asking: "Why should seniors pay for youth culture?"

I want books, stories, plays, poems and movies by and about seniors. I want art that honours our lives and experiences. Call me a grumpy old bat, but I'm tired of being schooled by writers half my age and younger than my children. I suspect too many publishing decisions get made by thirty- and fortysomethings who think seniors emerge for nothing but a 4:30 p.m. dinner at Swiss Chalet. Agents have said this to my face: "Older writers aren't relatable." I've been told no agent will sign me because I'm not a long-term cash cow: "You're not a good bet, Dorothy. Agents figure you only have maybe one or two more books in you before you die."

As for the overlapping Venn diagram of my senior and disabled communities, no one misses our missing numbers. Because disability increases with age, half of seniors over sixty-five are disabled. These three million disabled seniors are already 8 percent of Canada and 10 percent of adults. By 2036, disabled seniors will be 13 percent of the nation and 15 percent of adults. In short, disabled seniors are one of Canada's largest and fastest growing marginalized groups, but we are non-existent in the arts. The erasure of our numbers ensures erasure of our content. Without seniors who critique ableism and ageism, we have no role models of resilient senior anger. Instead, we are incarcerated in the public imagination as fading complacently off to dusty death.

What we see, we expect. What we expect, we become.

If the arts fairly represented Canada's numbers, we would never see any group of five artists that did not include at least one disabled artist and one artist over sixty. Instead, at entire festivals, I seldom see either. I give full credit to the Festival of Literary Diversity (FOLD) for hosting what I believe to be the first panel featuring a disabled senior writer. At my 2016 panel, Diverse Bodies: On Disability and Exclusion, I asked the well-read audience who could name a disabled senior writer. Three raised their hands. Other than me? All but one hand came down.

Today, no group of abled people under sixty should ever be called "diverse."

But in lip-service tokenism, I'm forever seeing "seniors and the disabled" tacked onto diversity goals of arts organizations containing neither. There is zero outreach, no discussion of affirmative actions needed to include a fair 26 percent of seniors and 25 percent of disabled artists. Don't tell me that artists are judged on merit. That implies senior and disabled artists can't create art of quality. Let's concede that seniors do retire. But let's also learn from our allies and call silencing and erasure by its name. The lack of senior and disabled artists is the result of keeping us out. We're erased by systemic ageism, ableism and inaccessibility of arts culture.

To build true diversity in the arts we can either argue for all marginalized communities to be represented in their numbers, or we can prioritize under-represented groups and ensure they get space beyond their numbers. Both approaches are valid. By either method, senior and disabled artists aren't getting anywhere near a fair share. All communities lose when disabled seniors are siloed and silenced. One erasure empowers other erasures. It limits everyone's future.

Imagine a world where we are all seen in our numbers. Where we all have books, movies, theatre, dance and art that rejects the stereotypes of aging, and the ableist tropes of triumph, cure or death. We'll all be enriched by arts that showcase authentically complex disabled and senior characters with struggles, lives and loves of their own. We all deserve to see seniors and disabled people earn space, employment, funding and respect supported by senior and disabled employers and mentors. We'll all benefit when younger abled artists consult seniors and disabled people, pay for their expertise and do the honest, hard work of research and empathy to include our perspectives. We'll all be happier when we get to create in our bodies, as ourselves.

Here's even more good news. Although I imagine every activist feels their fish is the one that needs frying first, numerically speaking, ageism and ableism are really big fish. Frying them up would feed us all. This is the truth at the core of Disability Justice: seniors and disabled people come from every identity. Increasing the number of disabled and senior artists won't take spots away from other groups. In fact, the opposite is true: a representative increase of disabled and senior writers would *increase* the representation of all other marginalized identities.

We all need to think about this: For fifty years, women have been politely asking to be published equally to men, and it has not happened. Politeness is the problem. Asking for charity and goodwill is the problem. Counting without demanding the numbers improve is the problem. In the 1980s, back when we saw only two genders, my generation of feminists backed down from demanding the quota that no gender fall below 47 percent of any area of employment. I see that as a critical error. It ensured there was no measuring stick, no quantifiable accountability.

Women of my generation died waiting.

Unless we adopt different tactics, unless we make collective demands, so will you.

In our millions, seniors grow poorer and face death increasingly alone. According to CARP and the Broadbent Institute, "fully 28% of single women seniors and 24% of single male seniors are living in poverty." Simply put, the way we treat disabled people and seniors now is the way we will all be treated. We're all melting like Frosty. We won't be cured like Tiny Tim. Whatever isn't done now will still be undone when you need it. In the long run – there's another lovely ableist term – abled people are only TABs: Temporarily Able Bodies.

This isn't to say, "Hey, young abled people, you need to end age-ism and ableism out of pure self-interest, because someday you'll be old and disabled, too." It's to say, we all benefit from caring for each other. Some people are born disabled. People can become disabled at any and every moment. Everybody is one short blink of years away from being an old, disabled body. Thanks to the late great Tommy Douglas, most Canadians get to have a disabled old age.

And that's a good thing. The alternative is far less attractive.

P is for Porn: Inspiration Porn vs. the True Inspiration of Stella Young

I wish I could say I found the courage to reach for Wenceslas by looking inside myself. But I'd be lying. I found it on the Internet. I found it in someone else. My third mother.

My mother never once said, "I love you." She never hugged me and she touched me as little as possible. My birth mother couldn't touch me without feeling her own pain. The first time I felt motherly arms reach out to hold me just as I was, to see me and tell me I was good enough exactly as I was, I was fifty-nine years old. The new mother reaching out over the Internet to hug me was thirty-two, half my age, a full year younger than my first-born child. Despite the fact I grew up in suburban Toronto and she came from the bush town of Stawell, Australia, I felt instant kinship with my virtual mother: the disability activist Stella Young.

We're both tiny redheads with expressive hands and foul mouths. We're both feminists, atheists, activists and knitters. We both became teachers, writers and comic storytellers. Her one-woman stand-up, *Tales from the Crip*, won awards; I coached winning improv teams.

Her heart's desire was to write the novel she never had growing up, one featuring a disabled teenage girl. My first novel, *When Fenelon Falls*, is exactly that, the story I needed and never had, the tale of fourteen-year-old disabled, adopted, red-haired rebel Jordan May March. I gave Jordan my disability. Stella was born with osteogenesis imperfecta, Billy's disability. I looked at her and saw his tiny, compacted body. She looked back at me with his blue-tinted eyes.

This time, I smiled. I saw her. I saw myself and I saw us.

Stella and I both had multiple corrective surgeries. We both eventually concluded we weren't the ones who needed correcting. When I heard her 2014 TED Talk, "I'm not your inspiration, thank you very much," like my NII, I played it until I could recite it. I wept and grinned for a week. It was as if I'd been struggling with a half-completed jigsaw puzzle all my life, then Stella said, "Sweetie, I think this piece goes here. And, darling, try that one there."

I finally saw the big picture. High and proud in her wheelchair, Stella declared, "I am not here to inspire you. I am here to tell you that we have been lied to about disability. Yeah, we've been sold the lie that disability is a Bad Thing ... It's not a bad thing, and it doesn't make you exceptional."

Stella used the word *porn* deliberately. She explained that sentimental stories and images of disabled people "objectify one group of people for the benefit of another group of people." I instantly had language for the impossible task I'd always felt was my job, one at which I'd always failed: "to inspire" abled people, "to motivate" abled people. As Stella put it, to exist for their benefit, so they could think, "It could be worse. I could be that person." I now had a name for every time Facebook asked me to "like" a child amputee tying his shoes, or a blind high school graduate. I finally understood why I didn't cheer for the football team that all faked it to let their disabled mascot score a touchdown, or the story about the pretty girl who gave her sister a kidney, which had no photos of the not-so-pretty dying girl who needed it.

In inspiration porn, the disabled person is reduced to the object, the silent prop.

The heroic captain of the football team leans down and asks "a wheelchair girl" to prom. A brave tech entrepreneur takes the "risk" to hire a disabled programmer. A mega-millionaire basketball star drops in with cameras and has lunch, once, for ten minutes, with a bullied, autistic child. In inspiration porn, the abled person is the hero; the disabled person is the second banana, the sidekick. What abled folks really "like" isn't the disabled person; it's how we make them feel. They like their beneficent moment of charity, wherein they reach down from on high to notice and patronize us, for ten seconds, before returning to their abled lives. These abled saviours get the microphone shoved under their noses while disabled people get no words at all. It's the abled experience that matters. Their voices fill news feeds, movies and books. We exist only so they can pat themselves on the back for looking at us and being seen with us.

Did Stella swallow that lie? Did she get silenced by its shaming?

Nope. She ridiculed the shit out of it.

She gave me the language to begin this memoir.

With wit and wisecracks, she debunked the traditional *medical model of disability*, which says we are disabled by our failed bodies, and embraced the *social model of disability*, which holds that disability is a social construct, that we are disabled not by our bodies but by ableism. The social model sees disability as a social justice issue. It's a matter of access and inclusion, not attitude. As Stella succinctly put it, "No amount of smiling at a flight of stairs has ever made it turn into a ramp. . . . No amount of standing in the middle of a bookshop and radiating a positive attitude is going to turn all those books into Braille."

I began calling myself a crip because she did.

She named herself to reclaim her power.

The more her vocabulary came out of my mouth, the more I agreed with her. I read every word of her online magazine, *Ramp Up*, and watched *No Limits*, the community TV show she hosted for eight seasons. Her best advice: "Disability doesn't make you exceptional, but questioning what you think you know about it does." Because she had no shame, because she rejected the very notion of shame, I could begin to shed mine.

Five months after her TED Talk, in *Between Us: Words and Wisdom from Women of Letters* (November 2014), Stella published "To my eighty-year-old self," a letter imagining how her disabled life would be rich and full, knowing "that I was not wrong for the world I live in. The world I live in was not yet right for me." The next month, at thirty-two years young, Stella died of an aneurysm. It was December 6: the day I signed my 2008 separation agreement, and the anniversary of the 1989 Montreal Massacre. So much death. For me, forever entwined.

But don't say Stella's early death inspires you.

She'd laugh in your face.

Please see what was inspiring: her glorious red polka-dot shoes, the abandon with which she danced in her wheelchair, her ability to laugh at discomforting truths, her vibrant affirmation that disabled people are so very ordinary – "I promise to grab every opportunity with both hands, to say yes as often as I can, to take risks, to scare myself stupid, and to have a shitload of fun."

In my favourite photo of Stella, she wiggles her trademark ruby slippers. But she absolutely does not look like she wants to wiggle out of her wheelchair. She knew what it took this Dorothy so long to learn: "There's no place like home."

I've tried to honour her by challenging inspiration porn. From the moment Stella first explained it, it felt as if she was speaking my true mother tongue. But given the insidious way inspiration porn intersects with abled privilege, it's not easy to confront it in your personal life.

When you're told you've offended someone, it's only human nature to be embarrassed. When you didn't intend to offend, when you're pretty damn sure you were trying to be nice, you get defensive. These are the reactions of abled fragility, responses I get when I explain to people that they're Internet pornographers when they click, like and share inspiration porn. My friends are teachers, writers, artists, unionists, feminists, educated thinkers all. Some agree with me when they hear my explanation: "Allies must make intersections, even uncomfortable ones, ones which ask us to re-evaluate our privilege and change our behaviour." Others shrug. I know that any agreement they offer me is lip service in their service, designed only to shut me up.

It's fascinating to me that these are the same folks who agree that the media creates another kind of porn: development porn – racist stereotypes that reduce the global South to starving naked children in mud-huts, or "jungle thugs" with machine guns and machetes. They agree that development porn is racist propaganda, produced by and for white audiences, to make colonizers feel superior. Then they jump on Facebook and post photos of disabled children. Burnt children, Down syndrome children. Cancer-bald children. Children disfigured by accident and disease. Children's bodies like pincushions, full of tubes and drips. Children clinging to teddy bears and to life. They tell me I must "like" it. If I don't type "amen," I have no soul.

These posts are often clickbait scams by data collection companies, but it's the "good" "charitable" intentions of ordinary people that concern me. When you "like" an ill or disabled "poor thing" who is a total stranger, when you know nothing about their life, family, home and history, or the condition from which they "suffer"; when you don't want to know, will never try to know; when all you want is a self-congratulatory spurt of good feels for having the courage to stare for two seconds and hit an emoji, then Holy Hypocrite, Houston, we have a problem.

This isn't charity, kindness or empathy; it's voyeurism.

It's pornography.

"But I repost it because they're inspiring! I'm not being insulting; I'm being supportive."

This is the reply I hear so often, a perfect example of ableism passing itself off as virtue. Exactly how is a passive, immobilized child in pain inspiring? How is illness, injury or the spectre of imminent death inspiring? They aren't. These children are on display as objects of pity. When big-hearted, healthy, abled you clicks an emoji to say you love them, it's not about them; it's about you. You *love* how they make you feel. Relieved. Separated. Grateful not to be them. Superior to them. They aren't inspiring you – *you* are inspiring you. You're inspired by your generosity, by being kind enough to see them for the two seconds it takes to send their photo along to someone else you hope will *love* them as sincerely as you do. It's the self-centred, colonial arrogance of the White Man's Burden, reconfigured as the Abled Burden.

And it doesn't end with children.

Inspiration porn also infantilizes adults.

Every day, on every kind of media, I get sent stories in which disabled adults do what Stella satirized as "amazing" and "inspiring" things. We play nicely with others. We get asked to prom. We go to prom. We dance. We walk and roll across stages to graduate high school and college. Sometimes, someone actually asks one of us to marry them. And we do so. We even have sex, give birth and parent children. Exactly why is any of this inspiring? Because deep in the superior ableist heart lies the belief that we are childlike, inferior and incapable. It's such a delightful surprise when one of us rises to the high bar of "normal" and does things abled adults take for granted. It also sends the message we're taken care of; we're no longer a burden.

Ask yourself this: Why is a bride in a wheelchair more inspiring than any other bride?

The standard romantic answer goes like this: "Wheelchair brides prove love is blind and inspire us all to look beyond our limitations." It is entirely logical in the ableist lexicon to be both blind and far-sighted in one sentence. The ableist hero in this "Not a Love Story" is the burden-assuming groom. The real moral of the story is the opposite of romance: we should be grateful for "charitable" men who will marry defective women, even those who can't cook and clean all day and ride them like the bucking stallions they are all night. Wheelchair brides personify the "I See No Disability" fiction essential to a world that benefits from refusing to see us. As one abled groom said on Facebook: "I don't see a wheelchair. I'm blind to it. I see the love of my life."

"I'll take, *Giant Loads of Fertilizer,* 'til reality do them part, Alex."

Buddy, if you don't see the wheelchair, she can't be the love of your life. Because she's a woman in a wheelchair. She doesn't need your denial. She needs you to help fight barriers: the ones on the planet, the ones in her mind and those in the minds of everyone else. Not seeing that is the problem. It's why the problem persists. Wheelchair brides, silenced and smiling, are Tiny Tims in veils and lace. They never complain. They're the template for other collaborators: the blind woman lawyer who claims disability is "no barrier," and "anyone who says otherwise is a lazy complainer." The CEO who describes himself as "wheel-chair bound," adding, "but the only disability is a bad attitude." The beaming super-crip athlete, "If I can win medals, anybody can!"

This is the real function of inspiration porn: to assert narrative control. Ableism accepts only two stories: disabled people can either die quietly or "individually triumph over" disability. Shrinking the narrative to the binary of death or cure ensures that the abled world sees only individual health problems, not a collectively marginalized community. Because inspiration porn also cunningly plants the lie that all disabled people can individually overcome disability if they really want to, if they just work hard enough, it absolves abled people of any responsibility to see systemic ableism, or to fight it with us. At its privileged, self-serving heart, inspiration porn tells abled people that once they perform sympathy, they are fully entitled to get off scot-free.

Do most abled people see or consciously agree to any of this?

Of course not.

The first perk of any race/gender/class/ability privilege is the power to be oblivious to your privilege. It gives you the power to diminish, trivialize and incidentalize the impact of your privilege, to reduce whatever tiny problems you're willing to agree your privilege might create to individual, isolated incidents that can be fixed by kindness and "a little uplifting goodwill."

I'm sure Stella would have a good hoot at the notion that we must be spiritually enriched by disability or we're doing it wrong. Sometime after her death in December 2014, a small voice I tried not to hear began whispering, "The way to honour her story is by telling yours. You need to come out as a disabled writer both inside and outside the book." I began asking myself if I could follow her example and claim my life in my body. I wanted to write the book I need as an adult, one that explores the intersections of ableism and aging. I wouldn't have had the words, the stamina or the daily cussing courage to write it without Stella.

But I knew I wasn't ready. Terrified by the exposure, by any public deconstruction of my closet, unclear and unprepared, I did what I have always done: I turned to books and friendly, wise librarians. For all of 2015, I immersed myself in the work of disabled writers. Following the vibrant and diverse disabled community on social media, searching out novels and non-fiction, literary and disability journals, I read nothing but disabled authors for a full year. Just as you can't declare yourself a nuclear physicist on the day you discover you're made of atoms, you can't announce you're disabled and then, *presto*, speak as a disabled spokesperson. That's profoundly arrogant and disrespectful. You need to take the long view of history, to seek out, learn from, respect and support the disabled community, past and present.

Yet again, I discovered good reason to thank the serendipity of a moment in history.

The twenty-first century Internet hasn't simply given disabled people a platform; it has made it possible to build an international, interconnected disability support network. With empathy, information, kindness, wit and solidarity, disabled activists across the globe reach out to make space for each other. It shames me to admit what I didn't see in my abled life: from feminist groups to unions, the green movement and grassroots organizing, my beloved, progressive left in all its activisms has always failed disabled people and seniors. Reeking of ableism, its community-building is built to keep us out. Its activism requires the money, time, ability, mobility, accessibility and stamina to get out of bed, out of the house, to and into meetings. To be seen and heard in the street. To walk, yell, stand and march for hours. To run in crowds and from the cops. Many disabled people can do none of that, but our activism is equal activism. Online, the disability community has built a vibrant and committed activist practice.

When I decided I wanted to do my bit to help change history, my own history kicked in. Wanting to work collectively in community, retired and missing my union life, I hoped to find an organization that integrated all my identities, one that had an inclusive and intersectional analysis. Unfortunately, some disability organizations are truly uninspiring. Some have no critique of capitalism and simply advocate for awareness and the opportunity to be employed consumers. Worse, some are headed by rich super-crips who seek only to build their brand and celebrity. Others focus only on one disability. Few have an intersectional analysis. Some leave out race, or pay mere lip service to misogyny, gender, identity or class. As a white woman, I specifically hoped to find a group that critiqued the enmeshments of ableism, ageism and white privilege. Instead, too many disability groups are run by, and for, young white people. I could find no organization with anywhere near a representative number of seniors. The group with the most seniors, one of the oldest American organizations, ADAPT, has no presence in Canada.

When I began to read about Disability Justice, I found true inspiration.

Coined by Sins Invalid, a group of disabled activists of colour in San Francisco, their work spoke directly to my improvising-unionist heart. Co-founded in 2006 by Patricia Berne and Leroy Moore, Berne calls it "a hybrid of community organizing and a performance." "The 10 Principles of Disability Justice" became my guide: Intersectionality, Leadership of Those Most Impacted, Anti-Capitalist Politic, Commitment to Cross-Movement Organizing, Recognizing Wholeness, Sustainability, Commitment to Cross-Disability Solidarity, Interdependence, Collective Access and Collective Liberation. These concepts also base the fledgling Disability Justice Network of Ontario (DJNO), the Hamilton group I joined, support and respect.

Eventually, I settled on accessibility as the focus that most interested me, and not just for personal reasons. The more I read, the more I began to see accessibility as an intersectional demand. Combining physical accessibility with e-accessibility, full accessibility for all ages, identities, incomes and the diversity of disabilities builds Disability Justice. We can't take a seat at the table if we can't get to the table. We can't transform the room if we can't get in the room. To be seen, heard, included and valued, to argue for all the demands of Disability Justice, to inspire and to lead, disabled people must be respected at the table. We bring a critical crip analysis to every issue: the climate emergency, city planning, carceral culture, police violence, poverty, education, housing and employment. None of these fights can be won without us.

In August of 2015, inspired by Stella and Disability Justice, I made my own hope.

I took Wenceslas out of the closet. The first place we went was the Scottish Festival, held each summer in beautiful downtown Fergus, Ontario. They do a fabulous job ferrying their largely senior demographic through the fairgrounds on golf carts, but I knew the standing and walking still required was beyond me. I wheeled Wenceslas to the car feeling as naked as another king, the one with no clothes. It would be the first time my daughter saw me with him. I feared being reduced in her eyes. She saw the new passenger in my back seat and grinned.

"Damn well about time, woman. Good for you. Now let's go meet some men in kilts."

I remember the unexpected freedom of that day. How quickly I could move around on the short grass, secure in the knowledge I wouldn't fall. I could feel my blood pressure dropping the instant I sat down, which I could do at any moment I chose. I zipped around at a speed I didn't know I still had. The safety and freedom of a walker made a happy summer day possible. But only if I kept my eyes on the lovely kilts, my lovely daughter or the ground, because when I stepped out with Wenceslas, I traded stairs for stares.

It all but ruined the victory. I had to pretend I wasn't being gawked at. Total strangers thought they had the right to tell me what my walker meant to them: "It's so heartwarming to see someone like you outside, dear," "We're so glad you aren't sitting at home feeling sorry for yourself" and, here it comes, "You're so inspiring." I told myself Stella's opinion mattered more. I told my friends, "A walker doesn't have to make you older. It can make you feel younger, more energetic, more confident." I told everyone, "Statistics Canada confirms that 22 percent of us will eventually use a mobility device. It doesn't end your life; it gives it back to you."

For me, a more accurate truth would be this: it gives you another, almost-able life.

I've always loved lingering in clothing stores, feeling fabric, admiring cut and style, pairing items in my mind. But when I tried to shop on a crutch, I couldn't browse. I could stand five minutes before I had to grab some garments, any garments, and head for the change room. I had to sit down before I fell down. I had no intention of trying anything on. I simply sat long enough in the change room to make it back to my car without throwing up or passing out.

Beau reduced grocery shopping to surgical strikes. I had to dive-bomb one aisle per visit. One day I'd get veggies. The next, cereal.

When a cashier eyed me up and down at the sight of nothing but red meat on her conveyer belt, I smiled, "I'm on the High Protein Vampire Diet. Everything raw. Preferably bloody." I always made a joke of it, but believe me, when your mobility shrinks a bit more each day, there's nothing bloody funny about it.

When I pulled Wenceslas from his box, he turned back the clock.

My first year with him was a shopping honeymoon. I couldn't afford to buy anything, but I could browse for hours because I brought my own seat. My brain cleared. Panic subsided. Pain dropped. I could think efficiently. In grocery stores, I stacked boxes flat on his seat and wheeled my giant edible *Tetris* to the till. I sat while my groceries got rung through, and kept sitting to pay. On my crutch, I couldn't carry more than two bags, but six bags, three to a side, fit along my walker's handlebars. I can buy whole meals. In equal nourishment, I can go to the movies. I can even wait in line at the movies without wishing everyone ahead of me would drop dead.

Without a crutch, I'm no longer Tiny Tim, but I'll never be Pollyanna. She's his female, American, inspiration porn doppelgänger, a perky little sunbeam from the 1913 novel by Eleanor H. Porter. Pollyanna plays "the Glad Game." She hopes for a doll in the missionary barrel, but when she gets crutches, she's "glad" because she doesn't have to use them. As a teenager, when she loses the use of her legs in a car accident, she is "glad" she has legs. This inspiring attitude not only leads to her being cured, it warms the hearts of her entire town. The 1960 Disney version won young actress Hayley Mills an Oscar for her inspiring, cripped-up portrayal.

Because I'm not a Pollyanna, I'll be clear: when you get a walker, it's a forced fit and a mixed blessing. Together, you may break barriers of distance and stamina, but you'll hit new ones: the inaccessibility of snow, ice, curbs, doors, stairs, restaurants, washrooms and, worst of all, the attitudes of others. You can know your walker is a boon and still have others treat it, and you, as a burden. When you see pity in countless eyes, it's a struggle not to see it in the mirror.

Here is my most sincere caution, and cause for pause: If you're losing mobility due to aging and you're still walking well some of the time, ask yourself if you're emotionally ready to use a walker full time, because you can't go back in time and give it back. It may start as an accessory, but it can quickly become a necessity. You get up one morning and you're another Almost; you're the Borg: part human, part metal. An enmeshed, hybrid being.

I am no longer a walker without one.

But rejecting internalized ableism and accepting that transformation can be inspiring. With Wenceslas, I get out more often. I'm a better listener, friend and mother. As pain and fear go down, patience, pleasant thoughts, love and laughter all go up. I have less fear of falling because nothing, and no one, can knock me down.

I'm literally a four-foot-ten rolling tank.

I'm sure Stella would approve.

Queasy and Quaking in My Boots

When my son came out in his teens in the '90s, our conversation went something like this: "So, Mom, I guess you know I'm gay?" Followed by, "Yes, dear, I was just waiting for you to want to talk about it." I'll admit that I cried a little. I was worried that he would find love and stay safe; a young gay man named Matthew Shepard had just been found beaten to death and left to rot on a fence. But my son has often said since that there wasn't one tenth of a second of doubt. He knew he would be loved, welcomed, accepted and cherished for himself.

Two decades later, when I started going out with Wenceslas, I was so nervous I feared I'd hurl into his basket. Many of my friends put me at ease with the time and space they offered. They listened, asked insightful questions, let me figure out for myself what needing a walker meant to me. Sadly, some of my friends couldn't even look at him, let alone call him by his name. I was newly hyper-visible, but they saw only their own embarrassment and denial. As the first of their friends on a walker, I'm obviously old. I brought the truth of how chicken they were of their own aging and mortality home to roost. I still can't decide who are worse: friends in denial or those kind friends who tried to define my experience for me.

"Don't worry, Dorothy. A walker changes nothing."

"Don't worry, Dorothy, I still see you. You're still you."

Suddenly realizing they'd gone to medical school, in the time-honoured privilege of abled folks instantly diagnosing disabled people, they said, "Don't worry, a walker isn't a death sentence." And, "Don't worry, you can still get cardio. Just walk fast." Even more miraculously, some discovered they'd gone to Hogwarts and could magically make a heavy metal walker disappear: "I don't see anything different. Don't worry, cheer up. It's all a matter of attitude."

It became very clear to me that they were all very worried and thought I should be, too. I felt their fear, felt their need to distance themselves from me as if I might infect them with decrepitude, might make them sprout a walker the way teens sprout zits. I also heard hypocrisy. Friends who call out *mansplaining*, saw no problem with their own *ablesplaining*. In similar instant judgment, they asserted that they knew better than I did; that they could override and dismiss me, advise and contradict me, erase my lived experience as if it counted for nothing.

I'm always fascinated by how ablesplaining claims both absolute authority and Six Degrees of Kevin Bacon. Abled people endlessly assure me they "know all about walkers" because their brother's ex-wife's neighbour's chiropodist's third cousin's gardener's granny had one. I see this distancing as purposeful, erected to keep their abled selves safely away from the great disabled unwashed. Yet again, it positions disabled people as rare creatures, distantly related not to them but to some other people out there, somewhere, the more distant the better.

The worst ablesplainers are those who apparently went to both med school and Hogwarts, because they are certain they can cure me. Sadly, these purveyors of magic nostrums and elixirs are mostly women. In feminized ablesplaining cloaked as wellness and self-care, they flog kale, yoga, weighted blankets, yoga, prayer, yoga, goji berries, yoga, going vegan or yoga. Most logically, every disabled person on the planet could be cured by going to vegan yoga to eat kale and goji berries in weighted prayer blankets. As eager as these women are to push their cures, they also maintain a safe separation. Yet again, they have a second cousin's boyfriend's next-door neighbour's babysitter's taxidermist's ninety-year-old great-aunt who had a walker, but now wins breakdancing awards thanks to . . . insert cure of choice here. Most likely also yoga.

One of the first things we teach in all anti-oppression work, from union committees to progressive improv, is the difference between intent and impact. Impact always matters more than intent and must be judged by those impacted. All those who intend to help by offering me "healing" do impactful damage. They're perpetuating the *cure trope*, so despised by disabled people, which assumes a cure is both possible and the only desirable goal. This revictimizes us. If abled people offer to heal us, but we're too lazy or unwilling to take their advice, then it's our own fault we're disabled. Needing to see me like a girlfriend with a broken leg, soon to be restored to their company at the top of the Great Ableist Chain of Being, these wannabe healers offer condolences for my walker. This is the worst assumption: that condolences are in order, that a walker must be something to be sorry for. Whenever I scratch this abled privilege, I get abled fragility. If I question their "kindness," they get teary. I've "hurt their feelings," when they were "only trying to help."

Abled fragility has ended friendships.

It ended one of ten years in ten minutes.

I was already grouchy when I picked Anna up at the subway, because I'd spent the morning shoe shopping and left empty handed. For many fat women, a love of fashion gets reduced to a laser focus on fashionable shoes. Shoe shopping is something they can do with their girlfriends where they belong, equally and without judgment. That has never been me.

This is how someone with no choice shops for shoes for all her life: Always alone. Afraid I'll see someone I know. In the little boy's section, in Walmart, in tears. With little boys and their mommies staring. I'm crying. Because it hurts to pull shoes on and off. Because self-loathing is my only choice. Because I'm trying on Ninja Turtles runners with Velcro. Forget colour. Forget style. Forget any notion of taste. If a shoe exists in my two sizes, if there's a 1.5 and a 2.5, if I can lace up and stand up, I have to buy them. Period.

I often shop in multiple stores without finding a double-casting. Either one size is missing or Herkimer feels great in a shoe I can't force fit onto Horatio. Girls' shoes are too narrow; I need boys' shoes, extra-wide. My sizes are hard to find because nine-year-old boys want grown-up shoes. Even when I find two pairs, I never know how long they'll last. Maybe a month. Maybe only a week until Horatio ruins his. He's never been beaten by a shoe; he always breaks them. He once split a shoe right off its sole on the first day I wore them. If I think shoes might last, I buy three pairs: one 1.5 pair for Herkimer, two pairs of 2.5 for the destructive Horatio.

I've been known to tell nosy clerks I have triplet sons: Herkimer, Horatio and Huckyou.

I never look at women's shoes – it's too painful. If I accidentally enter the women's aisle in Walmart, the colours, the choices, the sheer joyful fun of them make me want to scream obscenities. No, that's not all of it. Shoes made for adult women all stand for my mother. She and they make me feel like an unwanted, alien species. Fancy high heels make me hate any human woman who can wear them. They make me want to kill people, so I won't kill myself.

Do all you Sherlocks out there detect another change in tone here? You're right.

I've been holding back. Here's the truth: refusing to see my walker makes this redhead see crimson. At first, I tried to see it as being polite, as respecting my privacy. But that wore thin. After friends met Wenceslas, when I'd taken him to their homes, when they'd watched us navigate curbs, restaurants and movie theatres, after they'd watched us fall and still said nothing, when I raised the topic and they quickly changed it, I began to see their silence as selfish and self-serving. If they could ignore my walker, they could ignore their relationship to it. If they didn't have to address how my life had changed, they wouldn't have to admit their lives might have to change to spend time with me.

Their silence didn't protect me; it protected them from me.

My friend Anna had side-eyed Wenceslas once and said nothing. And I let her do so. A well-read feminist with a Sociology M.A., she was also a former athlete and a lifelong dancer. I'd always downplayed my disability with her. Somehow, in the place where we protect our closeted selves, I think I knew that if push came to shove, I couldn't count on her to push past her abled privilege. On the day I picked her up, when she spotted a Walmart bag in my car and "joked" about how I must be "going senile," I screwed my courage to the sticking point and said I'd been shopping there for years, even before my walker, since I got my crutch.

"Since your crutch? That's no excuse. It doesn't give you an exemption. The principled position against Walmart still applies to you. Of course, it does. It applies to everyone. Period."

"No, Anna. I'm telling you, as my friend, that those principled stands have always been contingent on being able-bodied. They don't apply to me. I'm coming out of the disabled closet."

The first thing she said was the only thing she should have said.

"What do you mean? I don't understand."

I'd been rehearsing the part of Outraged Disabled Senior for almost a year, trying to counter the lefty guilt I felt for patronizing Walmart, so I knew all my lines already.

"Yes, Walmart is evil. Evil with twelve accessible parking spots. Evil with a ploughed parking lot. Evil with a cart that holds me up. If the cashier doesn't get that I need to keep my hands free, at least when I ask for bags, they don't glare at me like I'm defiling the planet."

"Surely that's an exaggeration. Maybe you should just explain –"

"Maybe I shouldn't have to explain."

So, what does my feminist friend do? She laughs. Says I shouldn't personally appropriate the word *closet* from the queer community. She assumes she has the right to chastise me for personally inventing it, because she has made no attempt to educate herself, has no clue that the international disabled community has used the term for decades, with the support of disabled gay activists who talk about coming out of their double closet. But Anna does know this: She gets to tell me what to do. She suggests I exercise more. Increase my meds. She actually says, "The real pain is in your head." She doesn't want to see my intersectional self, an adopted bastard battling sexism, ageism, ableism, classism and chronic pain. It threatens her.

It threatens her belief that as a feminist, she is not, and cannot ever be, an oppressor.

It threatens her deepest fear: her able body cannot, must not, be the next to fall.

I know that some of her attitude is my fault. I have policed my own silencing.

So, this time, I decide to let her see the real me. Unfortunately, it's a red-headed moment. Pent-up anger comes out messy. I push on the accelerator and push back at her privilege.

"Are you actually trying to claim you know more about being disabled than I do?"

"I'm saying everyone can make the effort. Period. We should all buy local, patronize –"

"Snotty, elitist, expensive, inaccessible, downtown bookstores, like yours?"

It's a low blow and I don't care. When Anna had her hobby job in a bookstore, she spent every cent on herself. Her father was rich, as is her lawyer husband. They're childless. While her pampered Pomeranian is her baby, unlike my human children, Pattycakes did not require diapers, daycare or post-secondary education. For all Anna's life, money has never been an issue. She equally ignores my lack of it. Many friends insist that whenever we go out, they're paying the bill; it's the least they can do. Anna orders expensive entrees, several drinks to my none, and splits the bill fifty-fifty. She brags about leaving every penny to the humane society. I admit it: I'm jealous. I begrudge her well-coupled, financial, abled safety. I resent her smugness.

"What do you mean? It isn't inaccessible. It's near the subway. It's on a bus line."

"Anna, look at me. I can't use transit. I have to drive or stay home. At your store, there's no parking. The sidewalk is never shovelled, except for a narrow ribbon for feet. There's a huge step up, and a heavy door. The aisles are too narrow for my walker and there's nowhere to sit."

"That's not true! There's a chair at the back."

"I just told you I can't get to the back. The aisles are too narrow. And that chair? It's up three stairs, covered in cat hair and defended by a cat. Screw that. I'm going to Chapters."

"But there you go again. That's another betrayal of your politics. It's disgusting."

I think our friendship might have been salvageable had she not used that word.

It triggered my smelly teens, and my bastard shame of being dirty.

"Really? Well, when disgusting me can't get to Chapters, I fire up my Kindle and buy pain-free from Amazon. I live on twenty-fucking-thousand bucks a year. I won't be made to feel guilty for it. If you try to do so, you're no feminist. You're a rich, hypocritical, white bitch."

Well, that went well. Not my finest moment. Needless to say, livid lips sink friendships.

Anna took it personally. She should have. The ableism that bars me from books is very personal. I can't soft-pedal it to make friends feel better about themselves. Just as you can't critique sexism in front of a man in any way that exempts him, you can't critique ableism to an abled person in any way that exempts them. In this uncomfortable conversation, I'm not a feminist critiquing male privilege. Nor am I sitting in solidarity with Anna, listening respectfully to a BIPOC woman critiquing white privilege. That she would have respected. What she couldn't handle was this: I asked her to see her collaboration in my oppression. That was too much to ask.

A week later, she phoned to apologize by making a joke.

"I'm sorry, Dorothy. Can you forgive me for being such a moron? I guess I'm just blind to what you're seeing. But bygones. Let's just put it behind us."

I didn't point out that her apology used the ableist slurs of *moron* and being *just blind*. I knew that what she really meant was this: she would graciously permit me to exist, allow me to be seen in her company, as long as I was no challenge or inconvenience to her.

I paused as long as Archie. I made one face, then another. Then hung up the phone.

Abled folks don't get to decide what is and isn't ableism.

Or how to fight it.

Between the two of us here on the page, I'm really happy with our contract: your reading time in payment for my writing time. But I don't work for free.

And I don't owe anybody but you that education.

Restaurants, Ramps and Rodents of Unusual Size

Back in high school, I often wondered what it would be like to be old. I told myself I wouldn't be like the timid T.S. Eliot in "The Love Song of Alfred J. Prufrock," who asked: "Do I dare to eat a peach?" I remember thinking, "Eat one if you want to, silly wanker, but don't call it poetry." I figured I must be missing something. Was peach eating some kind of secret author smut code, like the one Ms. Dewsnap was always so eager to share in Shakespeare? Maybe Mr. Eliot was really asking if he could eat a fuzzy part of the human anatomy? Poetry indeed. But today, I get the question in its far less titillating meaning. A peach is inherently riskier if your hair is thinning like Alfred J. or, as I confess, like mine. When you can see right through to your scalp, you don't want to risk further humiliation by getting caught with peach juice dribbling down your chin. You don't want anybody pointing at you and saying, "No, Alex. I won't take *That Dribbling, Bald, Old Fool* for any amount of money."

You decide not to dare a peach. You settle for prunes.

When I turned sixty, I let my hair go grey. Some of it was a choice. I'd always vowed not to be one of those dye-job old ladies with hair as fake as Trump's Day-Glo orange fringe. I told myself, if you're lucky enough to get old, you should welcome the role and look the part. But being grey on a walker produced a profound change in the way the world saw and treated me. It really bit the prune. Literally overnight, total strangers kindly began teaching me how to use an elevator, a bank machine, a gas pump, my own cell phone. As a redhead on my own two feet, my ex was a thief on the run from an arrest warrant. As a grizzled old gimp on a walker, I felt new judgment: Dumped. Dried up. Sexless. Quite reasonably abandoned to die.

Back in my two-income life, I could drop a hundred dollars on my hair: a senior stylist, colour, highlights and a generous tip. Today, I'm at the mercy of dropout teenagers armed with scissors. I know better than to tell them I'm a teacher. I get shorn as short as a baby lamb because I need to make my $9.99 Senior's Special last three months. I've been stared at on crutches since childhood, but nothing prepared me for the reactions a fat, shorn, old woman on a walker elicits from strangers. It proves you one of two things: a decent human being or a snorting pig. Nowhere is this binary division more pronounced than when I treat myself to the once-a-month, mental health self-care of a meal in a restaurant, when I dare to dine disabled and alone.

Now, let me first say this assumes I can enter said restaurant.

Most rule themselves out thanks to outdoor steps, indoor stairs or a nasty ramp.

Abled people don't see the barriers right in front of them because they are not barriers to them. Sometimes, after phoning to confirm accessibility, I've arrived, taken one look at the steps abled staff swore weren't there, or at the Mount Kilimanjaro masquerading as a ramp, and had to leave. Too many ramps are built to an outdated code, a steep grade for pushed wheelchairs. Or to no code at all. Someone simply measured the space and built a slope, regardless of grade. On a walker, a ramp is scary, up and down. When I push up, my walker isn't taking any of my weight. When I head down, Wenceslas tries to rush out ahead of me. On more than one occasion, he has leapt from my hands into the street. Thank goodness he didn't hit a car, damage that would have been mine to pay. Or hit a child; that's damage I could never pay for.

But let's assume I can get in the restaurant door and let's praise all the good stuff first.

I've been moved to burbling tears by countless examples of generosity. Much of it from children. Their acceptance tells me that the othering of disabled people isn't natural to humans; it's learned behaviour. A four-year-old offered me their dolly to push in my carriage because they were sad mine was empty. A ten-year-old lay on the floor and tightened all of Wenceslas' wing nuts because they were going to be a mechanic like their dad. Tough teens with multiple piercings, with neck tattoos and torn T-shirts reading STRAIGHT OUTTA SCARBOROUGH have gallantly insisted that I please go first. A Junior B hockey team once bought me breakfast. Mid-mouthful, patrons have jumped up to make room for my walker to pass. Wait staff and owners have brought me free drinks and desserts because their darling gran had a walker. Total strangers have asked me to join them, or I've asked for the bill and been told it's been paid.

While I know some of these acts are layered with inspiration porn and paternalization, I choose to see the kindness of engagement. These are ordinary people who don't know how to help but want to do something. I see no reason to scream in their faces. I often try to have a conversation that makes them rethink my life. One we could not have if I was rude to them in any way. I see their willingness to engage me as a blow against ableism. I thank them for fighting it with me. I wish I could leave it there, with warm restaurant fuzzies for all. But I can't.

If I'm with friends, I get treated better. Perhaps it's instinctive: When I run with an abled pack, I smell good enough to be welcomed into the fold. Or, more cynically, perhaps it's because there are abled witnesses who'd be credible in court. Whatever the reason, when I'm alone, I'm not human; I'm a disgusting obstacle. People sprint across parking lots, not to open a door but to beat me through it. I've had parents push their kids ahead of me and drop the door on me with, "If we get in front of her, we don't have to look at her." I congratulated these role models, noting this was an excellent way to teach their children how to treat them when they get old.

When I stand in line, some folks won't meet my eye. Some pretend not to see me at all. They step up to the front and claim they were there before me. More than one maître d' has told me to go back outside in the rain or snow and clean off my wheels so as not to soil their clean floor. One well-dressed woman complained, not to me but to the waiting assembled, that walkers were unsightly and shouldn't be allowed in nice restaurants where good and decent people eat.

I rolled Wenceslas over her toes and asked her if she knew any.

Nine times of ten, servers take me straight to the worst table in the house, inevitably the tiniest and farthest away. It's like we're both caught in a loop, where the chicken blames the egg and vice versa. If single women, especially older single women, are reputed not to give good tips, maybe it's because wait staff keep seating us at the worst tables, ignoring us and serving everyone else first. Compare this to dining with my ex. At six foot four, in his tailored business suits with Senior Vice President panache, restaurants couldn't seat us fast enough. The best tables. The best service. Sommeliers on the run. Today, I'm a manless, short, fat, grey-haired, lame old biddy alone on a walker. Noting that none of my previous privilege was earned or fair, having lost all the perks bestowed by high-status coupledom, I still feel the difference acutely.

But I give each server the benefit of a doubt and my best smile. "I'd like a window booth, please." I can't use a chair because my feet don't reach the ground, get pins and needles, and fall asleep. When I try to stand, Herkimer and Horatio ironically refuse to sleepwalk. In a booth, I can reorient my body to prevent them from sleeping. I prefer a window, because folks with light-coloured eyes like mine are prone to photophobia: extreme light sensitivity. Window seats make debilitating headaches less likely, make it possible to accurately see the floor when I stand up.

I shouldn't have to explain any of this.

Staff should simply honour my request.

Too often, they look me in the eye and say there aren't any booths. When I point one out, they say they're reserved for large parties. When I say several have only two guests, they shrug. I have to get feisty, insist on my legal right to be accommodated. They often roll their eyes but magically discover a booth. If they head for the back, I won't play that game. I plunk myself down in the nearest window booth. If they ask me to move, unless they supply good reason, I refuse. One smarmy manager asked me to move to the back because, wink wink, "A walker doesn't fit the young and sexy image of my restaurant." I pulled out my phone, saying I was going to call the cops to be the young and sexy witnesses to my human rights lawsuit. Suddenly, I didn't have to move. Suddenly, I was sexy enough for a chocolate mousse on the house.

If I do politely follow the wait staff, it seldom occurs to them what is immediately obvious to me: the pathway between tables is too narrow for my walker. By legislation, by fire code, wheelchair clearance space between tables should be ninety-six centimetres, or thirty-eight inches. Size absolutely matters. If my walker at sixty centimetres, or twenty-four inches, won't fit, we all have a problem. I've had customers swear at me for bumping their chair, had diners refuse to move and tell me to go around the other way. Once, this lovely exchange occurred:

"Oh, my apologies. I just knocked your purse off the back of your chair."

The woman eyed me like an approaching enema. "So why don't you pick it up?"

Her husband smirked. "She can't bend over. Not with that fat ass."

It doesn't end once I'm seated. Servers grab Wenceslas. He folds up to a narrow fifteen centimetres and I need him in reach. When I explain I shouldn't have to infantilize myself and ask for help, that I should have equal chance to escape a fire, they blink like budgies. "All you have to do is ask, hon, and I'll bring it back. Right away, dearie. I promise. No problem."

Sometimes they want to kidnap him, whisk him away to that dreaded secret, second location. To make me give him up, with a straight face, managers quote the same codes they're violating in their crowded seating plans. I accept that in the interest of safety, sometimes a walker needs to be moved to the side. I can live with that. But I insist on two things: Wenceslas should not be grabbed out of my hands, especially not before I get my purse out of his bin; and he must be put where I can see him. Walkers sell for a quick hundred bucks online. They get stolen all the time. A friend had hers taken when she had to leave it outside an inaccessible washroom in the restaurant where she was celebrating her fortieth wedding anniversary.

The worst treatment I ever got occurred in one of the most expensive restaurants.

The immaculately groomed maître d' yanked Wenceslas out of my hands and hissed, "If you can't walk, what the fuck makes you think you can walk into my restaurant?"

I asked to speak to his manager. She listened then patted my hand. She said her grandma was hard of hearing, too. Said she was certain none of her exemplary staff would ever say such a thing. She stood up, offered me a free, non-alcoholic beverage of my choice, smiled and left.

Restaurants are supposed to be relaxing and fun, not demoralizing and humiliating. Sometimes I fight back; sometimes I don't. Sometimes I'm too hungry to be hangry.

I'm sure you're wondering, if she gets poor service, why doesn't she just leave?

Because it hurt enough to get there in the first place. Because I shouldn't have to run from bigots. Because I have no guarantee that the next restaurant will be any better. Because restaurants are the once-a-month self-care I really need to stave off isolation and despair, and I know this for sure: if I get back in the car, I'll just start crying and go home.

To simplify my life, I've boiled my decision to tip down to one thing: whether my server hands me the Interac machine, or attempts to teach me how to use it. If they treat me like an adult, they get a tip reflective of their courtesy and service. If they grab my bank card and insert it, or lean over my shoulder with, "Okay, dear, the chip goes in first. That's the little grey square on the bottom," I can easily do the math; their tip is zero. They get this verbal tip instead: "According to postmodern semiotics, the signs of my grey hair and my walker, even when read together, do not signify incompetence." If their face suggests I'm spouting gibberish that proves my senility, I tell them that the only tip I'm going to give them is the best one they'll get all day: "Stop assuming seniors with walkers are as ignorant as you're being when you think that way."

I'm paying for hospitality, ambiance and the expert meals I can't make at home. I didn't ask to be served patronizing humiliation. I'm sick of spending every moment tensed for another *Battle Royale*. I'd like to pick my battles without having them incessantly thrust upon me. It's exhausting. It requires a feisty bravado I don't always have.

Because older women like my grandmothers played such a revered role in my life, I find the double infantilization as a disabled senior twice as insulting. Echoing the messaging of adoption, I also know I'm not supposed to complain about the way I'm treated. Society likes its old people the way it likes its disabled people: served up to them in palatable bites, pat on the head cute, inspiring, sweet, silent and smiling. Tiny Tims with dentures.

In karmic full circle, I also see my own youthful, more abled callousness with new humility. I used to laugh about old people eating at 4:30 p.m., a laughter I hoped made clear I'd never do something so pathetic. The first time I patronized my local fish and chips shop for their Seniors' Special marked the moment I felt truly old. I'd skipped lunch, but it wasn't 4:30; it was at least 4:45. I opened the door and there they were – my peeps. A sea of permanently waved grey hair, highlighted by a few redheads of extraordinary hue. I did the math: seven canes, five walkers and three wheelchairs. I realized this grey army had good reasons for an early repast.

When most chairs are empty and pushed in, it's easier to move between tables. I don't have to ask anyone to move. Before the dinner rush, less-frazzled servers treat you like their own dear grandmothers. And I won't apologize for this: I like bland white people food. Less insultingly known as Depression survival cooking, or British working-class food. I enjoyed the meal my mother would have served in 1965: battered fish with tartar sauce, fat-cut chips, canned green peas, a crusty white dinner roll and rice pudding. It was comfort food and comforting.

So, please think twice before slapping your knee at old folks eating at 4:30. We may need a less-crowded spot for comfort and safety. We may not be able to shop that day, and be unable to afford expensive grocery delivery services. We may be too tired or in too much pain to make lunch. We may fear driving at night or being mugged in the dark. My own reason shames me, but must be included: many of us eat dinner early because we can't afford three meals a day.

Is it possible to gain weight on two meals a day?

You bet my poor, fat ass it is.

Starch is cheap. A diet of nothing but starch has little nutrition. Especially if Meal One is peanut butter toast and Meal Two is Kraft Dinner. On days I can't manage to make even that, I call my Pizza Pizza contact, Hazim, a most punctual and affable young man studying to be a gynecologist. When I say I put on weight, I mean the kind of poundage to make a sumo wrestler proud. It's no consolation that with poor mobility, poor nutrition and endemic poverty, most disabled seniors are diagnosed as obese. At four foot ten, I weigh 230 pounds. I'm twice what I weighed in high school, eighty pounds heavier than when I was pregnant. I could give birth to both my children at once and still spit out a pair of twins.

"Inconceivable!" shouts Vizzini from *The Princess Bride*. For once, using it correctly.

But I don't have a self-image problem. I know exactly how I look: like the Rodents of Unusual Size in *The Princess Bride*, I'm a Redhead of Unhealthy Size. I look like the Kool-Aid Man, round, red and stumpy with ineffectual arms and legs. In the interconnectedness of all things, weight gain means more pain, means being more housebound, more alone, more depressed and thus, more weight gain. I'm what doctors would call the Poster Gimp for the Morbidly Obese. Or would be, if I weren't too uncomfortable to have my photo taken.

I'm not fat-shaming myself. I understand that the fatphobia that creates self-loathing is a direct product of the male gaze, and of the valuation of bodies under capitalism, where women's bodies are only seen as having value if they are fit enough to work all day and hot enough to keep working it all night. What makes me uncomfortable is the math – my pounds per square inch. If a woman has size nine feet, Google tells me the surface of her feet will be 3.6" x 10" per foot, or 72 square inches. If she weighs 130 pounds, her pounds per square inch will be 130 ÷ 72, or 1.8 psi. My tiny fat feet, at 4" x 8" each, total 64 square inches. At 230 pounds, my already frail feet are enduring a crushing 3.6 psi, or twice the psi of an "average" woman.

I can no longer pretend to be tiny.

But I don't know how to stop getting bigger.

I once wrote a Sherlock story based on a case mentioned by Conan Doyle but never documented: "The Singular Affair of the Aluminum Crutch." When the good Doctor Watson indignantly defamed the lame protagonist with "I can't countenance self-pity, Holmes. It's unbecoming. Entirely Un-British," Sherlock set a cautionary hand on his old friend's shoulder.

"That is most illogical, Watson. I trust that as a medical man with a professional understanding of the human psyche, you shall see your error immediately. If I would pity a man in Condition X, then I become a man with Condition X, it logically follows that I must pity myself, or be a hypocrite. Self-pity is thus both entirely consistent and wholly required by logic."

So, yes, I sometimes feel sorry for myself and think I have the logical right to do so. I can handle the loss of mobility, the increase in pain and aging. What I can't handle is coping with them in poverty, knowing that suffering is caused by an able-bodied, pain-free man on the run from the law. A man who still gets the best seats at all the finest restaurants. In the summer of 2018, when I saved my pennies to go back to the Scottish Festival only to collide with a highlander, I pretended that being thrown flat on my back, yet again, didn't hurt me. I still make a joke of it, but his isn't the only manhood that has stepped over my face and gotten off scot-free.

I don't know how to save my own life.

I only know I'm running out of time to do so.

When I got my walker, I aged years in six months. In the mirror, I saw a stranger. A frail old lady. A fat old broad. It broke me. It shamed me. I stayed home. I self-medicated. I ate. I told myself I'd park Wenceslas at the door and never use him inside my apartment. Then I realized I could use his seat like a room service cart. Given my uneven gait, I've had to carry half-full beverages all my life. For the first time, I could fill cups up. I told myself I wouldn't use Wenceslas for anything else. Then I discovered he fit around the end of my bed, and it was probably a good idea to have him at hand in the middle of the groggy night.

It wasn't long before I wasn't taking a single step without him.

As pain grew, I bent over and walked leaning my elbows on my walker. I told myself it was a terrible idea. Bad for my neck. Bad for my back. But it took so much weight off my feet I couldn't stop. Lately, when I head outside, I have to remind myself I'm Homo erectus. Inside, I lean my head on my arms like a worn-out kid at the dinner table. I look defeated, old and feeble, and I don't care. Walking bent over slows me to a deathly crawl and I don't care. Because the next step is no step at all. It's a power wheelchair, one not yet purchased but already christened: Queen Mehitable the Inevitable. I'm not ready to bow to her yet. I'll fight my war of independence for as long as I can.

In that vow, I remind myself of one older woman I couldn't stand as a kid: my great-aunt Connie. She so resented her walker, she weaponized it. My dad put it best: "She'll roll right over you and won't even pretend it's an accident. She's one tough old bat." He grinned. "More than ready to come out swinging at anyone who dares get in her way."

If sports played any role in my life, I might have known my father meant a baseball bat. As the last of her generation, my great-aunt swung her dowager weight like a Louisville Slugger. But to preteen me, sports were a foreign language. When I imagined a "tough old bat," I saw a winged creature. Leathery. Brave. Aloft. Not a Dracula but a venerable vigilante, an elder judge soaring over her world. With sharp eyes and a sharper tongue, she wasn't going anywhere gently. If you're lucky, you'll get to be a tough old bat, too.

My father wasn't so lucky. He died at a young seventy-three, a month after my fortieth birthday, on the night of the moonwalk: July 20, 1995. He swam at dawn in Balsam Lake until he was diagnosed with myasthenia gravis, a neuromuscular disease. He went into the hospital that spring and never came out. On one of my last visits, to cheer him up, I mentioned the time I fell into his fish tank. He laughed, "Well, I guess soon I'll be the one sleeping with the fishes."

It never crossed our minds to put him out of his misery, but I do think that after three months of hospitalization, once he realized he'd lost that summer at the cottage, he simply lay down and died. My mother lived another sixteen lonely years without him. At ninety-one, admitted to hospital for observation after a mild stroke, she died alone on the hospital floor in March 2011. My birth mother died three months later, one week after my birthday.

I'm often asked how much of the rigid, distant mother in *When Fenelon Falls* is my mother, and now I have an answer. Her distance was all I saw at fourteen. But as you age, your vision changes. As my wise daughter put it, my mother's generation valued playing by the rules, only to have daughters who told them those rules were sexist, silly and sad. Our mothers wanted choices for their daughters, then resented us for having them. They realized not just that the parade had passed them by, but that the parade as they knew it was as dead as jumpsies.

As she aged, my mother's mental deterioration echoed Grandma Stobie's, only this time I was its target. Of course, our last discussion was about what I was and wasn't worth. The year I volunteered to host the family Christmas, she refused to let me borrow Grandma's silverware for the family meal. She shrugged and offered me a package of plastic forks. When I broke her silence rule, when I told her how much she hurt my feelings, how it made me feel like I wasn't really her daughter, she refused to speak to me for the last years of her life. And I let her do so.

When she died, my siblings decided they'd rather have the cottage to themselves than share it with an almost sister. And I let them go.

Sometimes a loss is no loss at all. Sometimes it's a welcome relief.

Sex and the Single Senior

Once I hooked up with my walker, I naturally started thinking about sex. It wasn't because the lovely Wenceslas generated some kind of granny pants surge in my libido. Quite the opposite. If my unisex uniform rebuffs the male gaze, my walker erases it. Put a walker in front of your boobs and *poppity pop!* they disappear. Most men don't see you at all. But there is a silver lining: being invisible makes it possible to see things you never saw before. Now that I'm as sexually neutered as long-ago mothers wanted Gerald to be, it clarifies sex as never before. There's nothing like not getting any to help you finally get it.

The first thing I saw differently was street harassment.

Having led decades of sexual harassment initiatives for both staff and students, I'd have said I knew what to expect when I went out in public with Wenceslas. I'd have been wrong. Worse than Jon Snow, I knew a clueless nothing. I became the target of potty-mouthed men.

A dapper man in a business suit mutters, "Lard ass. Get the fuck off my sidewalk."

A homeless man pushes his shopping cart into my bum. "Make way, cunty bitch."

On a hot summer day in the park, I'm approached by a well-dressed, blond, blue-eyed young man who comes right up to me smiling. My 1950s programing as a nice girl, my years of teaching, make me read him as a nice boy. I smile back. And he says, "Gimps really do it for me." He tugs on his fly. "Wanna watch me cum all over your walker?"

Other random men have kindly offered to impale me on, under and with my walker.

I've been called "a useless dumb cow," a "lazy, limping cow," a "faking, old cow," a "fucking, fat cow" and a "cocksucking cunt of a cow." I can only conclude that modern men have a primal hatred for cows. Or perhaps it's substitutional hate-speak for those with teats? Whatever vile combination of balls and entitlement motivates these men, the more I heard from them, the more I began to re-evaluate what I thought I knew. I began to unlearn and relearn.

In my teaching days, whenever my workroom discussed street harassment, I nodded in solidarity but always felt more imposter syndrome. I don't imagine I was the only woman walking on Earth who had never – and I mean not once – been sexually harassed by a stranger in the street. But it feels like I am. I let all my girlfriends think I understood it when it happened to them. But I didn't. I've never gotten a wolf whistle. Never been catcalled from a car or construction site. No strange man has ever hollered anything lewd or crude.

No pedestrian has ever thrust an erection in my direction.

Until I got my walker, I was a street harassment virgin.

How is that possible? Beats me. Street harassment is a universal experience for women. Friends, feminists, the media and academe all tell me what I believe true: every kind of woman gets harassed in public: young, old, skinny, fat, rich, poor, gay, straight, transgender, brown, black, white, Indigenous, abled and disabled. Any woman, all women. Just not this little bastard.

Of course, I've experienced sexism and sexual discrimination. Men interrupt me and mansplain things to me. For all my professional life, men took credit for my ideas. Men kissed up to other men, or simply were men, and got promoted over my head. Of course, men stared at my generous breasts. But if a polite request didn't work, I didn't care who they were, I always said, "Stop staring at my tits, or I'll start staring at your tiny cock."

And they stopped. Instantly.

But street harassment? I never got it. Not ever.

It's possible it happened behind my back, but I never heard it. In the bravado of youth, I believed I prevented it by a "don't you dare mess with me" glare. More realistically, given my glasses and being dumpy and short, perhaps men didn't process my approach as an assailable woman's body but as a nerdy kid's body. While no kind of clothing grants permission, without feminine attire or makeup, I didn't present the stereotypical image that men who erroneously feel they have the right to do so might comment upon. A limp is not sexy, and a crutch is not a come-on. When accessorized with Velcro running shoes, a "fuck me" dress ceases to be one.

So, why does Wenceslas suddenly bring out the smut boys? Why do men look at fat, old me on a walker and feel the need to ensure and broadcast my debasement? To send my dignity and self-confidence to the basement, where I sent the lovely Gerald so long ago? I don't know.

I think it has something to do with being more vulnerable and alone. Just the way children in orphanages, foster care, adoptive homes and the concentration camps on America's southern border all face higher rates of sexual violence, when I am alone in the street with a walker, I have no abled adult male relative to protect me and, like a trapped little child, I cannot fight or run. The "Let's stop sexual harassment and violence" webpage at Ontario.ca affirms that women "who live with activity limitations are over three times more likely to be victims of sexual assault than those who are able-bodied."

Conversely, I also I know this: I've always felt too ashamed to admit I've never been street harassed. How warped and irrational is that? Some part of me equates it with worth. A perverse proof that I'm desirable and valuable. Ergo, if I am not harassed, I am neither. There must be something so damaged, so intrinsically undesirable about me, that men want every other woman on the planet but not me. No woman asks for street harassment, or invites or deserves it. But I also remember how good, how sexy teenage me felt when Leo gazed through that long-ago bedroom window. He gave me sexual affirmation whether I wanted it or not. Today, this old lady can screw her courage to the sticking point and admit that part of me longed for that validation. Not the crude, insulting, creepy, touching or threatening kind. Maybe a whistle, or wink. Maybe once, just to see what it felt like.

Even when I knew it was wrong to want it, I still did.

Street harassment empowers men by reducing women to objects they can publicly rate at a glance. It reminds both parties that men control the definition of desirability. When men defend a wolf whistle as "a compliment," what they really mean is they're telling a woman in the quickest of animal shorthand that she is "fuckable." A cat-call says, that like some kind of broodmare, she still belongs to the youthful-enough, sexy-enough, abled-enough "I'd Do Her" Club. Fuckability is valuable. It's a judgment call that ageism and ableism teach women we should not only want to hear, but, deep down, be relieved, proud and grateful to keep hearing. My improv training says street harassment is a quickly established status contract. One with uneven power, by which men endow women. It tells women to feel validated by pursuit. It means we're not washed up, not about to be rejected and replaced with a sexier, younger model.

If I can admit a secret, irrational shame for never being catcalled, then perhaps abled women can admit to a secret scintilla of irrational reward when they are? If I can admit to being hurt by being left out of the abled fuck club, maybe abled women can admit they benefit from belonging to that club, that they know and accept that the male gaze that elevates them to that club does so only by keeping some women – fat like me, plain like me, disabled like me – out of it? Having spent my life with teenagers, I often see adults as taller teenagers, albeit with fewer zits and more facial hair. Adults still spend an inordinate amount of time and effort trying to stay in the club, jockeying for popularity, status and fuckability. Mean girls don't always grow out of it; they become mean women. Windy women stay predatory wolves for life. The rest of us get old and start asking, "Why did I fall for any of that crap? Why did I think it was important?"

I remember a time when it was important to me. In all my life, no one has ever called me beautiful. Not my family or friends. No date, boyfriend, lover, partner or husband. Never. So, I understand the need for validation, and why a woman might seek it. To be fully transparent, I also know my ideas about sex are tainted. Of course, people with disabilities are sexual beings; can and do have all kinds of stupendous sex in rewarding combinations, positions and places.

But I'm not, and never have been, one of them.

If you've been waiting for the juicy bits about my no-longer juicy bits, my apologies.

When I ponder my sexuality, I can't separate nature from nurture, or health from history. Has the trauma of adoption left me with attachment and abandonment issues? Yes. Can the shame of bastardy lead to adult sexual dysfunction? Absolutely. Survivors of childhood trauma can exhibit symptoms of PTSD for the rest of their lives. When I take the Adverse Childhood Experiences (ACE) test, I test off the scale. When I read about High-Functioning Depression, I'm looking in the mirror. And it doesn't take Dr. Ruth to see that being dumped so cruelly, in your fifties, right before double knee surgery, for a girl literally half your age, might take a teensy toll on your self-esteem. Might make it hard to ever trust a man again.

Yep. Been there, done that. Can't take off the T-shirt.

Because it's not all in my head. It's material.

My walker is a giant chastity belt, cold metal between me and any man I meet. The older I get the less attractive Man and His World tells me I am. The more mobility I lose, the more weight I gain, the more likely it seems that I'll never have intimacy again.Sometimes it's the greatest loss of all; sometimes it's no loss at all.

I've spent years wondering, "What if?" Will I ever know how free and confident my sexuality might be if I'd been taller, thinner and able-bodied? Been born into a more functional nuclear family? Been raised by my birth parents, or simply a mother that loved me? No.

Will I ever know how the trauma of infant sexual abuse has warped my sex drive? No.

Of course, everyone has the right to define their own identity, to their own names and pronouns, to be themselves in the world. Anyone who disagrees has all of Archie Bunker's bigotry and none of his humanity. But we also don't have to centre sexuality if we aren't so inclined. We don't have to pretend to have a youthful, abled sex drive, or a sexuality that defines us. For those of us who choose not to do the dating dance, sexuality may have less import. We all have the right to have sex, or not, in any consensual way we choose.

Did I never have much drive, or did I shut it down from child-hood, fearing I was doubly damaged, couldn't compete anyway, so it was better not to try? I'll never know. Am I repressed? Am I asexual: Someone who seldom experiences sexual attraction? Am I born that way? Made that way? Chose that way? Some or all of the above? Again, I don't know. When I read about asexuality, it fits. I'm likely a grey-ace or aroflux. Largely lithromantic. But the sheer volume of language about sexual identity overwhelms me. All I know for sure is that I seldom think about sex. I've enjoyed it, but never been driven by it. Never believed myself much good at it, or for it. When people trash their lives to bang the babysitter, screw the boss or hand a sexy con artist half their age their entire life savings, I'm disgusted by them and feel sorry for them. In my cold heart of hearts, they look ridiculous.

As a useful, intersectional, umbrella phenomenon, *lookism* doesn't get the attention it deserves. When you ascribe a positive or negative value based solely on the way someone looks that's lookism. Valuing "pretty" over "plain," respecting a tall man more than a short one, treating someone poorly dressed dismissively are all discriminations of lookism. Since the way we look is based on heredity, race, age, environment, class, income, health and ability, to ascribe intrinsic human value to these unearned attributes is participating in our own oppression.

The clearest example I've ever seen that even very intelligent people have fallen for this trap of ableist lookism occurred when *Jeopardy* superstar Ken Jennings tweeted, "Nothing sadder than a hot person in a wheelchair." Disabled Twitter exploded. Pretty young crips posted selfies at #hotinawheelchair. I respectfully think this was wrong-minded. There is nothing "sad" about plain, old, fat people in a wheelchair. There's nothing sad about wheelchairs, period. We can't fight ableism with lookism. Audre Lorde was right: "for the master's tools will never dismantle the master's house."

All traditional definitions of what is sexy and beautiful are definitely the master's tools.

An ableist, lookist, capitalist society will always place the highest value on disabled people who look the least disabled. Those who can move, speak, think, look and work the most like abled people are welcomed into the club and rewarded. This can make some disabled people more vulnerable to being co-opted by ableism. If disabled people buy into any lookist ranking of bodies in any way, it weakens disabled solidarity. While there is real worth in asking the world to see all disabled adults as vibrant, sexual beings; while it is important to take the position of Sins Invalid that every body is a good body; it is problematic to ask the world to see only some of us as desirable. Reinforcing ableism, "winners" can only win on the backs of "losers."

"Pretty," "hot" crips who post sexy selfies can fall for the trap of feeling pretty good about claiming membership in the ableist, ageist beauty club, because being attractive has material perks. "Pretty privilege" bestows unearned status and unfair access to social and financial benefits: increased salary, promotions, social standing and the ability to attract high-status partners. Claiming beauty like a personal brass ring pushes those who are old, fat, ill or have facial and cranial anomalies further into the "ugly" margins.

As disabled people, do we simply want a bigger slice of the beauty pie?

If so, then racist, sexist, ableist capitalism will shrug, laugh at us and quite happily give some of us some more of it, some of the time. Why is that good enough? And what does that complicity and collaboration cost us? As we say in improv, a word always contains its opposite. If we buy into the carrots of *cute* and *hot*, we're accepting and empowering the opposite, beating end of the stick: *plain, homely* and *fugly*. Fighting each other to be closer to the beautifully abled gods, being willing to step on and over those below you, only reinforces the Great Ableist Chain of Being and perpetuates the power of gods.

Worth, and self-worth, shouldn't ever be based on appearance, period. I'm attracted to wit, intelligence, kindness, a full voice and a hearty laugh. I've never judged bodies for hotness. The idea repels me. It's street harassment beyond the street. Centuries of objectification don't give women the right to repeat it, to stranger-rate men's bodies using the same ableist, ageist, classist criteria. If you find someone attractive, and it's appropriate to do so, please tell them. But rating strangers for hotness perpetuates the ableist gaze. If you declare that Stranger X is hot and hoot about it to your friends, you're practising ableism. Like the possession of the passive image in pornography, you're saying more about yourself than the object of your desire. You're declaring, "I'd Do That. I Deserve to Do That."

Of course, I might think this because I'm a wrinkled old prude. Or because I know I'd be a loser if anyone held a Hotness Measuring Stick up against me. But it might also be a matter of principle. Rankings of beauty use the instant, superficial, lookist judgments of homophobia, transphobia, racism, classism, sexism and ableism. Why is anyone who opposes any of these publicly rating anyone else's body? Beauty is the undeserved currency of healthy, well-nourished, medically privileged, ultra-abled, fashionably clothed and facially lucky young bodies. Often white, wealthy bodies. Endorsing any of that hierarchy moves us all backwards.

Why are any of us perpetuating any part of *any* hierarchy?

Just as the male gaze seeks to divide women, the ableist gaze seeks to divide the disabled community. Ableism pressures people with less-visible and invisible disabilities to identify more as abled than disabled, offers them status and benefits if they agree to do so. I'd like to gently remind disabled people who walk unassisted that I've been in your shoes. You get to make a choice many of us don't have. Now that I present as disabled, I can never again claim the status, safety, mobility, employability, access or benefits of passing as abled. When I could pass, I failed. I collaborated. I picked the wrong side.

I long to say, "Diverse disabled people of the world unite! We have nothing to lose but the Great Ableist Chain of Being." I long to see cross-disability community and solidarity.

But I'm worried. What roles do internalized ableism and lookism play in eroding our solidarity? Many less-visibly and invisibly disabled people have some kinds of abled privilege if they can pass as abled, at least some of the time. When you live betwixt and between, as I did for most of my life, it can increase the pressure to remain in hiding. I know the reluctances to leave the closet and have felt them all. The fear that identifying as disabled will limit your career and reputation. That you'll be "isolated," "pigeonholed," "passed over." Be "a burden." I long to help you reject this internalized ableism, to say a welcoming disabled community awaits. I understand there are times when disclosure is a risk, that to get or keep a bill-paying job, you might not want to disclose a disability at work. But I also believe Hillary was right: We're "stronger together."

You can quit the disabled closet without divulging any personal or medical detail. All you have to do, as the Internet pride campaign says, is #SayTheWord. I don't see it as a violation of our privacy. It's the opposite: the sharing of our expertise and credentials. I'll go further: it's every disabled person's job to help normalize disability. It is every disabled person's human right to claim and be claimed by our community. And here's the more difficult truth: those who stay in the closet do so on the backs of those of us who do not and cannot.

I truly welcome all those who identify as disabled in any way: less-visibly disabled, invisibly disabled, sick, spoonies, those living with mental health issues and/or chronic illness. But, I'm worried. Many online spokespeople for this important relatively newly self-identified sector of the disabled community appear to centre cure. Longing for a restoration to abled grace, and a return to their rightful place in the abled world, some grieve an individual fall from abled productivity, rather than rejecting the ableist capitalism that values only productivity. Disabled activists in multiple cities have noted that recent events advertised for invisibly disabled people have been posted without any accessibility information. Hundreds sign up without needing or demanding it. Some spokespeople flatly refuse to be called disabled, as if it's a dirty word.

Of course the wily beast of lookist ableist capitalism wants to seduce less-visibly disabled and invisibly disabled people by holding out the sweet carrots of belonging. They'll be seen as the best kind of Tiny Tim super-crip collaborators if they keep their mouths shut about inaccessibility. The ableist world will happily co-opt and use them, will claim it's doing a good job at "diversity," because it includes those with invisible disabilities. But all hierarchies divide to conquer. They "celebrate" individual winners to make us forget the societal structures that ensure the impossibility of collective success. It's time to ask this: Do we simply want a share of ableist privilege for some of us, or do we want ableism dismantled for everyone?

Because we bloody well can't have both.

I also want to say this to anyone who demands space, resources, status, funding and reputation as a disabled person but makes no critique of systemic ableism and offers no space and solidarity to the disabled community: Bite me.

I know I should have more empathy and patience. I fully admit that I have the scent of a reformed smoker about me. Now that I see the privilege of being able to pass as complicit and harmful, I want everyone to stop doing it. All disabled people who can pass, who can walk to events and climb stairs, who don't personally need any kind of accessibility, must choose between solidarity and selfishness. I'm so heartsick, so bloody sick and tired of watching you call yourselves disabled then blithely go off to attend, network at, perform in and get paid for arts events that ban other disabled people without the privilege of your presentation and mobility. It is self-serving, not solidarity, to protest an event's inaccessibility only after you have attended it.

Every step you mount is a knife in my back.

Any disabled person who won't come fully out of the closet to stand in solidarity with the disabled community for fear it will limit their career is telling me that they don't care if my coming out to defend them has limited mine. I understand the pressure to belong, to be seen to belong, to cling to whatever abled privilege you still have. I still have some. On good days, Wenceslas and I could climb a few steps. When the washroom is in the basement, I could leave at the drop of a drop. But I won't. My loyalties lie with those who cannot get in the door.

I will not sell out or collaborate. I will not be complicit.

I know I am uncompromising on this question. I believe someone has to be. As I've made clear from the start, I'm making an alphabet argument. It works like this: Imagine a continuum of support from A to Z. If the public is sitting at G or H, and you want to move their support along to M or N, you can't simply advocate for M or N. You must push to X, Y and Z. That way, more people will think it reasonable to move to M or N.

Working to help move everyone down the alphabet doesn't mean fighting every battle. I never speak for people with disabilities different than mine. I never demand accommodations for disabilities other than my own; I amplify the voices of those with that disability. Do I go to events that are wheelchair accessible but not fully accessible? Yes, I do. Because I've never seen a building, let alone an arts event, that is fully accessible, including my own home. But if any blind, D/deaf, sick, spoonie, chronically ill or mental health activists begin asking the public not to attend events that aren't accessible to them, I will do two things: Without debating or arguing, I will listen, and let them define what the word *accessible* means to them. Then I will immediately comply in solidarity.

But I can't, and shouldn't, speak for them.

I accept my limitations as an ally.

For example, I can't be "scent free." With no sense of smell, I don't know if my shampoo is scentless or stinks like a French *parfumerie*. I imagine it smells. In the logic of a capitalism that monetizes all trendy things, companies quite logically charge more when they leave scent out. But here's my truth about the financial inaccessibility I likewise don't have the luxury to ignore: I have to buy the biggest, cheapest bottle in the dollar store, no matter how it might smell. Please note I mention only shampoo. Conditioner is for rich people.

Especially for sexy, hot, young and abled rich people.

And I, thank goodness, am none of the above.

Travel and the Tick-Tock of Time

I used to love to fly. I've been to Paris three times, once with sixty students in tow. I've taken multiple teenage hordes on theatre trips to New York City. I've fallen in Central Park, on les Bateaux Mouches and, most spectacularly, when toppled by a rushing crew of schoolboys in ties and blazers, I bounced down the stairs of the British Museum. These days, I'm desperately seeking Scotland. When I visited it before knowing my history, I felt at home and an aching-almost. I wept like a willow when a guide explained *hiraeth*: a deep longing for a missing home. It echoed my version of Thomas Wolfe: You can't go home again if you've never had one. Each town, every glen reinforced what I didn't know: What part of Scotland was home?

Today, I'd love to see Kilcalmonell. To stand on the ground farmed by my ancestors. But that hope evaporates with each passing day. It isn't just the horror stories that flood social media about how disabled travellers are treated: wheelchairs lost and broken, passengers marooned by porters, patronized, insulted and dehumanized by airport staff. I can risk all that, but I can't risk this: I'm pinching every penny of my savings at a rate that keeps me alive for another two years.

A trip to Scotland would reduce that ticking time bomb to one year.

Travelling today costs me twice what it cost me as an abled travel-ler. I can't walk or take transit. I have to pay a taxi to go even a block. That's assuming one will stop for an old woman on a walker; many hit the gas at the sight of it. At a hotel, needing to sit on my walker at a moment's notice means I can't carry my bags and have to tip all who touch them. Hotels with accessible rooms that actually deserve the name and include roll-in showers tend to be more expensive. Given the exhaustion of being out all day and the inaccessibility of restau-rants, I need hotels with room service. To travel internationally, I'd have to hire a companion and pay their expenses as they get tickets, carry suitcases and handle all the details I can't manage. All these extra expenses effectively amount to a tax on disabled people, on those who can least afford it.

For me, money, energy and time have all but dried up.

Back in my teaching days, I could jump out of bed, shower, dress, eat a decent breakfast and exit the driveway, all in thirty minutes. That's the time having short, curly hair and going without makeup can buy you. When I heard women complain about needing an hour to blow-dry their hair and "put on their face," I kept my mouth shut but imagine my face said it all: "Shoot me now. If it ever took me that long to get ready in the morning, I'd stay in bed."

Today, it takes me over an hour to get dressed.

It takes me ten minutes to put on my bra, if that's what you can call the bi-normous, spandex hammock that hoists my bodacious ta-tas. Thanks to arthritis, I'll never wear a real brassiere again. I can't fasten hooks, in either back or front. In a fitting, forced-fit irony, in my sixties, I'm sporting my first item of sporting equipment. I have to play my sports bra real slow and call plenty of time outs. I can't get racy. When I'm damp from the shower, my skin is like wallpaper paste; I'm one sticky wicket. I've dislocated my thumbs and cracked two fingers trying to yank my over-the-shoulder boulder-holder over my boulders. I have to put one arm through. Wait. Stick my other arm through. Wait. Inch down one side. Wait. Rub my hands supple. Tug down the other side. Wait. And then ever-so-carefully begin nudging my fingers up under the band, slowly smoothing it flat round my back and under my breasts. If I bought a bigger bra, I could probably put it on with less risk to my hands, but no thank you.

"I'll take *Keeping My Nipples North of my Navel Whatever the Cost,* Alex."

Of course, my real struggle is the long-standing one: the daily negotiation of shoes. An aging Herkimer and Horatio won't go gently into any good morning. They're crochety old bats who often refuse to get dressed at all. If I don't get my shoes on in the morning, it's not a game afoot; it's game over. I can't book a movie, or dinner at a friend's, then wait until evening to put on my shoes. I have to trick Herkimer and Horatio when they're still half asleep, when they haven't had time to puff up and refuse. I must get shod at dawn and hold my breath, hoping it will be the rare day I can wear shoes for a whole day. When pain wins, my shoes have to come off, and stay off. If I had anything planned – seeing my daughter, meeting a friend, a doctor's appointment – my feet are Equal Opportunity Party Pissers. No matter the party, I have to cancel. No matter how much I've paid, want, or need to go, their two votes in our triumvirate are a veto.

Thankfully, Horatio has always liked to drive, and pride keeps him doing so. It's a superiority he lords over Herkimer, relegated to the role of snarky, back-seat driver. But lately, especially in traffic that makes him stomp back and forth between brake and accelerator, Horatio demands a pit stop. After being the reliable teacher who was always early, who saw being late as both selfish and a moral failing, it's devastating to have to pull off the road and make myself late. There've been more than a few messy cries, from having to give in and give up, having to wait until Horatio's screams subside sufficiently to let me drive back home to bed.

Having cancelled so many things, so many times, it's hard to make my own hope.

I put things on the calendar well in advance. I do absolutely nothing the day before. I take extra meds for two days before. But lately, my feet are less appeased by these offerings. Too often, I drive somewhere only to discover I can't get out of the car. It's hard not to retreat. Hard not to nip disappointment in the bud by making no plans in the first place. I've become an expert at talking myself out of joy. I tell myself it doesn't matter that I'm losing all the things I once loved to do when anything I might try to do today, I'm doing poor and alone. I know that's a capitulation. One I try not to make too often. One I have to make so often, it's demoralizing.

It would not be an exaggeration to call it life-threatening.

My poverty reinforces and exacerbates my poor health.

Even when I find something accessible to do, I worry about affording it. Friends often offer to take me to an art gallery, music festival or the local award-winning botanical gardens, but before I say yes, I start obsessing about the cost of gas, parking and entrance fees. Sometimes I've jumped through all the hoops. I'm up, showered, dressed and shod. I'm in my car driving somewhere I really want to go, but when I'm halfway there, I start to hyperventilate. I can't stop my brain from doing the math, from calculating that gas for this trip is costing me $3.17, money I need for food. If I go home immediately, it will only cost $1.59. So, I turn around, phone my friends and make excuses. I've become the one thing I swore I'd never be: my penny-hoarding mother, a woman whose refusal to spend money on me leaves me worthless.

In the mirror, I see the toll of loss and the little time left me.

I always expected to lose my mobility, but I was unprepared for the anguish of losing it slowly, fat, alone, old, poor and in failing health. A walker seduces you with the promise of physical security, by absorbing your fear, stress and pain, but over time, it chips away at the very mobility it first gave you. You trade a fear of falling for a fear of damaging your heart. I must walk at a speed that cannot be considered exercise. The more I use my walker, the less I want to walk at all. On my brightest days, Wenceslas permits me to do my shopping, have coffee with friends or see a movie with my daughter. On my darkest days, he leads me to a quicker death.

Ironically, I never talk about this because I don't want to further the "come to Jesus" ableist stereotype that my life is "suffered." Disability activists who reject the medical model of disability reject all words like *suffer*. We live full, authentic lives. We are not pitiable. We reject the doctors, hospitals, disability academics and big pharma, for whom our suffering is both capital and commodity. I seldom talk about my depression for the same reason I seldom admit my pain: it feels like a capitulation to the medical model. Because pain is not imposed by ableist society. It is not a social construct. Pain is my every breath. It most definitely cannot be changed by activism, rallies, Twitter campaigns, accessibility initiatives and human rights legislation. But to best defend my community, I know I must be more open about my mental health. I know I have to learn to say this out loud: "Yes, here at the intersections of poverty, fatphobia, ageism and ableism, the impairments of chronic physical and mental pain are a problem. I need help."

I've had to give up any kind of nightlife. I'm back home in bed before most people head out. I miss the dark. I miss the warm glow of patio lights and bonfires. I miss summer stars, sometimes more than I can bear. Thanks to the combined debarments of inaccessibility and poverty, I'm a drama teacher who can't go to the theatre, an improvisor who hasn't laughed in a comedy club for a decade. I spend every day the same: I sit in one chair to write all day then move to the chair beside it to knit in the evening. I chat on the phone and social media. Go to bed. Get up. Repeat. As savings evaporate, I try not to think about that day in the not-far-off future when I'll be forced to choose between eating and my Internet.

Simply put, writing is keeping me alive. I spent too much of my life unable to do it, and will not give up on it now. I know the answer to Langston Hughes' question, "What happens to a dream deferred?"

It spends every second of three decades working a triple day as teacher, mother/wife and unionist. It falls into bed so exhausted, there are no words left to dream

"I'll take *Books that Took Twenty-Three Years to Write* for no money, Alex!"

After a full scholarship to the Banff Writers' Colony in 1987, where I drank in every word from writer-mentors Rachel Wyatt, Adele Wiseman and Dale Zieroth; after publishing a few articles and short stories, I thought my literary fame and fortune was assured. Oh, sweet innocence of youth! The day Banff ended, my husband and I packed up our kids and moved to Ontario. Any hope of a writing life died in the interest of putting food in young mouths.

After returning to teaching in 1987, the novel I conceived in Banff, *When Fenelon Falls,* didn't get born until 2010, when a bona fide miracle virgin birth occurred: it got plucked from the slush pile and published by the venerable Coach House Books. I thought, "Finally, my writing life begins!" And it did. I had fabulous opportunities: reading at festivals such as Word on the Street, appearing on CBC Radio and meeting writers I'd known only in my dreams. I thought my Jessica Fletcher transformation from retired English teacher to globe-gallivanting writer would be permanent. I didn't know it would dry up like a raisin in the sun.

I don't for one second regret the family that delayed my first novel. My children embody compassion, creativity, intelligence, humour and commitment to a better world. My daughter became a social worker working in women's shelters and social housing. She's been an NDP executive member and union shop steward who also founded her own LARP. My son won flute scholarships and concerto competitions. He debuted at Carnegie Hall and became a respected international soloist and professor of music. Neither do I regret my teaching years, a rich legacy of improvisation and fighting united for quality education for all our children.

I do regret every second of the ten years between my novel and this book, years I was forced to spend trying to make a thief obey the law. Spending twenty-three thousand dollars on a lawyer. Then, unable to afford a lawyer, having to stand self-represented before a judge. All for nothing. When my ex fled the country, any illusions I had about Canadian justice died. It is no consolation to know I'm one of five hundred thousand victims of defaulted child and spousal support: some 3.7 billion is owed by Canadian deadbeat dads and spouses. When we do all the math, tally the generations of thieves like my grandfathers, the cost is immeasurable.

Try believing in yourself when lawyers, social workers and police officers shrug and say your life counts for nothing. Try having any life, let alone a writing life, on twenty thousand dollars a year. When I was cash-strapped as a student, young mom or striking teacher, it was temporary. Not now. As anti-poverty activists and poor people have long told us, broke and poor are different. My pension is fixed. My income includes my Canada Pension Plan, which I took at sixty. When I get my Old Age Pension at sixty-five, I'll get a whopping fifty-four more dollars per month.

"Yes, Alex. I'm told I have to take *Poverty and Disability* for the rest of my life."

And ding, ding, ding, it's Double Jeopardy! Of course, it is.

These double debarments leave me with one constant companion: despair. I often can't leave my bed. If I hadn't suicide-proofed my apartment, I wouldn't be here. The less I go out, the less able I am to do so. My balance is failing. Even with Wenceslas, I fall far too often. I'm increasingly barred from stores, concerts, theatres, restaurants and the homes of my friends. I've never seen either of my children's apartments; they're both up a flight of stairs.

As these losses accumulate, I negotiate between fury and despair. The fury I can share; redheads are expected to be angry. The despair I keep private. I know self-silencing is unhealthy. It's the stigma of internalized ableism that makes me ashamed, but I'm still ashamed. I know the world is eager to cast little-old-lady me as a burden, as fragile and childlike, needing the care and assistance of big, strong, young, abled people. I feel like I'm betraying my disabled community to admit that, yes, I am often fragile. I get so very tired. I often need help. I hold back from telling even close friends I'm depressed, because I know they'll pull out this ableist trope: "Well, of course you're depressed. You're bloody disabled, for heaven's sake!"

I absolutely don't want to hear one more "friend" tell me they'd kill themselves if they were me. This isn't unusual. It's the casually brutal ableism disabled people hear every day.

By 2016, I either had to fight my depression or succumb to it. When I committed to writing this book, I was a writer on a walker. I hoped to unite my disabled and literary communities. But despite my work as a feminist unionist, I was one naive newbie. It wasn't that I thought the accessibility war would be over by Christmas; I didn't think there'd be a fight. I thought my colleagues were so educated, empathetic, woke and intersectional that all I'd have to do was casually mention that literary events, readings, festivals, launches and retreats were all inaccessible, right across the country, and caring people would apologize and jump into allied action to fix it. I forgot about the entitlement of parking thieves and the lesson of Rosamunde: the Windys of the world will always exercise their entitled right to hurt all those they can get away with hurting. I forgot about the universal game-book of silencing and union bashing. When those in power don't want to hear the message, they always do two things: first they dispute the language of the message, and then they blame the messenger.

Unable is Not Unwilling; Unable is Not Unacceptable

"Just take a simple twenty-minute walk. How easy is that? Anybody can do it."

"This miracle machine combines the ease of skiing with the simple cardio of stairs."

"Work Like a Dog. Sweat Like a Pig. Look Like a Fox."

"Reach your potential. Better Body, Better Life."

"Jump like a frog, so you won't look like a hog."

"There are no reasons. There are only excuses."

"The best exercise is simple. Stand up and walk away from the table."

"Fast foods take you one place fast, to an early grave."

"Hang your swimsuit on the refrigerator door and the goodies you'll ignore."

"No matter how slow you go you are still lapping every lazy bum on the couch."

"You're not going to get the butt you want by sitting on it."

"Your body can do anything! It's just your brain you have to convince."

"Train insane, or face a future in pain."

"You can feel sore tomorrow. Or you can feel sorry tomorrow. YOU choose."

"The voice in your head that says you can't exercise is a LIAR."

"It never gets easier. You just get BETTER."

"Just Do It. No pain, no gain."

Does this list make you feel overwhelmed? Insulted? Humiliated? Defeated? Me too.

These weight-loss slogans sound like Dr. Seuss composing fitness fortune cookies on crack, but they're all real advice from posters in doctor's offices, the Internet, TV and well-meaning friends. Combining vicious fat-shaming with the Great Ableist Chain of Being, weight-loss advice sees fat people as animals. As for disabled people, it isn't that we can't move; it's that we're all a bunch of fat pigs, too stupid and too lazy to move.

Society pressures women to seek its unrealistic and unreachable definition of a perfect body. When you're a disabled senior woman in pain, it's a triple-barrelled misogynist-ageist-ableist attack. Each slogan, every moralistic word reinforces the lie that the barriers I face aren't real, merely the product of my own old, fat, lazy, shameful, stupid head. Of course, there are good reasons to encourage everyone to exercise. But I wish we could do so without erasing my lifelong struggle to walk, without using language that beats me into invisibility and worthlessness. Here's my Top Ten list: *When You Motivate Exercise and Weight Loss from a Smug Position of Abled Privilege, I Am Insulted When:*

1. Walking, or any movement of any kind, is described as "easy" or "simple."
2. Exercise is portrayed as normal, enjoyable and rewarding.
3. Every "inspirational" weight-loss winner is an able-bodied winner.
4. The able-bodied brag about and glorify the temporary pain of their exercise.

5. Slogans assume that anyone and everyone can, and should, "Just Do It."
6. Fitness enthusiasts claim that the only barrier to exercise is a bad attitude.
7. Pain-free able-bodied "experts" announce that pain is all in the mind.
8. Able-bodied quacks insist that exercise can, will and should heal or cure.
9. People praise *fitness* when they really mean *able-bodied excellence*.
10. People link health and morality: if you aren't healthy it's your own lazy fault.

An athletic friend once had the courage to train for my life for ten seconds. He asked, "How much pain are you in? Don't tell me, Dorothy. Show me. I want to feel the reality of it."

I did the first thing I could think of. I grabbed his arm, twisted it around his back and pushed, hard, to equal the ever-present pain in my feet.

"Okay," he yelled, "I get it. You can stop now."

I didn't. I said, "Not yet. Now walk. Now talk. Now think."

"I can't. Stop it. I'm not kidding."

I wasn't either. "Now smile. Be nice to abled people who aren't in pain. Spend every second, pretending you aren't in pain. Smile at people who tell you it's all in your head."

He regained his footing and pulled away. "That wasn't cool. I didn't ask for that."

I shrugged. "Exactly."

For me, exercise is like pouring a bathtub of pain into a bucket already full. My fitness goal can't be improvement. It can't even be main-tenance. My only goal is one I can never tell if I achieve: degeneration delay. Is adding more pain to my life worth it? Especially when much of the motivation to be fit comes from the lookism and fatphobia that

I reject but by which I will always be judged. Men will always look at my walker before my face, or even my boobs.

In full disclosure, I must also admit this: When my ex dumped me, I went on a food campaign to ensure that no man ever hurt me like that again. If I made myself undesirable, I wouldn't have to risk another betrayal, because no man would want me in the first place. I see fat as armour, as safety, but I know it restricts and endangers my life.

I have not entirely given up. In 2015, once I unpacked in Burlington, I found a new family doctor. She looks impossibly young, but is knowledgeable, dedicated and kind. When I told her I wasn't sleeping, she sent me to a sleep study. When I stopped breathing multiple times a minute, they prescribed a CPAP machine. Alone in my bed in mask and hose, I'll happily look and sound like Darth Vader's wheezing granny if it keeps me on the right side of the Dark Side.

It never occurred to me that renting would also endanger my life.

After my ex left me in 2007, using the proceeds of our family home, I had enough for a down payment on a tiny wartime house an hour outside of Toronto. One I had to sell when he stopped paying the first time. I rented throughout two years of court proceedings. When the judge ordered my support payments recommenced, desperate for equity I'd eventually need as income, I scraped together just enough for the down payment on a small condo farther from the city. When my ex stopped paying again, I had to sell yet again; without my court ordered support income, no bank would renew my mortgage. Forced to move four times in six years, it took me three months to find an apartment I could afford in an accessible building with underground parking. I had to move far out of Toronto, two hours away from my daughter, to find it.

When my doctor referred me to my Local Health Integration Network (LHIN), which coordinates community health services, the risks of renting became clear. An occupational therapist came to my apartment to tell me what the scars on my arms already knew: I had to stop using the stovetop. If I cook sitting on my walker, beyond burns, I risk yanking boiling pots into my face. Noting I needed a roll-in shower, not just a plastic seat in the tub, all she could do was suggest a special grab bar. It cost eighty dollars. She wrote up a full page of safety and accessibility renovations, all of which would be tax deductible in my own home, then shrugged, saying, "The chances of any rental company agreeing to any of these renovations are zero."

She suggested I apply for Assisted Living.

It takes three years to get a spot.

Next, LHIN provided four visits with a physiotherapist. She gave me low-impact exercises I can do on low-pain days. She suggested an under-the-desk cycle. It cost four hundred dollars, but I can do it sitting on my walker. I can also do TV arthritis exercises, if I turn off the sound. As for the perky young thing who tells me that with "only a little bit of effort" I can be "healed and whole, a better, reborn, brand new me," I'd happily cure her potty mouth with a fistful of kale.

The LHIN also sent me a Personal Support Worker (PSW) for two hours, twice a week. Because no one can push a walker and a Wet-Jet, she sweeps and washes my floors. Because my laundry room has top-loading machines I can't reach into, she does my laundry. Because I've cracked three arthritic fingers wrestling with a fitted sheet, she makes my bed. Her first job is to chase down anything on the floor. When carrots I'm trying to chop jump out of my failing hands, it's all I can do to yell, "You're dead to me!" at their gleefully escaping little orange behinds.

In short, seniors and disabled people desperately need doctors and caretakers that take us seriously. We equally need self-care advice that isn't ableist and classist, that doesn't pass itself off as a substitute for good medical and community care, that doesn't blithely advocate buying something, "going for a simple walk" or "treating yourself to a mani-pedi." As if I could drop a week's groceries on colourful toes. As if I'd ever take my socks off for a stranger. My self-care consists of congratulating myself when I make it the forty-seven steps to my toilet. It's a race I often lose. Of course, my physical degeneration affects my attitude, but it is absolutely not affected by my attitude. It's material.

Of all the material realities I've revealed here, only one embarrasses me: my diapers.

When I told my doctor I'd attended a literary event in a bar so crowded I couldn't get to the washroom unless I turned Wenceslas into a snowplough and rammed people and tables aside, and had instead peed myself on my drive home, she did her best to console me. She said many teachers who never get to pee when they need to, many women with high blood pressure, who'd had exuberant 1980s episiotomies, often need pads, even surgery, later in life. Hence the explosion of Poise Pads and adult diapers. But after wetting the bed into my teens, it feels like I barely got over that shame before I began doing it again. Today, I pee when I laugh, when I sneeze, when I stand up. Forget pads. They leak. They slither down your leg. Enough said.

To channel Stella, "No amount of grinning at my granny pants will ever keep them dry."

But here's the good news: if you missed buying stock in Facebook, rush right out and invest your every penny in adult diapers. As boomers age, somebody's going to get stinking rich. Adult diapers cost about a dollar each. Fat people like me pay more, as there are four more in an "S" package than in the "XL" for the same price. Don't buy the dirt-cheap ones. I refuse to explain it, just don't. Nighttime diapers are worth over a dollar, because then I might need only one. When even my ULTRA-Nighttime-Defense diapers leak, I tell myself every woman curls in a fetal position around the wet spot.

But the cost is no joke. If I use one per day and one at night, it's sixty dollars a month.

If I need two in a day and two at night, that's $120 a month.

When you did your retirement planning, did you include the cost of diapers? I sure didn't. Diapers are one of the reasons I eat twice a day.

Exercising in a diaper gives new meaning to the word *infantilizing*. It is absolutely no fun at all. I certainly don't want to "just do it."

Do you understand my loathing for organized sports a little better now?

I've held my scorn in check throughout this book, but just this once I'll trust you with it.

Just as fashion models normalize and fetishize the 1 percent of bodies that can ever be that tall and thin, professional sports normalize and fetishize the 1 percent of bodies that can ever be that abled. Beyond deifying those gods, the real function of organized sports is to organize our cultural reaction to competition, force and violence. They tell us competition is normal, desirable and fun. They tell us wining and losing is inevitably human. When we agree to worship the male athletes at the top of the Great Chain of Being, we normalize, reward and validate men's will to hurt. We agree to equate force and violence with winning masculinity.

Since I first presented the idea in a Sociology of the Family course back in 1975, it has been infuriatingly clear to me that organized sports also function as ongoing war-readiness propaganda. As a Canadian, I'm specifically expected to cheerlead the supremacy of white, male, winter-warrior privilege known as hockey. We agree to pay our athlete soldiers with the incomes of small countries because war is expensive and we must win at all costs. When the public agrees to take sides, when we identify with hometown teams of athlete-warriors in uniform, when we cheer "munch 'em, crunch 'em, get 'em boys," when their win is our win and only our boys deserve to win, sports become home-front, war-readiness training. In short, we've all been had. We've been organized into worshipping the multi-billion-dollar baby of capitalist, patriarchal ableism at its violent, distracting, mind-numbing, hero-worshipping, war-simulating worst. In June of 2019, when the Toronto Raptors won the NBA championships, when my hometown erupted in V-day frenzy, I despaired for those who believed "we" had won something. No, we all lost our ability to think past the manipulations of ableist capitalist propaganda.

"That felt pretty good, Alex, but I'll take *Olympic Overkill*, just for fun."

The "world-unifying" Olympics spits in my face when the separate-but-never-equal Paralympics are an inspiring afterthought. When the Rio 2016 Paralympics ran a "No such thing as can't" campaign, showcasing super-crips who "gloriously defeat" disability, I longed to lock them in a room with non-stop videos of Stella, until they understood the depth of the apology that they owed to all us regular crips. The Olympics' real function is to dramatize war between nations on a global scale. The Paralympics' real function, like the Invictus Games, is to distract abled folks from the harms of ableism and war by glorifying grown Tiny Tims, the grateful, beaming, collaborationist, athlete-soldiers who have become doubly victorious by "vanquishing" disability. By enshrining individual competition, the Paralympics tell us that top tier respect is reserved for disabled athletes who see themselves as lone individuals who have met their heroic responsibility to work themselves to exhaustion to be as abled and unburdensome as possible.

Spreading their fancy fantails, these boasting guppies happily show off for personal gain.

Whenever abled people tell me to "accentuate the positive" and "celebrate good news stories," I hear them telling me to be a super-crip guppy. Not happening. I'm not going to smile and say thank you for not stealing my fridge. I simply expect abled people to be decent humans and not steal my fridge. If you've stolen it for decades, I'm certainly not going to grovel when you finally give it back. Being grateful for charity, celebrating charity, is the wrong focus. Echoing *A Christmas Carol*, it centres abled people when they grant or give us something they've always had. Teachers had to drop the celebratory multicultural model to do openly anti-racist work. Let's not make the same error fighting ableism. I welcome the good news of dedicated space, prizes and awards for disabled people, but we must also confront systemic ableism directly. We must see and name the barriers and the harm.

I'm not a peacemaker or a conciliator. I'm a redhead. Like Stella.

Of course, there are things real disabled people and seniors can't do. For me, increasingly so. Thanks to the dastardly trio of arthritis, osteoporosis and poor nutrition, I've lost two inches in height. I can no longer reach the second shelf of my kitchen cabinets. While I used to be able to take Wenceslas shopping, now I can only use e-carts, restricting my choices to Walmart and the one local grocery store that has one. When pretty super-crip collaborators tell inspiration porn lies, I can only echo Stella and Audre: Are we satisfied watching a few super-crips "defeat" disability, or do we want to dismantle the power and privilege of ableism for all?

Because, yet again, we can't have both.

We can't hang on to one and achieve the other.

I've left the most unacceptable bit of exercise "advice" for last. It's such a nasty, snide, backhanded insult, I don't even know where to start. I do hope you enjoy it:

"You are far too smart to be the only thing standing in your way."

No. In collective victory, my disabled community and I are finally strong enough to see that every single person who can stand benefits from standing in our way.

V is for Victory and for Venom

A few blocks from my apartment stands a beacon-shaped memorial to Terry Fox. It's next to the bench where I sit every day I can, dreaming of my lost Balsam Lake, drinking in the changing colours of Lake Ontario. Commemorating kilometre 3,582 of Terry's Marathon of Hope and the date he reached Burlington, July 13, 1980, it reads: "Even if I don't finish, we need others to continue. It's got to keep going without me." I believe many Canadians are still running with Terry. Not just in once-a-year runs organized by "men calling for charity," but by fighting ableism every day. For chronically ill and disabled people, there is an urgency to do so. As it was for Terry, the Reaper is our ever-haunting Ghost of a Christmas Soon to Come.

Today, I also realize this: some people want me dead.

It's not a realization I faced easily. As a disabled bastard, even before I heard the word *cinching*, I knew in the words of Audre Lorde I "was never meant to survive." But when I first heard disabled activists cite the fact that Hitler wiped out hospitals and sanitariums as proof that the rise of racist white nationalism could produce a twenty-first-century cleansing, I dismissed that as alarmist. I saw myself as too much the historian to fall for such rhetoric. I disagree, for example, with an ultra-left friend who believes this: "Since most abortions are of bastard children and of fetuses diagnosed with disabilities in utero, women have become the murdering dupes and criminal accomplices of capitalist patriarchy, willing to kill their children because they won't become abled workers, or because a man won't acknowledge their paternity."

I want to be clear: Abortion is not euthanasia. Euthanasia is the murder of living human beings. Is euthanasia fuelled by eugenics, the belief that some bodies are more worthy of life than others? It took multiple, repeated examples in the news to convince me I had personal reason to fear this. It took the cumulative weight of things I had never set together on the scale.

Here are the five events from only the last few months that affected me most:

The first seems pop-culture harmless. Based on a bestselling novel by Jojo Moyes that sold six million copies and hit number one in nine countries, the 2016 blockbuster movie *Me Before You* grossed $207 million worldwide. When banker Will Traynor is paralyzed after a motorcycle accident, this young, mega-rich, handsome, smart, funny, well-educated white man decides a disabled life isn't worth living. Despite having a loving family, despite being able to buy the best of assistive technology and health care, despite falling mutually in love with Emilia Clarke, the lovely Khaleesi from *Game of Thrones*, Will travels to Switzerland to end his life.

Please let me first clarify my position on Medical Assistance in Dying (MAID), made possible in Canada in 2015 by Bill C-14. Disabled people do not need to be infantilized or protected from our right to consider that choice. We do need to be protected from all others, from family, caregivers, doctors, nurses, hospitals, institutions and governments – anyone who may want to make this decision about us, without us. We need good health care and community care. We need governments that fund life with dignity, so we don't give up and want to die. We all need to oppose the very notion that seniors and disabled people are burdens with "a duty to die."

When Will Traynor accepts that duty, when he calls disability a "half a life," one it would be too selfish to ever ask an abled person to share, when ending his life is portrayed as brave and self-sacrificing, abled audiences fell for it hook, line and Kleenex. Friends I expected to know better called it "romantic" and "deeply moving." When I said it was the worst of inspiration porn, so dangerous in the absence of disability-positive messaging, even when I argued no one would ever defend a movie where any other marginalized person kindly killed themselves to unburden their oppressors, my friends shrugged. I heard the voice of my father, a half-century unchanged: it's "better to put someone like that out of their misery." I heard what fans were really saying: If a life of privileged disability isn't worth living, how can ordinary disabled lives be worth living?

There is but one Sherlockian conclusion: they aren't.

On July 26, 2016, in Sagamihara, Japan, nineteen disabled people were stabbed to death by a former employee of a residential care facility. He wanted disabled people dead because "it would be good for the country to be rid of the burden." Some Japanese media called their worst massacre since WW II a "hate crime." Canada called it "heart-wrenching," called the murderer "clearly deranged." Even my most-woke friends, quick to see the hypocrisy that any murderer of colour is "a terrorist" while any white mass murderer "simply has mental health issues," told me I was overreacting to call this mass murder an act of ableist hatred. On social media, disabled people feared and mourned alone. This attack got none of the attention of Charlottesville, Paris or Orlando. There were few "hearts and prayers," no Twitter campaign. When I posted about it, few of my friends could rouse enough empathy to push an emoji button. That's when I got it: This is the apathy of abled privilege. When disabled people are murdered, abled people shrug.

I felt the punch of a similar hateful hand in the 2017 story about a home for unwed mothers in Tuam, Ireland. For three decades, the same Catholic Church that shielded pedophile priests tossed bastard babies into an unconsecrated, unmarked mass grave. In the sewer system. Eight hundred of them. Babies just like me. Godly nuns chucked us into the garbage, whether we were dead or not. Apparently, bastard burdens, like disabled burdens, are not meant to survive.

This fourth example hit closest to home, knowing I will soon have to live in one:

My former Western roommate comes from a farm near Woodstock. I've always equated the best of small-town Ontario with her generous and compassionate United Church faith. In June 2017, Woodstock nurse Elizabeth Wettlaufer pleaded guilty to eight counts of first-degree murder. For over a decade, in three care facilities, she'd been deciding that disabled senior lives weren't worth living. Like all terrorists, she claimed to be doing the Lord's work. As quoted in the *Toronto Star*, June 1, 2017, God called her to kill Michael Priddle, sixty-three, because "Huntington's is a terrible disease," and the "surge" she felt telling her to kill "must be God, because this man isn't enjoying his life at all." Yet again, the media saw an "unstable" lone wolf. There was no discussion of ableism. No hate crime. No hatred. And no lesson to learn.

In this fifth example, the scales of disbelief finally fell from my eyes: With Trump's election, as the party of big business paid for tax cuts for the rich by dismantling heath care, I got called a "pre-existing condition." On Twitter, I saw disabled Americans grow fearful, then terrorized. Cuts in health care meant they would sicken. They would die. And they did. In preventable deaths caused by inadequate health care, the disabled community lost activists Carrie Ann Lucas and Bill Peace. But when activists from ADAPT fought the repeal of Obamacare in 2017, reporters saw "poor souls" being dragged from wheelchairs, not an organization with chapters in thirty states fighting since 1983. There was no mention of disabled history.

That was my eureka moment: I realized that I'd fallen for my oppressor's history.

Yet again, I'd been kept from my own history. I never heard the word *disability* in all my years at Western, but of course the white-washing and erasure of BIPOC, working-class, women's and queer history also applies to disabled history. It's all perpetrated by the same white, colonialist, male, middle-class, abled historians. It would take volumes to reclaim it all.

Let's just say there are some things we all should know.

In Canada, the forcible removal of Indigenous children to residential schools is the racist, genocidal arm of the colonial paternalism that saw generations of illegitimate and disabled children sent to orphanages and asylums right across Europe. Canada has always quite happily monetized poor little bastards. From 1869 to 1948, one hundred thousand poor but not-always-orphaned British Home Children were swept from the streets and orphanages of London, Dublin and Glasgow, to be sent as indentured servants to Canadian farmers and factory owners. Some of these little bastards were treated well. Some were adopted. Some never saw a school. Some were starved, beaten, assaulted and left to freeze to death in alleyways and barns. All these mass kidnappings were led by a church and state that smugly claimed to be saving souls and lives.

Ableism and racism conspire to justify and reinforce carceral culture. Racialized people and disabled people have been stereotyped throughout history as both childlike and subhuman, as both sweet-natured and violent. These legacies continue to cause harm, to feed racist and ableist beliefs that those who are not white and abled need to be feared and locked up. Indigenous and disabled communities have also been exploited by fakers and thieves. To paraphrase Indigenous critique, "settlers have been playing Indian since they landed." Europe also has a long history of hoaxers pretending to be disabled, from Roman circuses to medieval mummers. For sympathy. For attention. For publicity. For personal gain. Generations of P.T. Barnums offered up fake rodeo Indians beside fake "Dog Boys" and "Siamese Twins." Beyond the frauds, many circus freaks were exploited marginalized people who could find no other employment or housing. Be it a travelling jail or one of bars and bricks, a cage is still a cage.

Canada began building asylums even before it was a country, the first in 1839.

It built one of the world's largest in 1896, the Orillia Asylum for Idiots. It was still open in 1967, Centennial Year, housing an astounding 2,600 inmates. It was closed by a winning 2009 class action suit, charging "systemic physical, emotional and sexual abuse against disabled children since 1945." Marilyn Dolmage's affidavit "described residents being kept in caged cots, having all their teeth removed for 'safety reasons,' and being held upside down with their heads under running water as a punishment for not eating." Yes, Canada has waterboarded disabled children. The government formally apologized for decades of abuse and paid a small settlement to survivors. It's a true forced-fit of our history: Orillia, home of the great humorist Stephen Leacock, has a home for disabled children with 1,400 unmarked graves.

Canada erased disabled people who were born that way, but began to care for white, male soldiers who were made that way. When troops returned from the carnage of WW I with blindness, amputation, shell shock and "nervous conditions," the War Amps raised awareness and support. Then came WW II. In "racial cleansing," the Nazis began sterilizing disabled people as early as 1933. By 1935, the effectiveness of propaganda protesting the cost of keeping disabled people alive escalated to the active euthanasia of disabled children. This began before the war, in 1939. The wartime Nazi euthanasia program, Aktion T4, eliminated "life unworthy of life." In Schönbrunn, it ran the mass gassing of the entire population of nine hundred patients in a hospital for "the mentally defective." Aktion T4 murdered one hundred thousand disabled people, bringing the pre-war and wartime total to the murder of 360,000 disabled lives.

We all need to know that the eugenics movement was not confined to Germany.

As a term invented in France in 1883, meaning "good in birth" or "noble in heredity," eugenicists sought to ensure the "selection of the fittest." Churchill, Roosevelt, George Bernard Shaw and Helen Keller all supported eugenics goals. In 1919, US high school teacher turned eugenicist Harry Hamilton Laughlin advocated compulsory sterilization for "the 5 D's": all the "degenerate, deficient, dependent, delinquent, and defective." Many states passed legislation based on his criteria. As head of the Eugenics Record Office, Laughlin testified to congress as to "the extra levels of insanity" in immigrants, resulting in restrictions to the Immigration Act of 1924. In 1936, he won an honorary degree from Germany for "the science of racial cleansing."

Formed in 1930, the Eugenics Society of Canada had many prominent members, including four of the Famous Five feminists in the "Persons Case": Emily Murphy, Louise McKinney, Irene Parlby and Nellie McClung. From 1928 to 1972, the Alberta Eugenics Board sterilized 2,800 "unfit" women and children. Without their consent, it disproportionally sterilized Indigenous women incorrectly deemed "mentally unfit." Again, it took a court case, that of Leilani Muir, to bring this atrocity to light. Ontario and BC passed similar sterilization acts. Forced sterilization wasn't banned in Canada until 1986, and may continue illegally today.

In the Canada 150 celebrations of 2017, settler Canada celebrated the state it built on the backs of marginalized peoples. If your Canadian history does not include the Sixties Scoop, Butterbox Babies and Barnardo Boys, it should. Before anyone claims pride in Canada, please learn all its legacy. Change was never charitably granted. It was demanded and fought for.

The Canadian Human Rights Act of 1977 forbid discrimination against disability by the federal government. The full prohibition of discrimination against disabled people waited until the Charter of Rights and Freedoms in 1982. The disability community continues to fight on many fronts: education, housing, poverty, employment, inclusion, medical and legal care.

The Accessibility for Ontarians with Disabilities Act (AODA) passed in 2005, mandating a barrier-free Ontario by 2025. I don't know any disabled person who thinks it will happen. The law provides few inspectors and small fines for non-compliance. Businesses appear to have taken a cynical wait-and-see approach rather than spend money on even tax-deductible renovations.

Bill C-81: The Accessible Canada Act of July 2018 is our first national accessibility law, but applies only to the Federal Government and takes four years to implement. It's earned increasing critique by the disability community for its lack of specificity, funding and enforcement. Given that a full 60 percent of cases before the federal Human Rights Commission are filed on the grounds of discrimination against disabled people, enforcement of existing policy is critical. In December 2018, Canada acceded to the Optional Protocol to the United Nations Convention on the Rights of Persons with Disabilities, giving disabled Canadians recourse to file a UN complaint if our convention rights are violated.

Because eugenics isn't long-ago history; it's still alive and kicking in daily life.

Its normalization starts with cruelty and abuse. Disabled children are bullied five times more than abled children. Disabled children of colour, disabled queer and transgender children, ten times more. It leads to discrimination. Some 80 percent of disabled people are under- or unemployed, dependent on charity, living below the poverty line. Doubly marginalized disabled people are most at risk. Disabled people face higher rates of sexual and physical violence. Jails have become racist, ableist warehouses replacing mental health care. It ends in murder. Murder by poverty. Murder by medical neglect. Murder by cutbacks and underfunding. Murder by the state. We all know the police disproportionately shoot people of colour. Did you know that some 50 percent of police shootings are of disabled people? And more than murder gets normalized. Valuing and ranking bodies for capitalism, eugenics thinking gets us all to buy into the daily disparagement of "crazy" and "lame," and the "slow feet don't eat" venom masquerading as witty wisdom. Eugenics enshrines Darwin's "survival of the fittest" in every breath of daily life.

Consider the twenty-five-year still-running "debate" over the 1993 murder of twelve-year-old Tracy Latimer. In 2001, after many appeals, Tracy's father, Robert Latimer, got a life sentence. He served seven years. In 2008, he won day parole, and then full parole in 2010. In 2018, still insisting he'd done absolutely nothing wrong, he applied for a full pardon. As if child murder was a debate with two equally reasonable sides, in July 2018, the *Globe and Mail* ran two opinion pieces, one calmly explaining why a man who murders his child "deserves" a pardon. Apparently, Tracy is still seen as "life undeserving of life," an injured animal that a caring man can freely put down.

Eugenics likewise empowers the straw bans of 2018. Not seeing us in our numbers has long permitted abled people to ridicule products seniors and disabled people need, to call peeled oranges, pre-chopped vegetables and sock assists "useless products for lazy people." Many disabled people depend on straws for their very survival, for medication, hydration and nutrition. When governments began banning plastic straws without consulting disabled citizens, it took an army of activists explaining non-stop that, no, we know for certain that neither paper, metal nor bamboo straws work. Plastic straws don't collapse or degrade in hot liquid. Plastic straws can be positioned, don't chip your teeth or cut your tongue, palate or oxygen mask in a muscle spasm or seizure. We were consistently clear: plastic straws are the only choice that works for all.

But abled folks were more moved by a viral video of a sea turtle with a straw up its nose, than the right of disabled people to eat and drink. Celebrities like Justin Trudeau and Margaret Atwood leapt on the straw ban bandwagon. Disabled activists rightly called it misdirected, guilty-liberal performative activism: straws account for about .05 percent of plastic waste. Focusing on individuals using straws lets corporate polluters off scot-free. But the social media push back got brutal, telling disabled folks who couldn't "drink properly" to bring their own straws or stay home. To which, at #SuckItAbleism, disabled black activist Imani Barbarin tweeted: "Imagine if your solution to segregated lunch counters and restaurants was for black people to bring their own chairs. Now apply that to straws and disabled people."

This casual eugenics, seeing my community's right to eat and drink debated and dismissed, didn't infuriate me; it terrified me. It gave me insomnia, worsened my panic attacks, made me afraid to leave my apartment. I had to avoid social media. I couldn't bear the hate of ordinary people openly saying that if it would save sharks and sea turtles, "cripples could go ahead and die." Of course, capitalism found a way to capitalize: companies monetized straws, making disabled people pay for them, or they saved money by not serving straws and infantilized us yet again by making us ask for them. My social media feeds are full of disabled people being refused straws at restaurants because abled wait staff inform them that they don't look disabled enough. This smug slacktivism would be laughable, if it weren't so dangerous.

Because the belief that disabled people are costly burdens doesn't end with straws. In its own deliberate dismantling and privatization of health care, Ontario's Conservative government is going to "reorganize" LHIN because the services that help keep me alive, that help seniors and disabled people live with dignity, are to quote Nazi propaganda "too expensive and financially inefficient." Years ago, when I first learned that the Ontario Disability Support Program (ODSP) pays disabled people below the poverty line, I said, "They don't care if we live or die." Now I see it more clearly: "They want us dead."

I've often pondered how capitalism has successfully made us fear death. To see it as unfair. Just as teenagers think they'll live forever, too many adults seem to believe they deserve to live abled and pain-free forever. They feel shocked, betrayed and punished when they become ill or disabled. That's the brainwashing of ableism. Why would anyone think our bodies are infallible? Because it suits the capitalist narrative. If long-lived good health is the norm and illness and disability are aberrations, it greases the wheel of cuts to health care. If a loss of productivity equates to death, then becoming disabled is a demotion to be avoided at all costs. No wonder some would rather risk killing their children than vaccinate them.

Do abled people hate us because when they look at us, they see the inevitability of their own demise? I don't know. I do know that disabled death is seen as inevitable. As the climate crisis creates floods and wildfires, we get "sad stories" of empty wheelchairs, left behind because there was no plan to evacuate seniors and disabled people. No one calls it murder. In the second decade of this century, in the worldwide ramping up of hatred, we're in a fight for our very lives.

In the global rush to perfect and monetize gene editing, many countries, medical institutions and universities are also puppy-dog eager to pour big bucks into keeping more disabled people from being born. The CRISPR/Cas9 permits genome editing, the choice of "desirable" inheritable characteristics and the eradication of "unfit, undesirable" ones. Just as biologists have genetically modified food, just as my father selected guppies to ensure resplendent fantails, we'll soon be able to edit the human embryo to create genetically modified humans. While gene therapy may be welcome treatment for life-ending diseases such as cancer and muscular dystrophy, gene editing can also be used to alter DNA to prevent disabilities. Who decides who is "fit"? Who decides which disabilities are "life unworthy of life?" Equating disability with disease, weaponizing the medical model that sees disability as a "burden" to be eradicated, using the new god of technology to birth beautiful, neurotypical, perfectly abled designer babies, both normalizes and emboldens eugenics.

Many people radicalize out of personal experience. Not me. I'm a historian by nature and nurture. Only once I understood ableism as a collective historic injustice, as eugenics, as the monetization of systemic bigotry and hatred, could I begin to get angry for the one, lone individual that is me. Today, I get it: disabled history is everyone's history.

Disabled people were not meant to survive.

But we did. And we do. And we will.

This gives me the courage to share a memory I've never shared. In the summer of 1973, before I left for university, I went to the opening day of the Canadian National Exhibition. At the midway, I came face to face with a monkey – not a cute little circus monkey in trousers, but the latest attraction of the Freak Show: "Pookie the Monkey Girl." A girl in pink. The blush rose of my coming home outfit. The barker said this girl was seventeen, said she was tiny because she was "retarded and damaged by birth defects." He brandished what he called her "long monkey arms and legs." She started to cry. He said nothing could be done for her except the kindness of charity. Then he produced Bibles for sale to the crowd, claiming every cent would go to her care.

When newspapers revealed that Pookie was "retarded" but only five years old, she was removed from the Freak Show. The Children's Aid kindly informed her working-class single mother it was illegal to display her child for personal gain. When she asked how else she was supposed to pay for her expensive, multiply handicapped daughter, no one answered.

What did I do? I stared. I saw Billy and Gerald. I saw another broken little bastard and I saw myself. But I pretended I saw nothing wrong. At least I didn't laugh along with the crowd. But I still cannot forgive myself for what I did next. I shrugged. I turned my back and walked away with my abled friends. I needed out of there pronto because "Pookie the Money Girl" sounded too much like my father's nickname for me: Pooch, and sometimes Poochie.

I abandoned her, but she never left me. I still look in the mirror and see our hybrid haunt: "Poochie the Monkey Girl." Today, I can finally apologize and give her the credit she deserves. She fuelled every thought I ever had that became the Great Ableist Chain of Being.

I refuse to call either of us Pooch or Pookie.

All human children have human names.

Wondrous Won't Always be Wonderful

We all ask how our parents met. We want their love story to be one.

But I was raised with stud guppies. I know they behave badly. Sometimes, guppy sex is consensual, the result of a courting dance. Too often, the male guppy indulges in what fish enthusiasts, not coincidentally all male, call "sneaky mating." It's forced copulation. The male corners the female and thrusts his gonopodium at her urogenital pore. Guppy mothers give birth to some fifty fry every thirty days. Once inseminated, female guppies store sperm in their ovaries, where it can continue to fertilize ova for up to eight months. Accordingly, sneaky guppy fathers can continue to produce non-consensual off-spring even long after they are dead.

When I was fifty-five, I met my frail, octogenarian birth mother for the first and only time. She told me all I know about my father. She met him at a dance in Toronto in the Hurricane Hazel fall of 1954. His name was Jim Stanley and he was perhaps a little older than my mother's jitterbugging age of twenty-three. He was tallish, with dark curly hair. He came from a musical family. He drove a Stude-baker. On their third date, en route to another dance, they stopped at his house to introduce his mom to his date. And after the dance, he raped her.

I imagine it was in the Studebaker. I see a black car, iced with glittering chrome. I see a tartan blanket on leatherette seats. And, as in every young man's car of the day, there's a hula girl on the dashboard. Whether I want to see it or not, her skirts get set aquiver.

Half a century later, I watched as fresh pain wracked my mother's eighty-year-old face.

"Please, don't ask about it. It was vile. Everything about it is disgusting." When it registered to whom she was speaking, her consolation came too little and immeasurably too late, "But at least you came out of it."

When I quoted my NII, told her it said my father was a bricklayer, that I'd spent all my life looking at postwar buildings, wondering if he had built them, she frowned. "No, he came from a musical family. I don't remember anything about bricks."

When I asked this stranger what my children and I deserved to know, if I inherited my disability from her, she dropped a furtive glance to my stunted feet. "Nobody in our family has your birth defects. As for his family, I've no idea. Nice girls, we didn't talk about such things."

To be a nice girl, to prioritize her pain, I didn't ask again.

Until now.

The truth hasn't set me free, but it has reset my thinking.

About my parents' "Not a Love Story": About a mother who refused to be one and a father never told he was one. My NII says the Children's Aid left phone messages for him. There's no record of how often they called, or what message they left. My mother did not call or write. She enabled his evasion. It was best for her. Immediately after becoming pregnant, she met and married another man. I was born three months after their wedding.

Of course, my nicely married mother gave her little bastard baby up for adoption. Of course, I'm still angry. She abandoned me. Chose some strange man over me. Ran off to sunny California to raise two healthy, legitimate children. What might my life have been, what might I be, if I'd been raised with them? In a family that was at least half mine? In a place I could swim year-round. A place without snow. I remind myself it was 1955. No one kept babies like me. I want to forgive my birth mother but still hear what she said in the one moment we were alone.

"I don't remember much. I barely remember Hurricane Hazel, and I'm pretty sure you were conceived during it. But I can't be certain, because after that horrid night, I had electroshock therapy." She paused, averted her eyes from mine. "For depression."

"I know. My records say you were 'hospitalized for insomnia and depression, and had numerous shock treatments which affected your memory.'" Shock zaps me before I can stop it. "But now you're saying you agreed to shock treatments knowing you were pregnant with me?"

"Everyone said it was for the best."

"Certainly not the best for me."

To her credit, she didn't lie. "You're right. All I can say now is I'm glad you didn't die."

Did electroshock cause my feet? Or, was it my mother cinching her belt in shame, doubly hoping I would die? Doctors still aren't sure. Medically, half a family tree is but half an answer. Personally, half a tree is a miracle. It gives me Scottish ancestors. Today, I have family photos, even if they're only headstones, right back to my great-great-great-great-grandparents. Being able to claim this family heals half my heart. But only half. Somewhere out there is my birth father. He is the last barrier between me and my human history.

Please hear the words I did not value myself enough to say for half a century.

I want my father. I want him, rapist warts and all.

I'd like to know something, anything, about him. Little things. Human things. His birthday. His middle name. Where he grew up.

His favourite books and movies. His favourite pizza topping. What kind of music did his musical family play? I'd like to hear his story and to tell him mine. My mother reduces him to one criminal moment, then expunges his very existence. I cannot. My rapist father exists in full-blooded, three-dimensional forever for me.

He is half my DNA, half my vital medical history and half my family tree. His story is my ethnic and cultural heritage.

His history is my children's legacy.

My babies still face having babies as I did, with the fear of birth defects unknown. And we aren't the only victims. My father's parents are my grandparents. His siblings are my aunts and uncles; their kids are my cousins. His children are my brothers and sisters. None of the extended Stanley family did anything wrong. Why are they deprived of me and me of them? Why does a stranger's crime have no statute of limitations for me?

The moment of my conception polices all the years of my life. My genealogical research proves that the state took me from a family of bigamists, con artists, thieves and abandoners to whom I was related and gave me to a family of bigamists, con artists, thieves and abandoners to whom I was not related. The Stanleys may be a dream come true, or toxic through and through.

But they are my family. I'd like to meet them.

Because children of rape grow up. We're not perpetual infants who need permanent protection from difficult truths. For any other crime, as my father's adult daughter, I could still negotiate a relationship with him and the rest of his family, if I chose to do so. The decision to know him or not should belong to me. Not to the courts.

And, with respect, not to my traumatized mother.

I support a woman's right to choose, but I also embody Audre Lorde's dark truth: I know I was never meant to survive. If my mother had known safe, legal access to abortion in 1954, I would have been one. Even today, adults born of rape remain frozen in the public imagination as unwanted children.

That stigma still makes strange bedfellows.

Century-old law and modern feminists both infantilize me, ignore my adulthood and reject my right to choose. To "protect" me, Canadian law gives me no access to my father and him none to me. Too many feminist sisters have likewise decided for me that all rapists are incurable monsters who must never have any access to their children. To protect my mother, they erase me. Why is it so hard for intersectional feminists to see that my life intersects with my father's? If I suggest they've got it backwards, that it's not about his rights to me but my rights to him, I too often hear knee-jerk accusations of anti-feminist high treason:

"You sound like a chest-beating Men's Right's Activist."

"You're betraying rape survivors. You're perpetuating rape culture."

"The very idea you might want to meet the man who raped your mother, that's sick."

It appears the law, my sisters and my stuck-in-1954 mother all agree: I'm "disgusting."

Screw that. I chose my truth over their retelling of it. Adults born of rape are rape survivors; everyone has betrayed us. My human rights aren't contingent on whether the sex that spawned me was consensual. I reject any law, any feminism, that shames and silences me, that appoints gatekeeping strangers to decide what I can or cannot know about my own family. Folks with extended families and full family histories have no right to tell me how to handle having nothing and no one. If you're legitimate, if you grew up with relatives, if you knew even one of your parents, you have blood privilege. Please stop talking and start listening.

If you want to know my lived experience as an adult born of rape, ask me.

Here's my answer: let's all look past conception. I begin there, but I don't end there. Like everyone else, I get to hold both my parents responsible for me. I believe survivors, but refuse to perpetually demonize my father, or deify my mother. Rape does not give either party the right to use a breathing child for healing, redemption, vengeance, harm or denial. I have two parents. I'm not my mother's transferable property. I'm not the Canadian state's disposable chattel.

Feminists centre survivors; the law centres crime. It's time to centre the living child.

What really perpetuates rape culture? When we let rapists escape fatherhood scot-free.

Call a man a monster, he remains one. It's not enough to hope rapists become better men; we must demand it of them. Just as every child has the right to DNA confirmation of their paternity, all fathers have a right and a responsibility to know they have a living child. Whether or not the courts ever grant him any access to that child, every father must pay child support. Enabling evasion only perpetuates patriarchy. It's no protection or kindness to abandon raped women and their children to struggling, single-income poverty. All paying fathers should be able to petition the court for some form of appropriate contact with their children. Children born of rape should be able to petition the court for their full family and medical history. When they are legal adults, they should decide if they desire any kind of contact. No other crime automatically and eternally keeps a father from his child, and the child from their family, culture and history.

Let's reject the lie that fuelled the racist, forced, genocidal removal by the Canadian government of some twenty thousand Indigenous children and sent them to white families in the Sixties Scoop: children are not slates that can be wiped clean and handed to another family to write on. It's time to debunk the damaging fantasy that stranger adoption is the fairy-tale answer. It produces higher rates of depression, divorce, alcoholism and suicide. We need choices that decolonize adoption and value family connections. Visitation, shared or full custody, could be awarded to grandparents, or to extended family. Possibly even to a rapist father who can prove he has taken full responsibility for his crime and the child he has fathered.

I know this will enrage many of my feminist sisters. But we must not be hypocrites.

Countless Canadians are the product of non-consensual sex.

In 1954, a musical young man had an enticing hula girl on his dashboard. All his buddies agreed: nice girls need convincing. He'd dated this nice girl twice. Spent a fortune. When they slow danced, her breasts teased more than his heart. On their third date, when she agreed to get into the back seat and under the tartan blanket, he figured they both knew exactly what it meant.

How many millions of us were conceived this way? When "No" didn't mean no. When it didn't get said, heard or heeded. When consent didn't matter to a sperm piercing an egg?

Especially sixty years ago. Especially last week.

It's rape. I'm not saying it's ever acceptable; I'm saying it happens all the time.

In the enlightened second decade of the twenty-first century, I'm asking: Why do we still have a double standard? Why are we still punishing only some of us who were born this way? Bastards. Those of us whose parents weren't married. Married parents can be all kinds of bad news: bullies, addicts, abusers, pedophiles, con artists, criminals and rapists. Raped wives give birth. But children of marital rape get to know their parents, no matter how ill, immoral or just plain evil they may be. Legitimate kids get to play any family card life deals them. It's only bastards like me who never get to see our cards, let alone play them.

It is equally hypocritical to assume our cards are always and only bad. Dare I say it? Throughout history, generations of rapists have made excellent fathers.

Some of them may be your relatives.

Are you the product of sex in a Studebaker?

Only the hula girl knows for sure.

Let's reject the 1950s secrecy and shame that has cost me my family. It's time to let adults negotiate adult lives. I'm in my sixties. My birth mother died months after we met. I've scoured the Internet, celebrated and cried with countless adoptees desperate to find their birth families, but can't find a Jim Stanley in 1954 Toronto. My father is likely dead. He'll never see my face. He'll never know there was a little red-headed girl, a young mom, a drama teacher, a disabled senior, longing for him, bereft but too ashamed to say so until it was too late.

I know my parents' love story isn't one.

But I propose a kinder ending.

Mom and Dad: I grew old missing you. Without you, despite you, I raised myself. I spent over half a century trying to forgive you. I hope you made penance and found peace.

I'll always wonder what you did on the other twenty-five thousand days of your lives.

Here's what I'd tell my double-casting of parents: Broken feet and a broken bloodline did not have to break the girl. But they did. I spent all my life blaming myself until I heard Robin Williams in *Good Will Hunting*, when he holds tight to young Will, holds him up to let his grief out, won't let go until Will believes it: "It's not your fault. It's not your fault. It's not your fault."

So, with this book, with my children beside me, I'll stop falling for that lie.

It's not my fault. Not one word. Not one bone. Not one bottle. Not one scar. Not one limp. Not one single fall. Not one hole or drop of blood. Not one abandonment or betrayal.

None of it. None of it. None of it is my fault.

I am hereby uncinching myself.

X-Rays Cast Light Down to the Bone

I've always loved Victorian and Edwardian architecture. Warm red and orange brick. Playfully patterned, like quilts for houses. Because my NII said my birth father was a bricklayer, I researched bricks and the buildings they built. Before I explain my work as a disability activist, anyone who holds any kind of event in a Victorian-Edwardian building needs to understand this: these "charming" buildings were built during the Ugly Laws. That's an umbrella term for municipal laws that sprung up all across North America in the last half of the nineteenth century dictating who could and could not be seen in the streets. Ugly Laws, typified by the Chicago City Code of 1881, made it illegal for people to appear in public who were "diseased, maimed, mutilated, or in any way deformed, so as to be an unsightly or disgusting object."

Making it clear that the state that dispensed the carrots would also eagerly beat with sticks, Ugly Laws authorized the police to arrest and incarcerate unsightly poor people. Ugly Laws targeted beggars, often those made beggared because they were old, alone, homeless, racialized and/or disabled. Ugly Laws also kept those other unsightly burdens – disabled people who weren't beggars – out of the public eye. Families didn't dare put their Billys in baby carriages; disabled people didn't leave home. Stigma, shame and inaccessible buildings ensured they stayed there. There's no reason to make buildings accessible when it's illegal for ugly disabled people to be in the streets. Ugly Laws remained on the books until after WW II, when governments grudgingly conceded that disabled veterans injured fighting Nazis had earned the right to go out in public.

Today, if you attend events in inaccessible buildings, you're perpetuating the Ugly Laws.

In 2016, Wenceslas and I started reaching out to my literary community, hopeful for what Disability Justice calls "our collective liberation." Instead, I found Sisyphean despair. I'd get a Facebook invitation to a literary event and my moment of pleasure would quickly die. In 2016, none of these invitations had any accessibility information. Apparently, it's not the least bit rude or unkind to invite someone to travel two hours to your reading, expect them to pay for gas and parking, all without checking to see if they can get in the door when they arrive.

I trust you understand that I can't just show up hoping an event is accessible?

I have to know days beforehand to adjust activity, rest, medication, budget and shoe wearing. No accessibility information leaves me two choices: let the Ugly Laws win and stay home, or become Sherlock Crip Holmes. When I sleuth out a venue's website, it often also has no accessibility info. Having to investigate, inquire after and wait for the permission of abled people to attend is infantilizing and insulting. It's not acceptable to post accessibility info as an afterthought, or only when asked. I've seen tickets sell out before accessibility info gets posted.

How much clearer could you be that we are second-class citizens, neither invited nor welcome? Afterthought access and access on demand are not access. Many disabled people are so tired of constantly having to phone up and inquire like a child if they can please get to sit at the grown-up table that they've drawn a line in the sand: they refuse to attend any event, store, restaurant or bar that doesn't have accessibility info already posted.

In 2016, if I took this principled position, I could go nowhere in the world of CanLit. Sick of sleuthing, wanting accessibility information routinely made public so no one else would have to sleuth, I began posting directly to public Facebook invitations: "I'd love to come to this fabulous reading! Please post accessibility info." It surprised me when organizers were surprised, when I was repeatedly asked to define *accessible*.

Surely it was their job to know and follow the the Accessibility for Ontarians with Disabilities Act? And to know the meaning of words?

In Ontario, to qualify as *fully accessible,* a building must be AODA evaluated to meet a long list of exacting criteria, including adult change tables and Braille signage. *Wheelchair-accessible* venues include e-doors, no stairs outside or inside without an elevator, an accessible washroom with e-doors, a stall with wheelchair clearance, grab bars and reachable sink, soap, towel or blower. This list falls far short of what buildings must have by 2025 to be "barrier free."

But the arts community loves its charming Ugly Law bars.

So many literary events are held in them.

Many have steps at the door and more inside. In the typical Victorian-Edwardian practice of banishing dirty things, washrooms are down a steep flight of stairs in the basement. In 2016, a full seventeen of the nineteen literary events to which I was invited were not wheelchair accessible. In 2017, I was barred from twenty-four of twenty-nine. In 2018, twenty-one of thirty events banned me. The number of inaccessible events is actually higher, because I counted each reading series only once. For the last three years, I estimate that maybe 10 percent of literary events in Toronto have been wheelchair accessible. As for being fully accessible: given the lack of provision for D/deaf/HOH readers and writers via ASL and captioning, for low-vision and blind people via large print, Braille and care stations for service animals, and for the neurodiversity community and those living with mental health issues, via relaxed presentation modes and quiet rooms, it's safe to say the number of fully accessible literary events that have ever been held anywhere in North America is zero.

We see this sign on every door: "Ableds Only. No Disabled People Need Apply."

I experience inaccessible events collectively. Having experienced childhood slurs as snakebites, as an adult I carry an accumulation of venom in my body. But I'm constantly reminded that my abled literary community wants me to see inaccessible events individually, as unfortunate exceptions. One organizer said, "Sorry my series is inaccessible, but just go online, I'm sure there are plenty that aren't." Well-meaning friends say, "Don't worry, I'm sure there'll be an accessible event next week." I recognize these empty assurances. I've heard them before.

My son spent some lonely years as a single gay man in a small college town in Ohio. When he told colleagues there was no one out of the closet to date, they all said this: "There must be. Just keep looking." He believes this reply came from two places: a sincere hope he'd find happiness, and an equal investment in refusing to address the community's pervasive homophobia. When I first told colleagues there were few accessible literary events in Canada, they parroted that denial, "You just need to keep looking." I guess if you couple the belief that disabled people are few in number, with the idea that plenty of accessible events must already exist, you can do what I did at the freak show: shrug and walk away with your abled friends.

I want to stress that event organizers are writers I deeply respect, often my friends, and progress has been made. Several important series – Brockton Writers Series, Pivot Readings, and Rowers Reading Series – have all moved to more accessible venues. They all have my respect and thanks. I equally appreciate my board colleagues at Canadian Creative Writers and Writing Programs (CCWWP), who struggled

with me to find a wheelchair accessible venue for our 2019 confer-
ence. Some abled writers, often women of colour with whom I've
worked on diversity issues, have taken a public stand that they won't
attend any inaccessible events.

But too many in all the arts know their events are inaccessible
and shrug.

When I post an accessibility inquiry online, I'm often messaged
for my phone number. Why? Organizers don't want to reply in
public. No one wants to admit in writing that their events are inaccessible. On the phone, I've been told to stop being "a whiner" and
"a publicity-seeking complainer," to "stop trolling for inaccessible
events so I can pick on them." I'd love there to be none to find.
Internationally, disabled activists in America, Australia and the UK
all confirm my experience: disabled people get left out until we point
it out. When I point it out, I too often get an "explanation" that isn't
one; it's ableist entitlement in action.

"We're sorry our series isn't accessible, but we can't leave our sig-
nature venue."

"We're sorry we're inaccessible, but we have a very busy volunteer
committee."

"Our event is semi-accessible. Only the bathroom is in the
basement."

I began seeing this insulting invented euphemism, this attempt
to redefine and control the language of accessibility, after I'd been
advocating for it for about a year. In the same lazy, performative,
self-serving slacktivism that produced *handicapable*, some organizers
thought it their right to invent their own disability language. They
began calling their events "partially" or "semi" or "mostly" accessible,
as if that was their duty done and something to be proud of. There's
no such thing. Either a person in a wheelchair can independently
access the entirety of the venue or it's not wheelchair accessible. Any
organizer woke enough to know accessibility is an issue should be
woke enough to provide it. Thank you for coming to my TED Talk.

Instead, I can't count how often I've heard: "Will you hunt down an accessible venue for us to consider, maybe for next year?" In teacher-pleasing goodwill, I used to volunteer to do so. After consulting my disabled community, I stopped. I reject any notion that I'm not sincere about accessibility unless I personally labour for free to provide it. It's an organizer's job, not mine.

This request repeats a pattern the international disability community finds both typical and deeply offensive. Even in progressive arts and social justice groups, abled organizers first expect us to wait until accessibility is convenient to them. When they agree it's "a problem," they expect us to give free expertise and labour to solve it for them. When they do maybe half of what we advise, they turn on us for our ingratitude, call us "difficult" and "too demanding." In my literary community, too many reduce "the problem" to me "being a problem." If they accommodate me once, they figure they're done. This arrogant noblesse oblige will continue as long as abled people see accessibility as charity they can grant, or not, as they personally see fit.

It isn't. Accessibility is everyone's responsibility.

Legally and morally.

Since 2016, I've taken responsibility non-stop. Thanking and amplifying accessible events. Doing sensitivity readings. Providing accessibility assessments for literary events including Word on the Street. Writing for literary and disability journals. Being an invited speaker at the Toronto Disability Pride March three years running. Joining disability panels at Writers in Dangerous Times, Momentum: A Disability Justice UnConference and the Canadian Writers' Summit. Serving on the Accessibility Advisory Committee for FOLD. Discussing linking funding to accessibility with arts councils. Mentoring disabled improvisors. Writing a monthly column for and serving on the board of CCWWP. Working with CCWWP to get the Writers' Summit to begin including captioning, aka CART: Communication Access Real-time Translation. Much of this is free labour, and costly to me. I pay for parking, gas, food and sometimes hotels. In the expensive city of Toronto, I have to wear more diapers and skip more meals. Any day I do any kind of activism leaves me too exhausted to do anything else.

But here's what exhausts and hurts me most of all: inconsistent allyship.

Some "allies" think it acceptable to be supportive in the spotlight, then regress when the spotlight departs. In 2017, when I saw that the well-funded International Festival of Authors (IFOA) was co-sponsoring a panel at an inaccessible movie theatre, when I realized two panelists were already on record as refusing to appear in inaccessible venues, I contacted them and they immediately stated they would not appear unless the event relocated to an accessible venue. This is true allyship: taking a stand against IFOA, a place many writers dream of appearing.

My request was based on an old axiom of the theatre that is still true today: if there ain't no talent, there ain't no show. As "the talent," this is how fast writers could end inaccessibility if they wanted to do so. At the risk of sounding like Nancy Reagan, we could all "Just Say No." Of course, the organizers instantly found another venue. One organizer called it "a turning point in their allyship." And, equally of course, these same organizers held their very next event right back at the same inaccessible theatre. They're still there. Over two years later.

To my face, "allies" have said, "I like accessible events, but I don't limit myself to them."

Sadly, the arts community can be equally dismissive of financial inaccessibility. At launches and readings, I can't buy the books. And I can't explain why. I congratulate authors, but feel gutted with shame to have to pick up a book, praise it and put it down. I hope my colleagues don't take it personally, don't think less of me when I leave empty handed, but imagine they do. Writers regularly post pics of a stack of books purchased at an event. Five twenty-dollar books total one hundred dollars. Just as I can't buy books, I can't support any of the arts community's fundraising campaigns. I'm relegated to silence during any discussion of dressy arts events, and often find the expenses of makeup, shoes and dresses discussed totally classist and prohibitive.

Are we accepting the subtext that money makes someone a "good" colleague? There's no critique of the class privilege this purchasing requires and broadcasts. Some events address financial inaccessibility by asking solvent members of the arts community to buy sponsor passes for those who can't afford entrance. However well-intentioned, that strategy only reproduces the burden-charity model. It won't make permanent or equal space at any table for my communities.

Because I want to be clear: when I'm asking for financial and physical accessibility it isn't just about me. I didn't personally invent the tactic of asking both organizations and individuals to stop doing inaccessible events and to relocate in accessible ones. It's the three-pronged approach – organizational, legislative and personal – that the international disabled community uses in Australia, America and the UK. After thirty years of activism, groups like ADAPT know we must fight on all fronts.

But in Toronto, it shouldn't be a fight. No disabled person should be told it's "too hard" to find an accessible venue in a city of 6.5 million people. When I point out disabled people must eat, drink and defecate somewhere, when I suggest accessto.ca, which lists two hundred accessible venues, when I say one Toronto launch earned everyone's respect by relocating to an accessible venue two days before their event and Vancouver's Growing Room festival relocated in twenty-four hours, some organizers are encouraged. Some believe venues are "too hard to find," because then they don't have to look.

I'm not buying it. Former students who are now event planners tell me new AODA-compliant venues often offer slow, mid-week nights for free. But even if accessible venues do cost more, are you telling me I'm not worth it? Do you actually expect me to agree that *any* economic argument justifies excluding the disabled community? When I asked one organizer if their venue banned Muslims or transgender attendees, would they continue to use "expense" as a justification, he shot back, "Of course not. We'd never ban them in the first place."

When organizers admit their event is inaccessible, I get empty "apologies," all centring me, as if they've convinced themselves I'm the only rare and exotic creature they're keeping out.

"We're sorry you can't come. We feel really bad about it. You'll be missed."

"We're so sorry you can't come. But we're discussing it, behind the scenes."

"We're so very sorry you can't come. Maybe someone will live tweet it for you?"

Since the Women's March offered a virtual march, some events have attempted an end-run around accessibility, offering online inclusion, or live tweeting, to justify exclusion. Separate is never equal. Events must accommodate my disabled person, because I'm a person. Telling me a live feed is "good enough" says I'm not "good enough" to be there in person. If I'm not in person, I can't ask questions, congratulate, discuss, share and network. I get less than half the fun. Time and time again, I hear, "We feel guilty. We're so sincerely sorry. Maybe next year."

Anyone who is "sincerely sorry" stops doing what they feel guilty about and does better.

Instead, I get yelled at, sworn at, patted on the head and threatened.

One organizer phoned me up, invited me to read, praised his accessible venue, then added, "The other writers will read from the stage. It's up a few stairs, so you can read from the floor." When I asked that all writers read from the floor together, he bristled. "No. I can't do that. That insults and demeans them, doesn't it? There's a stage. They have every right to use it."

I explained that we need to change the prime image of a writer as someone standing to read. I added that any stairs to a stage or the use of podiums or bar stools not only tell me that nobody expects disabled writers to get on the stage, it also says abled writers will stand together to keep me off their stage. It says I'm expected to accept a second-class, back-of-the-bus status. It tells disabled people they can be passive, paying listeners, but never working writers.

This sorry man yelled, "At least I gave you a fucking chance." And he hung up.

In a stupendous feat of circular logic and denying our numbers, another writer said, "If I start getting disabled people coming to our readings, then I'll start worrying about our venue being inaccessible. But not until then. I'm not going to make changes for some mythical people."

While I am fairly certain I am not a hobbit, she is definitely a bigot.

I get email from bigots all the time. An organizer of a local reading series, declaring herself an ally, wrote she was "personally committed to accessibility," which she defined as "when they had grants, they used accessible venues, when they didn't, they made compromises." She "respected anyone who chose not to offer inaccessible events." Then concluded, "Just launch your own accessible reading series. That solves the problem."

Can you imagine these insults casually sent off to a member of any other marginalized group?

Of course not. But I'm sure we all deeply respect those who "choose not to offer" sexist, homophobic, transphobic or racist events. I wanted to ask, "What makes you think you can dispense my human rights, or not, out of the charitable goodness of your heart, on those rare occasions when you magnanimously feel flush with cash?" But I know the answer: Charles Darwin, Charles Dickens, the Industrial Revolution, Ugly Laws, governments, schools and urban planners that segregate disabled from abled, and generations of collaborating super-crips and Tiny Tims. In short, all the players in the enmeshment of capitalism and ableism.

If ableism in the arts is often passive-aggressive, troll ableism is openly aggressive. I've been their target since 2016, when I argued that the UBC Accountable letter demanding "due process" for a fired UBC instructor failed to understand that unionized teachers have already won excellent due process: negotiated employment contracts, the right to grieve dismissal, union-paid legal representation, independent provincial arbitration and protections of labour and privacy law. I wasn't surprised when these same "due process," "free speech" types lashed out at the very idea that disabled people can, or should, speak freely. The same cowardly bullies who hide behind cartoon profiles to mock preferred pronouns see no irony in how they reveal themselves as smugly stuck in 1950s hate when they respond to my request to stop using ableist slurs by calling me "a flaming retard," and "cuckoo as Cocoa Puffs." We all know the measuring stick with which they've anointed their abled, white, cis, middle-class, male selves.

But a weenie by any other name is still a dickhead.

Unfortunately, too many organizers sound too much like trolls.

I got a call from one who didn't appreciate being asked on Facebook if his event was accessible. It wasn't, but he didn't want to discuss that. He wanted to shoot the messenger: "Dorothy, you better watch yourself. You need to tone it down. Maybe if you came to the event, and talked to us personally, we'd all respect you more." When I asked him where we would have that discussion, in the street? When I asked him if he would seriously drive two hours to talk organizers into letting him in, not to that event but maybe next year, he got nasty.

"You're turning yourself into the Accessibility Nazi, a total sniper. You're hurting all of CanLit. That gun will backfire in your face. I promise you that. And you'll deserve it."

The term *white women's tears* explains a tactic of white privilege: when white women are accused of racism, they centre themselves, claim victimhood, insist they've been attacked, cry, then attack in retribution. Disabled activists of colour have also called out "the abled fragility" of "abled tears" as a tactic of abled privilege. It's about appointing your abled self both gatekeeper and judge, to decree that because you don't like tone or tactics, you're entitled to see yourself as attacked, to correct, shame and attack the disabled messenger. In my experience with abled fragility, abled men skip the crying part and simply start punching.

Ironically, I hear the same lines men used to silence my generation of feminists, the same words BIPOC friends say are still used against them. I'm told to "catch more flies with honey." To not be "so strident," "bossy," "bitchy" or "browbeating." That I should "drop my all-or-nothing approach." I should be "patient and polite." It's as if abled fragility took a page straight out of Sexist Silencing 1963: it hears a disabled woman's assertion and calls it aggression.

No abled person has the right to dictate tone or tactics to the disabled community.

I have every right to use the terminology and arguments used by my community.

I don't need to be polite when I'm defending my very right to exist. Friends in the disabled community sometimes think I'm not assertive enough. Many see arts communities as smug coteries of vain, self-absorbed ableists who need the wake-up call of picket lines of crips in wheelchairs blocking their inaccessible events. But I guess I do sound pretty radical, if I'm the only disabled activist you know. If you don't read or follow others. I'm grateful for all assertive activists, for the many listening opportunities gifted me by BIPOC writers. I'm especially thankful for activist writers of colour, for Indigenous Twitter, for all who struggle and resist.

Unfortunately, some young writers want to explain intersectionality to little-old-lady me like wait staff explaining Interac, as if I'm too doddering to get this new-fangled thinking. When we agree that Kimberlé Crenshaw did not mean any overlapping identities but specifically oppressions that reinforce each other, like classism, racism and ableism, we have rich, fascinating discussions. I'm most interested in listening to artists who have an activist practice in the world. I'm not interested in being told I must be patient and kind. They're the kind of smug bullies who use the word *nuance* to mean "make your point more palatable to me or shut up."

I hear my mother's bruising, white-gloved voice telling me to be a nice girl.

To whom should I be kind? To be kind to my disabled community, I need to call out ableism as clearly as possible. To be kind to my aging senior community, I cannot be patient. I must embody and voice our absence. Now. Not next year. To be kind to myself, to respect Stella and this book, I have to fight for my own right to be seen and heard. I reject any notion that I must be a kind and cheerful Tiny Tim when I protest my own oppression. No privileged group in history has ever willingly given up their privilege because the oppressed asked nicely.

In 2017, I joined forces with two disabled writers, Bronwyn Berg and non-binary writer Jane Eaton Hamilton. We collaborated for weeks, hoping to craft a #CripCanLit pledge "kind" enough to get many signatories. This was its heart: *In active solidarity with readers and writers with disabilities, I will not plan, book, promote, read at, speak at, fund nor attend any inaccessible literary event.* We got some instant signatories. We appreciate and thank them. We also got some most disappointing, ablesplaining responses. Some colleagues spent ten seconds on Google and tried to argue that 20 percent was too high. We got many private messages, writers saying they "supported the pledge in theory" but couldn't sign it because it would "isolate" them, "keep them from friends' readings" and "prevent them from networking for job opportunities." They obviously didn't care that all of that happened to us all the time.

Days after they signed the pledge, some writers posted about running an inaccessible event, rationalizing it as "close enough." They kindly volunteered to walk us disabled folks down the block to an accessible washroom. Really? I refer anyone who thinks I can have a long-distance relationship with a kybo to a certain Christmas Eve. If you don't want me anointing your floor, provide a toilet.

I'm disgusted to have to explain this. Even once. My dignity is not a debate. These organizers did relocate, but the damage was done. The mood shifted. All three of us in CripCanLit got unfriended, ghosted and sent some nasty private messages.

But what response was the loudest and the most hurtful? *Crickets*

So many friends and allies, writers with whom we support other causes, ignored the pledge entirely. It left us asking: How can anyone defend the indefensible? What makes progressive artists think it's acceptable to ignore, or speak over, disabled people? Is there a hierarchical "virtue of the oppressed" that makes some artists think they can cherry-pick which oppressed groups they will support? To decide that the oppressions they personally recognize and/or experience supersede all others? That isn't intersectional. If you buy into a hierarchy that believes any one oppression is less important than all others, you are part of the problem.

In 2018, we began to hear a whisper campaign that claimed Crip-CanLit was "targeting" writers. The very use of the word *targeting* is problematic. Sending the same words to everyone – "Please do not organize, read at or attend inaccessible events" – isn't "targeting." When you target someone, you take aim at them to hurt them. Asking someone to stop hurting me is not *targeting* them. Calling it targeting is buying into the ableist trope that disabled people are inconveniences and burdens, that when we ask abled people to respect our human rights, we are *hurting them*. It's abled fragility and abled tears to blame the victim then claim victimhood for themselves.

Let's turn that ableist trope on its head. If you are personally invited not to organize, read at or attend an inaccessible event, lucky you; it's a compliment. It's an honour to be asked. A disabled person is taking their time to ask you personally. They're hoping you are the principled kind of person who might support our community, not just with "likes" but with action. If Indigenous activists ask you to check your settler privilege, if BIPOC activists ask you to check your white privilege, if disabled activists ask you to check your abled privilege, it's all an invitation – to join the solidarity party on the right side of history.

As a unionist and lifelong NDP supporter, I come from solidarity culture. I can't count the boycotts, picket lines, rallies, demonstrations, motions of support, fundraisers and petitions I've supported because others asked me to help fight something that hurt them. No one gets asked to help more than unions. Unions offer bodies, time, space, resources, publicity, expertise, solidarity and funding. Would it ever occur to unionists to say these requests "target" workers?

Of course not. Being invited to solidarity is always an honour.

Let's be clear: If you run an inaccessible literary event, you're telling this unionist that you won't let me into my workplace. You're admitting that you only hire abled people to earn the income, reputation, learning, sharing and networking, all vital to our growth and employment as writers. If you take a job in an inaccessible building, it's akin to crossing a picket line. Worse, it's like being a scab. When disabled workers are locked out of readings, festivals, launches and retreats, when these workplaces are being publicly protested for illegal discriminatory hiring practices and unsafe working conditions, abled writers have a choice. Like men accepting their preferential hiring to the exclusion of women, like white people internalizing the belief that they are entitled to any job they want, an abled scab will shrug and say, "But I can work there safely. I can get paid and enjoy myself there. I have bills to pay. So I'm going to put myself first."

Capitalism tells scabs it's good to be a survivor in the survival of the fittest.

Scabs will work for an employer who practices discriminatory hiring because they're on the carrot side of discrimination. Buying into capitalism's vision of the arts as a dog-eat-dog system of scarcity, they're willing to undersell their labour for conditions that aren't safe, fair, inclusive or equitable. Why? Because they individualize. They find some way to tell themselves they personally deserve to be one of the dogs with one of the bones. Take it from this old picket captain:

you're not just taking disabled jobs; you're supporting an active, conscious, bigoted ban on disabled people. It's Ugly Laws writ small. It's eugenics with a shrug.

Nowhere is this clearer than in the privileged, abled defense of "beloved independent bookstores." I appreciate the contribution they have made to abled emerging authors, abled diverse authors and abled small presses, but as I published on All Lit Up and in FOLD's 2018 program, when I surveyed twenty Toronto independent bookstores, not a single one was wheelchair accessible and none had plans to change that. Before anyone praises "beloved" bookstores for promoting "diversity," please note this: conservatively speaking, these twenty stores collectively host thirty-some promotional events per month, or 360-some events a year. That's over three thousand events over the last decade. None of these events have been accessible. This is how inaccessible bookstores ensure the exclusion of 25 percent of the adult population. It's how they reinforce the lie that we are few in number, therefore books by disabled writers won't sell. They do sell, and would do even better if we had equal access to the workplaces and events that promote, publish and sell them.

Of course, capitalism and ableism are enmeshed and invested in each other.

Of course, it might cost businesses something to stop benefitting from the Ugly Laws.

But it is not my job to brainstorm solutions to ensure the profit margins of stores that don't value me enough to let me in the door. Inaccessible independent bookstores could do several things right now at minimal cost. Build permanent ramps at your doorsteps. Temporary ramps are dangerous, and not always insurable. Adjust your aisles to wheelchair passage width of eighty-one centimetres, or thirty-two inches, to follow fire, health and safety codes, and AODA regulations. Publish accessibility information online. Most importantly, host all public events somewhere other than your inaccessible store. It's a negligible cost to secure a free accessible venue and pay one employee three hours' wages, a cost offset by books sold there.

It infuriates me that anyone falls for the sob story that bookstores make so little money that they deserve exemption from the law and should get to violate the rights of 25 percent of the adult population to ensure their profits. It is beyond belief to me that writers scale flights of stairs to attend standing-room-only events and openly excuse it as defending some higher calling of literature. It confounds me that the same people who would never side with Conservative politicians, would never claim that "financial efficiency" justifies hurting any other marginalized group at any time, will argue that a store's profit margins justify harming disabled people.

Why is banning disabled people ever acceptable to anyone?

A close writer friend suggested, "Dorothy, you're endangering your career by calling out inaccessible readings and bookstores. None of them will have you when this book comes out."

I made a face like Archie and stared at him until he got it.

"Right. Sorry. If a venue is inaccessible, you can't appear there anyway. Got it. What am I thinking? Yeah, you might as well name names."

Why haven't I done so here? Because this isn't about individuals. It's about systemic ableism. It's about privilege trumping empathy, about standing on the wrong side of history with Donald Trump and Doug Ford. To date, no abled white writers, no abled male writers, no abled agents or literary organizations except FOLD, no abled publishers large or small have taken a principled position to refuse to attend or hold inaccessible events.

There have been some recent victories. When the writer is disabled, or when an abled writer insists, events get held in accessible spaces and excellent accessibility info gets posted from the start. This is both encouraging and bittersweet. It proves my approach to ask individual writers for active allyship was correct, because accessibility is being provided when an author demands it. Sadly, this reinforces accessibility as "optional charity." It centres the request of abled writers, not the rights of the disabled community. It also proves organizers have learned how to do accessibility right, but if the next author doesn't demand it, they'll go right back to not doing it at all. Inconsistent allyship and bystanding is the problem. We all must be the solution.

I believe the word is fully out. Any writer, organizer, store, series, festival, retreat or event that wants to stop profiting from our exclusion has done so. Everyone else should have their funding pulled. No one should get taxpayer money to run, or appear at, any inaccessible event. *Discrimination by ability* violates all city, provincial and national arts funding regulations, not to mention the Charter of Rights. I'm soul-deep tired of repeating this to people who know this but choose not to act on it.

One of my oldest union friends, a gay man of colour, read this chapter and summed it up like this: "When you read all these excuses together in one place, they sure sound pretty damn lame." He clamped his hand over his mouth at the word. When I giggled, we both laughed.

To get real change, we must ask this: Do we want to see capitalism continue to offer its paternalistic, colonizing "kindness," to continue to siphon off and absorb a few, token, anointed, marginalized artists, or do we want all formations of the arts deconstructed and rebuilt anew?

Because, yet again, thank you Ms. Lorde and Ms. Young, we can't have both.

When anyone asks why men, cisgender people, heterosexuals, the financially secure and white people won't see, own and check their privilege, I know exactly why. For the same reason abled people don't see, own and check their abled privilege: they're getting too much out of it to give it up. They're munching the carrots and swinging the sticks. They can't imagine a world where carrots and sticks aren't theirs by right. They like being comfortable, happy, well-fed carrot eaters. If you are young and abled, why aren't you demanding accessibility for seniors and disabled people? Because you benefit from our exclusion.

All young people. All abled people. All of the time.

Dear young, abled readers of this book, please let me remind you what a small thing I'm asking. I'm not asking you to share my disabled senior life. I'm not asking you to avoid all the places I can't go, or to battle ableism with your every breath. Guilt free, with impunity, please continue to visit your inaccessible bars, bistros, banks, bakeries, basketball games, ballets and barbershops. I want your privileged, abled life to go on oblivious and unchallenged, except for the few short hours when I'm asking you to move down the alphabet with this: Please do not organize, appear at or attend inaccessible literary events. Please be a good human and relocate.

I'm already a limping little bastard banned from heaven. I've been told all my life that I can't belong in my birth family, my adoptive family, my shoes, my clothes, my sexual identity and every step of the walking world. So, no, you don't get to ban me from anywhere else.

It's the core principle of Disability Justice: nobody and no body left behind.

Y Chromosomes and Why They Always Matter

For sixty years of my life, I thought I'd live and die a bastard alone. I was wrong. Just as my father discovered late in life that he had half siblings, so did I.

I took an Ancestry.ca DNA test in 2016, and have since retested at three other sites. My genetic background reads like that of many settlers: My roots are Scottish, Irish and Western European, with a dash of Scandinavian invader thrown in for red-headed good measure. My miniscule 0.4 percent "Native American" DNA could come from anywhere in North or South America, and suggests one ancestor some seven generations ago. Of course, that doesn't give me any conceivable right to call myself Indigenous. My genealogical research reveals I'm descended from the king of medieval Wales. While I'm pleased as punch to be related to a badass Prince of Powys named Gruffydd ap Madog, I won't be claiming that throne anytime soon.

While I recognize all the reasons to be wary of testing companies, and share concerns about who will use our data, and for what purposes, I also believe the rights of adoptees must be central to any discussion of DNA testing. We must not throw thousands of bastard babies out with the dirty Big-Brother-Big-Pharma bathwater. DNA testing offers us a last-chance lifeline we get nowhere else. Having joined several adoption rights organizations over four decades, having met countless adoptees torn from kin and culture, please understand this: knowing anything at all about your family is blood privilege. If you know your parents' names, if you had them in your life and/or had their stories through extended family, you had what I did not, and still do not. Even in my ripe old age, this little bastard still has to take whatever I can get.

One of my best friends, seized in the Sixties Scoop, had his Indigenous family, history, culture and heritage all stolen from him. He tried unsuccessfully for thirty years to follow the government falsified paper trail to his birth parents. He found them a month after DNA testing. His parents had been looking for him all his life. I likewise have enormous empathy for all the real adoptees represented in Ancestry ads so excited to learned something, anything at all, about their families. Given sealed and altered records, there are countless adoptees for whom a DNA pie chart is the sum and total of everything they know. It may be all they ever know.

I always took delight from my NII, which told me I was Scottish.

But it was an uncertain, almost-comfort, knowing many adoptees have discovered that some, all or none of their documents are true. I had no idea what glen, what clan or which side of the Battle of Culloden my family fought on. Believe me, when you're Scottish, that matters. I had to wait half a century to learn it was the right side: My birth mother's clan McLean sided with Bonnie Prince Charlie to spurn the colonizing English invader. It was a thrill to discover the McLeans fought beside the McLeods, the clan of one of my oldest friends. But for all the years I lived without my birth family, did I have the right to embrace Scottish culture in general, to get as imperfectly close to my stolen family, history and heritage as best I could?

Perhaps, if you aren't an adoptee, you don't get a seat at that table.

The Adoption Council of Canada cites seven million, or one in five Canadians, as touched by adoption: adoptees, siblings, family members and birth relatives. Watch even one episode of *Long Lost Family* and the damage of this theft and loss becomes clear. The Facebook page DNA Detectives has 119,000 members, with 1,100 joining each week. It's a place to mourn and celebrate the search for our missing families. Adoptees use both DNA and genealogy, recognizing neither are magic umbilical cords, only imperfect tools.

In 2016, a "close family" DNA match popped up on Ancestry.ca. I corresponded with a lovely woman who proved to be my second cousin, via my birth mother. In 2017, a second "close family" match appeared. The high centimorgan count indicated she was likely my half-sister. Imagine the jolt of joy I felt when I realized this: because she did not also match my birth mother's relative, this sister and I must share the same father. I had such hopes that she would want to meet me. That she could tell me all about him.

Sadly, I found my sister Denise too late for both of us.

Through emails with her husband, I learned all I will ever know about my sister. She is adopted. She was also born at St. Michael's Hospital, five years before me. Her birth mother was also working class: a domestic servant from Ireland. Denise is a retired Social Worker with an M.S.W., who worked in the same field as my daughter: youth homelessness. She was an avid reader and red-headed fighter for justice. Her name is on the Hall of Recognition at Ottawa City Hall as a United Way Community Builder. But I will never meet her; she will never know me.

Denise lives in a care home where zipping around in her wheelchair has earned her the affectionate nickname of "the Roadrunner." She has a rare form of dementia, Posterior Cortical Atrophy (PCA), which is the progressive deterioration of the back of the brain. It takes your ability to read and write. Despite the heartbreak of finding a sister I'll never know, I'm so very grateful to know my sister lived a happy life. I told myself finding her was enough.

Then I spent the Christmas of 2017 preparing for open-heart surgery and preparing to die during it. Google says our chances of kicking the proverbial bucket on any given day are one in two hundred and fifty thousand. Chances of surviving an aortic valve replacement are 98 percent, which sounds great until you get up that morning with a one in fifty chance of dying that day.

Herkimer and Horatio have never kicked anything.

Bucket-kicking ain't on our bucket list.

Two years of shortness of breath and dizziness should have been obvious clues, but I attributed them to pain. Then, on April 26, 2017, a twinge in my left arm became a jackhammer in my chest, became sweating, disorientation and gasping for breath. I'd just had steroid shots in my feet and knees, and they always give me a fever. I phoned Telehealth Ontario to ask if this was a more adverse reaction. The nurse called an ambulance, confirming what I feared: I had all the classic signs of a heart attack. A frightened night in the hospital, two EKGs, a chest X-ray and two blood tests later, thankfully, I had none of the markers of a cardiac event. The ER doctor said it was likely a severe panic attack, aggravated by high blood pressure, fever, dehydration, poor nutrition and exhaustion. He told me to avoid stress entirely. And he sent me home.

Later that day, on April 27, I could find no comfort on my bench beside Terry Fox. I know any heart can fail, but I didn't expect it to be *my* heart. Every wave of a slate-grey Lake Ontario waved goodbye. Left me despondent. Feeling the broken stones of rock bottom. Then I received an email from Wolsak and Wynn offering to publish this book. That karmic kindness keeps my heart beating. It moves me to be as honest as I can here, knowing it's the last chance I may have. It's so very improv to deepen the drama and raise the stakes. I love being a deadly serious running joke that won't run for long, one with both a pun and a pop-culture reference.

Go ask Alex. I think he'll know.

Of course, it wasn't just stress. A cardiologist, an electrocardiogram, an echocardiogram and an angiogram later, I had a confirmed diagnosis of aortic stenosis. My badly calcified aortic valve needed immediate replacement. It's congenital; I was born that way. At least this time it wasn't injury done to me. My surgeon came from Leicester and sounded so much like Grandma Palmer I took it as a sign from a loving Jesus I did not believe in that he might not want to suffer this little bastard to "come unto Him" just yet. But I prepared for the worst: putting my affairs in order, telling my children what I needed them to hear and giving them the chance to do the same.

Then, because my life insists upon being chock full of coincidences no one would ever believe in fiction, in December 2017, days after learning I needed life-saving surgery, I found another half-sibling match on Ancestry.ca: my brother Don. In excited emails and phone calls, I learned he was born and adopted in Toronto, then moved back to his family's rural Francophone community in New Brunswick. Like my dad, Don worked at an oil company most of his life. He's an electrician, a hockey coach, a husband, father of two and grandpa of four. I have a new sister-in-law, two new nieces and four great-nieces and great-nephews. And I'm his big sister.

Here's what you don't get to say every day: I'm one week older than my little brother.

We were both born in St. Michael's Hospital. Our mothers could have met in the maternity ward, never imagining the extraordinary: they had both birthed the same man's child. Don's mother was also a domestic servant, a nanny from Chile. In 2018, months after finding me, he found and met all his Chilean family. They were never told he existed, but welcomed him warmly. He's also met a Toronto woman, also adopted, who is one of the children raised by his mother. She has welcomed him as extended family and told him many stories about his mother.

It appears our stud guppy father authored more than one "Not a Love Story."

According to Don's NII, his mother met our joint birth father when he "offered her a ride home from church." This could have been the Sunday morning after the Saturday night he impregnated my mother. Did both our birth mothers feel the rough, unwelcome scrape of a tartan blanket in a Studebaker? Only the hula girl knows for sure.

Chatting with my son, Conor, I didn't expect an answer when I asked this question.

"That's three little bastards so far. I wonder how many of us there actually are?"

Without missing a beat, he said, "Forty. I'm betting on forty."

I like to think he inherited Archie Bunker's trenchant comic timing from his mother.

I know my children and I will always welcome every one of my missing brothers and sisters. I'd love to know our numbers. Regardless of how we arrived on planet Earth, we're here. I'll take the truth of my family history every time. It is authentically mine.

Of course, if any life can throw yet another curveball, it's mine.

Literally twenty-four hours before open-heart surgery, I almost found my father.

Emphasis on *almost*. After I finished the chapter in this book about living without him, when I should have been relaxing and staying calm, a "close relative" match popped up on Ancestry.ca, one also related to Denise and Don. I spent an entire sleepless night right before surgery analyzing centimorgans, searching Ancestry records and family trees, desperate to see how we were related. But this Sherlock didn't have enough data to solve the case.

Politely, cautiously, I contacted the mystery match and watched my phone like a pot set to boil. But when they rolled me into my six-and-a-half-hour surgery, where they would stop, repair and restart my heart, my match had not replied. I'd said all my goodbyes. I'd made peace with being implanted with a chunk of dead cow. I'd made my daughter my literary executor for this book in case I died on the table.

I succumbed to the anaesthetic furious and terrified – to think I had come this close to my story but might still die that day without it.

When I came to after surgery, I didn't want my daddy; I wanted a milkshake.

The kids say I told them, "I'll just power this down, and then we'll get outta here."

In full-blown hospital dementia, every cell of my being believed the Hamilton General Hospital had been magically transported to 1920s Chicago where Al Capone and Bugsy Malone were out to kill me. From the next bed over, I kept hearing that the pope had died. If gangsters could get to Il Papa, they could certainly get to me. My kids had to tell me more than once, "No. Your neighbours are speaking Tagalog. It's a name you're hearing. The pope didn't die."

I knew Bugsy and Scarface had gotten to them, too.

Two days after surgery, upon recovering what passes for my wits and my wit, my kids gave me my phone. My mystery match had replied during my surgery. My children had endured an agonizing two days, in more ways than one. They didn't feel they had the right to open the email. But not knowing if it was good news or bad, welcoming or rejecting, they were also afraid to let me read it mere hours after open-heart surgery. With the patience of all redheads, I opened it immediately. Together, we found my first cousin. His mother is my birth father's sister. Like Don, like Denise, like me, our cousin was born in St. Michael's Hospital. This time two months before me, in the spring of 1955. He is a freelance writer with a son named Connor.

My cousin's emails tell Don and me everything we may ever know about our father.

He did begin as a bricklayer, but became a builder, ran his own successful construction company. He married and had three children. My cousin describes his uncle Jimmy as quite the character, an opinionated poet, storyteller and ladies' man who wrote long, entertaining poems in phonetic Scottish. He knew "The Cremation of Sam McGee" by heart. A proud member of the Royal Canadian Navy, he joined up to fight Hitler at eighteen. On October 14, 1944, his ship, the HMCS *Magog*, was torpedoed by a German U-boat in the St. Lawrence. Pulling dead comrades from the water haunted him for life. Although he distrusted governments, and called 9/11 a hoax to ensure war, in his retirement he ran for alderman. My cousin called him a generous, loving father. He assured us that if Uncle Jim had known about us, he would have treated us as his own.

Thanks to the wonder of Internet photos, I found a father who looks like me, but I'll never meet him in person. My birth father, James Daryl Stanley, died some three months before I found him. His sister, my aunt, died two months later. Don and I never met either of them. My cousin told us that he would pass our email on to our half-brother, but we have yet to hear from him. We remain hopeful. We all have lifetimes of stories to tell each other.

On May 24, 2018, I met my brother Don.

I looked into his blue-grey eyes and saw mine.

♿

Zephyr: The Breeze that Airs My Closet Blows Us All Some Good

In March 2019, on the one-year anniversary of my surgery, I got the all-clear from my cardiologist. A lovely zephyr, a sweet breeze from Earth not Zephyria, warmed my life that day. Finally believing I was going to live, I figured I should start doing so. I threw open my closet, breathed in all my intersecting shames and secrets. I made a conscious decision to celebrate the fact that life has made me an angry person. Righteous anger is one of the finest of all human emotions. It reaches beyond the self to rage for others. It's feisty, red-headed change.

Please permit me to share this question to summarize all I've learned: Do we want to build a mass movement for change, or do we want to go to brunch with our five best friends?

Because, yet again, we can't have both.

As I learned at the Women's March of 2017.

As first posted in every host city in North America, the Women's March sorely disappointed the disabled community: it had zero accessibility information. We were unwanted and erased. My social media flooded with disabled women posting responses from March officials in all their hometowns, ranging from apology and action to apathy and insult. After contacting the Toronto organizers, they addressed accessibility with true sincerity.

Was it insulting to have to ask, to be nothing but an afterthought yet again? Always.

Did that give me the right to put my nose in the air and refuse to attend? No, it did not.

I paid to attend. In more ways than one. I rented a hotel, as I couldn't safely drive home after a painful day in the cold. And I bought a wheelchair. She's a transport chair, a step between a walker and a power chair I never expected to take. She's another forced fit, another gain and loss. Now I can go long distances, but only if I surrender all autonomy to someone pushing me.

Wenceslas is jealous, but Herkimer and Horatio love her to bits. She's quite spiffy. With elegant ergonomic handles and tartan upholstery, her name is McAlmost.

Echoing my first trip out with Wenceslas, I had to avoid the stares so as not to spoil the victory of the day. Marchers kicked my feet, raced to cut in front of me. They congratulated "someone like me" for "getting out of the house." They talked to my daughter about me, refusing to look at me. Marches are inherently ageist and ableist, doubly so in winter. I saw few wheelchairs or walkers. I don't remember a disabled or senior speaker. But I'm glad I marched as a fully out-of-the-closet disabled senior. I'm forever proud to have been in a Women's March of sixty thousand with my daughter.

But here's my point: all allyship is always uneven and combined. If we want a mass movement, we must reach out beyond our five best friends. I marched knowing full well that few marchers would have my back the next day. They won't see or support my daily struggles. I can't expect them to become my Brienne of Tarth, a pledge knight from *Game of Thrones*, sworn to defend me for her lifetime. They'll continue to "like" Facebook inspiration porn and attend inaccessible events. Hell, they'll steal my accessible parking spots. But it's entirely ultra-left to throw your hands in the air and refuse to join the imperfect struggles of an imperfect world.

Here's the key: while working together, my community and I will keep asking, "Please see us in our numbers. Please stop erasing and banning us. Let's all reject the carrots and the sticks. Let's all do better." Each and every day, I remind myself, "Dear Fat Lady, it's not over until you stop singing. As long as we chose to sing in a fully diverse choir, someday, a collective song will be born. Disability Justice really does mean harmonic change for all."

My disabled community truly inspires me.

It's with love and care that I ask for more.

I recognize, appreciate and honour the work of personal solidarity and consciousness raising that online disability activists have given long hours of their lives to perform for free. I have learned so much from their individual support, empathy and expertise. But, in this era of a climate emergency that portends planetary extinction, of escalating attacks against the disabled community, when ableist hatred works hand in hand with attacks on other marginalized communities and the rise of racist right-wing nationalism, we need more. The powers that be would like nothing more than to keep us siloed off in a sound bubble commiserating with each other. They'd love to reduce social media to nothing more than a place to let off steam.

We must not fall for that.

We must outwit and outplay ableist capitalism.

I believe that collective campaigns are crucial to our survival. When disabled people ask/complain/demand individually it only cements the notion that the world is being asked to accommodate this one, lone, rare, exotic disabled person. When we act alone, we hand abled people the chance to blame the messenger and ignore the message, to label us individually as pushy, bitchy, demanding and selfish. They accuse us of centring ourselves because they don't see we are centring our community. No one looks at me asking for accessibility and thinks, "Holy Expletive, Batman! This request represents some 25 percent of the planet. We better take it seriously." Too many look at me and think, "How can I perform individual sympathy for this one cranky little old lady but use as little of my time, energy and resources as possible?"

If we act in our numbers, if we ally in our numbers, we cannot be ignored.

I long for the disability community to move together beyond what Trotsky would have called reformist politics. A reformist demand is one that extends democracy but does not fundamentally challenge the organization of society, or the role and power of the nation-state. Disability rights groups that focus on such things as inclusive hiring, voting and housing laws are making reformist demands. Transitional demands, however, call for a fundamental change that moves us toward socialism. Disability Justice is transitional. It demands a complete redefinition of the intrinsic value and worth of human bodies. It rejects all the old hierarchies of carrots and sticks: capitalism, colonialism, classism, racism, misogyny, fatphobia, homophobia, transphobia and ageism. When human value does not depend on the ability to produce, to labour and consume, everybody belongs. Nobody, and no body, gets left behind.

To achieve Disability Justice, we need collective campaign solidarity, organized from the grassroots community level through to national and international levels, united in protest with other progressive groups and causes. Together, in a united front, we need to make proactive, collective demands on the state. I recognize the irony that I only understand this at a stage in my life when I am physically far less able to do that work. But I do believe that justice is achievable.

It is what I long for now that my life is no longer like a brand-new box of chocolates. Today, this old lady knows exactly what she got. At birth, I got doubly shamed. As a child, I got repeatedly cut open. At fifty-three, I got a crutch. At sixty, a walker. At sixty-two, a wheelchair. I might see sixty-five before I have to bow to Queen Mehitable the Inevitable.

Do I respect the limping journey of my aging, disabled body? Yes.
Do I love both my disabled and literary communities?
Truly. Often madly. Always deeply.

But would I rather have been born abled, or disabled without pain? Absolutely.

Sherlock Holmes would say it is entirely illogical to love pain. If magical aliens landed, I'd want them to heal me in a heartbeat. If I could live an abled life, I'd to so without a second's guilt. Do I see this as a betrayal of our fight for Disability Justice? No, I do not. A person can, and should, fight for justice for all, whether they are disabled or not.

My allyship with my body will always be uneven and combined. I will not take personal responsibility for ableism. I won't take responsibility for not being personally able to bash it all down. I also refuse to see pain and incapacitation as some kind of higher calling. I won't claim "the virtue of the oppressed," or participate in any kind of inspiration porn. Because there are no magical aliens. Every night as I head off to bed, I worry that I'll have a heart attack in my sleep, die with this book incomplete. The next day, I sit and write again for ten hours non-stop, pausing only to eat crap and crap, both of which I fully realize brings that death closer. I kept waiting for an epiphany, for a moment of searing insight through which pain would be illuminated as redemptive, possibly even ennobling. And that was the last bit of internalized ableism to fall.

Not going to happen. Pain is just pain. It sucks.

The next day, it sucks again.

For all my life, I thought my attitude toward pain should be something I could fix. Something I should be strong enough to fix. When I couldn't, I thought it was my fault. Wrong again. Pain is damage. It's material. I can't transform damage. It's as fused as my bones.

Finally, all the forced fits of my life fit into the life that is mine.

Today, I appreciate how all my identities – bastard, child of rape, survivor of infant sexual abuse, adoptee, mother, teacher, unionist, senior and impoverished, disabled writer – twine together. Being raised by a fighting-not-to-be-working-class family is an invisible marginalization with material repercussions. People see an educated, well-spoken white woman and wrongly assume a middle-class life. Everyone assumes I grew up knowing my mother's name. Being deaf in one ear is increasingly marginalizing. My good ear has deteriorated. Unless I can see faces to lip-read, I struggle to hear. My son's deep voice is audible. My daughter's sweet voice results in me bellowing, "What?" To which she rightly yells something unprintable back. In short, this little woman is growing deaf on the poverty line and will likely die under it. Aging in disability, poverty and depression is a quadruple marginalization. And an eager killer. But for now, the Beatles' song I still sing to Herkimer and Horatio rings true: life goes on.

I'm proud to say I've broken abusive cycles and healed a family wound. My children know I love them. I hug them, kiss them and tell them every day. We've had our fallings-out, but we share our adult lives. For a full seven months after my surgery, my daughter gave up her life to come and live with me. I can never adequately thank her for the nursing, bathing, dressing, cooking, cleaning and putting up with a daily exposure to *The Young and the Restless* and crusty old me in my tiny apartment while she slept on the couch. Simply put, she saved my life.

All that spring and summer, Severn pushed me and McAlmost on our favourite walk, past the Terry Fox memorial to the Burlington waterfront. We always breezed right past a large Royal Navy memorial facing Lake Ontario, dedicated to ships lost in both world wars. Then the wave hit. Just as my missing sister Denise has her name on a memorial wall, there it was, carved in stone, on another wall, mere steps from home: my lost father's lost ship, the HMCS *Magog*.

In that same summer of 2018, when I'm sixty-three, yet another DNA match appeared on Ancestry. It was the youngest son of my absconding red-headed grandfather, Charlie Maclean. It was my birth mother's half-brother, my seventy-two-year-old uncle, only nine years older than I am. He and his brother are cattle ranchers near Lethbridge. Married for fifty years, he has two children. His son is the family genealogist, a history buff who works at a local museum. In short, I've learned enough of my almost family history to be almost content.

And who knows what surprises await.

My birth father may continue to bless me with siblings, even long after his death.

Anticipating my own end, I've done my best in these pages to offer a long overdue apology to Billy, Gerald, Edwina, Rosamunde and Pookie. But in daily life, I'm quite happy to be an unapologetic old bat. I never wanted to be a sweet old lady, powdered, meek and dainty. Bah, humbug! I'd like to have more of my hair, but in another serendipitous moment in fashion history, all the top models are dyeing theirs granny locks grey, so I'm strutting my own catwalk.

"Our next model is Dorothy, sashaying toward us in mix-and-max items from her chic Wenceslas-meets-Walmart collection. Her look begins with classic black track pants, topped by a fetching purple fleece hoodie with sizzling snowflake embroidery. She accessorizes this Go-Get-Em-Granny ensemble with snazzy, white Reeboks sporting racy, silver laces that match her shimmering, silver locks. With a shiny black purse tucked in her smashing walker, she's dressed to hit every bar in town. It's a wonderful life that depends on Depends. Smell ya later, alligator."

Last, but never least, I'd like to tell a real joke. It's been my favourite for forty years, and only as I was searching for an ending here, did I realize it's more than funny. It's a tall tale where disability is the victor, not the victim. It sounds best when told aloud. Please feel free to do so.

On a typical *Hockey Night in Canada*, Big Red and his buddies walk into a bar.

After a few drinks too many, they start betting on the game in backslapping wagers. When Red loses big time, he pays up and weaves his unsteady way up to the bar.

"Hey, Mister Bartender. I'm Big Red. Bet you five bucks I can bite my left eye."

The bartender shrugs, "Okay, buddy. You wanna lose another bet, I'm happy to help."

Red yanks out his glass eye, pops it in his mouth, bites it, then returns it to his face.

The bar applauds as the head-shaking bartender hands over five bucks.

Red grins. "Hey, Mister Bartender. Betcha twenty bucks I can bite my right eye."

The bartender thinks it through: "This guy can't possibly be blind." So, he agrees.

Red pops out a full set of false teeth. Bites his right eye. Restores choppers to mouth.

Again, the crowd roars.

Again, the beaten bartender hands over the cash.

At closing time, a swaying Big Red yells, "Tell ya what, Mr. Bartender. I feel bad 'bout taking your money. Wanna earn it back? See that blue bottle wayyyy over there at the end of the bar? Betcha ahunnered bucks I can pee in it from here and not miss a drop."

Now, the bartender is out a full twenty-five bucks.

He shrugs again.

"Okay, I'll call your bluff. You're on."

Red drops his pants, aims his dick like a firehose, pees up one side of the bar, across the mirror and down the bartender's shirt. Everywhere and anywhere, except in the bottle. The bar hoots and hollers as he zips up, yanks out his wallet and hands over five twenty-dollar bills.

The bartender laughs. "Why are you're smiling? You're out a hundred bucks."

Red winks. All trace of inebriation vanishes. "Well, Mr. Bartender, every Saturday night my buddies and I, we pick a different bar. We make a few small bets. Then we convince the whole bar to make one big bet. And, presto, every time, we win a thousand bucks."

"No way? How? On what?"

Big Red drains his only brewski and smiles. "Our bet is simple and always the same. That, by the end of the night, I can piss all over the bartender and he'll laugh."

Here ends my not-so-tall tale about redheads getting the last laugh.

If my story has touched and tickled you, if seeing me get naked helps you expose your secrets and find your own righteous anger, likewise, bravo. If some of you barkeepers have laughed as I vented in your direction, well done. A joke is only as good as its audience, and you have been splendidly game. Please take your purposeful laughter home with you.

I'll be at home, too.

When you are a retired, grey-haired, single, short, poor, lonely, adopted, fat old woman bastard on a walker, deciding to like and value your aged, disabled, degenerating self is a revolutionary act. Today, when I look in the mirror, I acknowledge what I have lost, but more importantly, I see the proudly disabled, community-connected senior life that I have gained. In this body, I'm worthy. Experienced. Accomplished. Creative. Analytical. Feisty. Resilient. Always willing to investigate the big picture. I'm worthy precisely because I'm flawed. Bossy. Impatient. Demanding. Quick to judge. Convinced I'm always right. Profoundly surprised when I discover I'm not. It was 1973, and I still haven't gotten over the shock.

All of this is me. I accept every serious and unserious cell of me as mine. This little old lady has finally fallen for the perfectly imperfect woman I get to name.

I call her Myself.

There once was a little girl who stayed awake all night chanting the alphabet because it was the most powerful thing she knew, and she hoped it would protect her. It didn't. But as the years passed, its power grew, until one day an old woman on a walker used the alphabet to honour the little girl she had been, to tell her story from A to Z.

I love the word *recollection*. To remember. To recollect. Reorder, redefine, re-empower.

Will my story help other somebodies like me spell out their own recollections?

"Cue the music for Final Jeopardy, please, Alex."

Because, yes, justice always begins in the form of a question.

Acknowledgements

How can I thank all the friends, loved ones, colleagues, comrades, mentors and allies of seven decades? I can't. My thanks and gratitude extends far beyond those acknowledged here.

I'll begin with teachers. Dear Miss Heath, Mrs. Gray, Mrs. Smith, Miss Van Norman, Mr. Bleeker, Mr. Adamson, Mrs. Gosse, Mr. and the lovely Ms. Dewsnap, you are the reasons I became a teacher. To the two teachers that gave me the gift of believing in myself – my grade ten Man and His World teacher, Barry Marynick, and my Western mentor and friend, Professor Craig M. Simpson – I can never repay you, but tried to do so with each student I taught.

To my three decades of teaching colleagues, your collective excellence, your friendship and solidarity, made a life in education a pleasure. As parents, as citizens, we owe an unpayable debt to all who have ever served in teachers' unions. My personal thanks to my OSSTF executives and all District 13 members who defended education during the Harris attacks. Especial thanks to Marianne Froehlich, Nancy Henry, Cara Sullivan, Dale Nevison, David Lomax, Dave Griffin and Wayne Hingston, whose friendship, solidarity and teaching excellence made me a better teacher and a far better person. To our infamous PRSS second-floor workroom – Nancy Turner Malcolmson, Tara MacKay,

Miriam Lowney Bosonello, Barry Mager, Alyson van Beinum, Gretchen Cornish, Natalie Passarello, Mark Lebourdais, Andrew Okaeme and Robin Maharaj – it was my honour to share your teaching days, and your engagements, marriages and babies over fifteen years. Thank you.

Next, I'd like to truly thank a catalogue of librarians – from those half a century ago at the Alderwood Public Library, to Western, to city and school librarians in Vancouver, La Crete, Calgary, Ajax, Oshawa, Pickering, Uxbridge, Toronto, Mississauga and Burlington – my deepest appreciation for your indefatigable and invaluable service to youth, to learning and to hope.

I equally want to thank my over three thousand students for the opportunity to be a small part of your journey: especially my extraordinary classes of OAC English and Writer's Craft and decades of grade ten Drama. To the joyous family of improv in ADA2G1, ADA3G1 and all my teams that played at the Toronto improv games, it was my pleasure to laugh with you every day. It was the privilege of my life to witness your growth as human beings.

Those who know me will be surprised I want to thank two administrators: Principal Bob Dockstader and English/Drama department head Nolan Taggart. Their deep expertise and caring professionalism made it possible to remember why we despised all the flunkies and failures who followed them after the Harris attacks, when the only criteria to become an administrator was a grunting obedience to authority and how much anti-union ass you could kiss.

In deserving counterpoint, I'm delighted to thank my friends, regretful only that I can't thank you all. In chronological order, I'll thank a few for invaluable times: Gail MacCallum, Jim Stobie, Susan Koswan, Jill Burling, Garth Riley, Richard Gubernat, Steven Fradley, Mark Worthington, Bonnie Crawford, Rosa Forgione, Sonja Dodich, Deborah Agnew, Ann Campbell, Sandy Szuba, Lahring Tribe, Peter Gubbels, Tim Platts, Tom Nunn, Heather McLeod, Pam Singer, Linda Grant, Edith McKay, Byron Nelson, Alina Karpova Raskin,

Nicholas Dipchand, Madeleine Jullian, Janet Berkman, the Victoria Creek Book Club and my CCWWP colleagues.

It is likewise impossible to thank all those in CanLit who have shared their work and wisdoms. The kind support of Rachel Wyatt extended far beyond the Banff Writers' Colony. Bharati Mukherjee took me aside after the birth of my daughter and urged me not to give up. Special thanks goes to my Coach House editor, Alana Wilcox, for plucking *When Fenelon Falls* from the slush pile and publishing the first novel in Canada with a red-haired, adopted, disabled protagonist. For this book, Diane Terrana offered expert guidance at a critical time. FOLD's Jael Richardson and Amanda Leduc supported me at my lowest and continue to shine a daily beacon of principled hope that true diversity justice can be built together.

My abiding thanks to all in Disability Justice and CanLit whose daily tweets, activisms and discussions informed the book, many of whom also so kindly agreed to read and comment on all or part of it, including: Jane Eaton Hamilton, Bronwyn Berg, Janet Berkman, Alice Wong, Julie Rak, Gabrielle Peters, Carrianne Leung, Jónína Kirton, Sarah Jama, Farzana Doctor, Sonya Huber, Adam Pottle, Judy Rebick, Margo Tamez, Sally Chivers and Amanda Leduc.

Noelle Allen of Wolsak and Wynn accepted this memoir when it was but a baby guppy. For her faith in me, for her guidance, expertise and the greatest gift you can ever give someone – telling them exactly what you really think – my gratitude always. My thanks also to Andrew Wilmot for his meticulous copy-editing, to Ashley Hisson for proofreading and publicity, to Marijke Friesen for the fabulous cover and interior design, and to all the caring team at Wolsak and Wynn.

For further reading of the work of disabled writers, I recommend two excellent lists: one by Leah Lakshmi Piepzna-Samarasinha in *Care Work: Dreaming Disability Justice*, and "Black Disabled Woman Syllabus" by Vilissa Thompson on her blog, *Ramp Your Voice!*, at rampyourvoice.com/2016/05/05/black-disabled-woman-syllabus -compilation/.

I offer my thanks and my greatest respect to #CripCanLit colleagues Jane Eaton Hamilton and Bronwyn Berg for their costly commitment to Disability Justice. I want to thank all those with disabled boots on the ground, especially the co-founders of the Toronto Disability Pride March, Melissa Graham and her late partner Kevin Jackson, and Sarah Jama and her team at the Disability Justice Network of Ontario. The online international family of disability activists is legion and growing every day. I urge everyone to follow #Disability Twitter, for the daily work of countless worthy voices. Please read their work, refer and hire them, for their extraordinary experience and expertise.

It will forever be a wonder to me that I get to end this book by thanking my family. I had to wait until my sixties to find my brother, but he was worth the wait. I thank Don Doiron, his wife Anne, my new nieces Melanie and Ginny and my four great-nieces and great-nephews, for the warm welcome they have given me and my children. It is likewise my pleasure to thank Nolan Pearson, Cory Price and four-legged family members Willow, Odin and Jimbo for loving my children. Conor and Severn, my love and thanks to you for letting me be the complicated, imperfect mother I was and loving me anyway. Beyond me, without me, despite me, you have become two of the finest humans I have ever known.

To all the somebodies out there like me, living in adopted, disabled, aging bodies, thank you for reading this book of my heart. I most sincerely hope it helps you to fall for yourselves.

Onward.

Dorothy Ellen Palmer is a mom, binge knitter, disabled senior writer, accessibility consultant and retired high school drama teacher and union activist. She grew up in Alderwood, Toronto, and spent childhood summers at a three-generation cottage near Fenelon Falls.

For three decades, she worked in three provinces as a high school English/Drama teacher, teaching on a Mennonite Colony, a four-room schoolhouse, an adult learning centre attached to a prison and a highly diverse new high school in Pickering. Elected to her union executive in multiple capacities, she served as Branch President and Picket Captain. While coaching for the Canadian Improv Games, she created and toured staff and student improv workshops to fight bullying, racism, sexism, sexual harassment and homophobia.

Dorothy sits on the Accessibility Advisory Committee of the Festival of Literary Diversity (FOLD) and is an executive member of Canadian Creative Writers and Writing Programs (CCWWP) where she writes a monthly column on disability for the newsletter.

Her work has appeared in: *Nothing Without Us, REFUSE, Wordgathering, Alt-Minds, All Lit Up, Don't Talk to Me About Love, Little Fiction Big Truths, 49th Shelf* and *Open Book*. Her first novel, *When Fenelon Falls* (Coach House, 2010), features a disabled teen protagonist in the Woodstock-Moonwalk summer of 1969. She lives in Burlington, Ontario, and can always be found tweeting @depalm.